Pocket Dictionary of
BUSINESS
ITALIAN

MILENA SELLITRI-VAN KRAAY

Series editor: C.G. Geoghegan

Hodder & Stoughton

A MEMBER OF THE HODDER HEADLINE GROUP

British Library Cataloguing in Publication Data
Kraay, Milena Sellitri-van
Pocket Dictionary of Business Italian
I. Title II. Geoghegan, J. Y. III. Series
453.21

ISBN–0–340–59574–4

First published 1995

Impression number	10	9	8	7	6	5	4	3	2	1
Year		1999	1998	1997	1996	1995				

Typeset by Wearset, Boldon, Tyne and Wear.
Printed in Great Britain for Hodder & Stoughton Educational, a
division of Hodder Headline Plc, 338 Euston Road, London NW1 3BH
by Cox & Wyman Ltd, Reading.

INTRODUCTION

This Pocket Dictionary series is designed for the non-language specialist who needs to find the meaning of a common word used in a business context. The series helps the user read a report or business article in the foreign language and is a useful tool in the preparation of brief reports, faxes, telexes or letters. Selected with general business activities in mind, the words have been chosen for their frequency of use in everyday business dealings rather than for their popularity in theoretical or academic business studies. The list of words has been compiled by analysis of the business press and of business documents. Special attention has also been given to terms in marketing, sales, import and export, finance and accounting, personnel management, transport and distribution.

The Italian to English section gives the translation, or explanation, of words or expressions commonly found in business and general communication in Italy. This section is designed to help the user understand foreign language communications.

The English to Italian section provides a general purpose business translation for English words used in business activities. The aim of the section is to help the user communicate effectively in Italian using the most widely acceptable translation for their needs. The translations are selected for their value to the non-specialist user and are sometimes more general than those in the Italian to English section.

HOW TO USE THIS BOOK

Where a word has more than one common meaning these are indicated by the numbers 1, 2, 3 and so on. To help make these different meanings clear the common area of use is often indicated in brackets. For example:

> **carry** *vb*, **1** (on a vehicle), transportare. **2** (with your hands), portare. **3** (have in store), avere uno stock; **carry a stock of . . .** , avere uno stock di . . .

When you are looking for a possible translation of a word you need to check the part of speech. Be wary of *fixed phrases* or standard business phrases, as you might not be able to understand these by translating the individual words. You will generally find standard or fixed phrases listed under one of the key words they contain. For example:

> **elettronico(-a)** *adj* **. . . scambio dati elettronici**, EDI, Electronic Data Interchange

It is advisable not to use a translation out of the context indicated, as a word may have a number of special meanings. This is a general business dictionary and for very specialist terms you might need a specialist dictionary, such as a dictionary of accounting terminology and practice, or a dictionary of public relations terminology.

A word can have many different meanings according to the context, part of speech and gender (in the case of nouns). Grammatical and contextual information about the word, or expression, is given in the entry.

Abbreviations and symbols

Here are some of the abbreviations used to indicate the area of use of a word:

acct   accounts
admin   administration

agric	agriculture
comm	commerce
comp	computer
corr	correspondence
cv	curriculum vitae
electr	electronics
eng	engineering
fig	figurative
fin	finance
gen	general
geog	geography
imp/exp	import/export
ins	insurance
maths	mathematics
med	medicine
mktg, sales	marketing, sales
naut	nautical
offce	office
pers	personnel
techn	technical
telec	telecommunications
transp	transport (includes distribution)

Grammatical abbreviations

adj	adjective
adv	adverb
conj	conjunction
n	noun
nf	noun, feminine
nfpl	noun, feminine, plural
nm	noun, masculine
nmpl	noun, masculine, plural
pl	plural
prep	preposition
vb	verb

Occasionally it is not possible to find an exact translation or equivalent for a word or phrase in another language. Similarly it can be difficult to find an exact equivalent for certain official organisations or institutions. In all of these cases the symbol ≈ is used to indicate *roughly equivalent to, roughly the same as*.

ITALIAN — ENGLISH

A

abbassamento *nm*, **1** (gen), lowering, fall. **2** (fin, mktg, sales), downturn

abbassare *vb*, **1** (gen), lower, **abbassare i prezzi**, lower the prices. **2** (fin), downturn

abbonarsi *vb* **a . .**, (a journal, a service), subscribe to . . .

abbonato *nm*, subscriber

abbozzare *vb* (plan), outline

abilità *nf*, **1** (potential), capacity. **2** know-how. **3** skill

abitazione *nf*, home

abituale *adj*, usual

abnegazione *nf*, self-denial

abuso *nm*, abuse; **abuso di fiducia**, abuse of confidence

accaldato(-a) *adj*, heated

accelerare *vb*, accelerate, step up, speed up

accendere *vb*, light, switch on

acceso(-a) *adj*, on; **essere acceso**, be on; **la luce è accesa**, the light is on; **il computer è acceso**, the computer is on

accesso *nm*, access; **avere accesso**, have access; **vietare l'accesso**, deny access; **avere l'accesso alla rete**, access the network

accessorio *nm*, accessory; **accessori** *nmpl* **auto**, car accessories

accettabile *adj*, acceptable; **condizioni** *nfpl* **accettabili**, acceptable conditions

accettare *vb*, **1** (gen), accept. **2** (law), agree; **accettiamo i termini del contratto**, we agree to the terms of the contract; **accettare un'opzione**, take up an option

accettazione *nf*, acceptance; **accettazione con riserva**, qualified acceptance

acciaio *nm*, steel; **acciaio laminato**, rolled steel

accludere *vb* (corr), attach, enclose; include; **accludo una copia della fattura**, I enclose a copy of the invoice; **si prega di accludere . .**, please include . . .

accogliere *vb* **(un visitatore)**, meet intentionally (a visitor, a customer); **accogliere un cliente**, meet a client

accompagnare *vb*, accompany; **il nostro direttore sarà accompagnato da . .**, our manager will be accompanied by . . .

acconto *nm*, **1** (part payment in advance), deposit; **pagare un acconto**, pay a deposit. **2** (part of amount due for a purchase), instalment

accoppiare *vb*, match

accordare *vb*, grant; **accordare una licenza**, license

accordo *nm*, agreement, understanding; **arrivare ad un accordo**, reach an agreement; **essere d'accordo**, agree; **mettersi d'accordo**, agree, reach agreement; **alla riunione ci siamo messi d'accordo di . .**, at the meeting we agreed to . .; **accordo di compensazione** (imp/exp), barter trade, countertrade; **abbiamo raggiunto un accordo**, we have reached an understanding

accreditare *vb*, credit

accusare *vb*, accuse; **accusare ricevuta**, acknowledge receipt; **accusare qualcuno (di un delitto)**, charge somebody (with a crime)

acquirente *nm/f*, buyer, purchaser

acquisizione *nf* (fin), procurement, acquisition; **fusioni e acquisizioni**, mergers and acquisitions

acquistare *vb*, 1 buy, acquire. **acquistare esperienza** (CV), gain experience

acquisto *nm*, purchase; **acquisti** *nmpl* **all'ingrosso**, bulk buying; **acquisto a rate**, hire purchase; **OPA (offerta di pubblico acquisto)**, sale of equity to existing shareholders

adattare *vb*, adapt, adjust, tailor; **adattare ai nostri bisogni**, adapt to our needs; **adattare alla situazione**, adjust to the situation; **possiamo adattare il nostro servizio in funzione dei vostri precisi bisogni**, we can tailor our service to your exact needs

adatto(-a) *adj*, suitable; **un luogo adatto**, a suitable location

addebitare *vb*, charge, debit; **è da addebitare sul conto**, it is to be charged to the account; **si prega di addebitare il mio conto**, please debit my account

addestramento *nm*, training; **centro d'addestramento**, training centre

addestrare *vb* (pers), train

addetto *nm*, 1 attaché. 2 (pers), in charge; **addetto agli acquisti**, person in charge of purchases, buyer

addetto(-a) *adj*, employed

aereo *nm*, aircraft, plane

aereo(-a) *adj*, air; **difesa aerea**, air defence; **per via aerea**, by air; **carico aereo**, air cargo; **nolo aereo**, airfreight

aeroplano *nm*, aircraft, plane

aeroporto *nm*, airport

affare *nm*, 1 business. 2 deal; **affare fatto**, it is a deal; **buon affare**, bargain; **fare un buon affare**, get a bargain

affari *nmpl*, business; **come vanno gli affari?**, how is business?; **uomo d'affari**, businessman; **donna d'affari**, businesswoman; **viaggio d'affari**, business trip; **fare affari con . .**, do business with . .; **giro d'affari**, turnover

affermare *vb*, affirm, maintain

afferrare *vb*, seize; **afferrare un'opportunità**, seize an opportunity

affetto(-a) *adj* **da**, affected by

affidamento *nm*, trust, confidence, reliability; **fare affidamento su . .**, rely on . .; **affidamento su un prodotto**, reliability of a product

affisso *nm* (mktg, sales) poster

affittare *vb*, let, rent, lease (to someone); **affittare uno stand**, rent a stand; **affittare uffici**, rent offices

affitto *nm*, rent; hire; **camere in affitto**, rented rooms; **macchina in affitto**, hire car; **in affitto**, on hire; **prendere in affitto**, hire; **cessione contratto d'affitto**, leaseback; **pagamento affitto**, rental

affrancare *vb*, (corr), frank; (put a postage stamp, tax stamp or rubber stamp), stamp

affrancatrice, macchina affrancatrice *nf*, franking machine

affrancatura *nf*, postage

affrancato(-a) *adj*, paid; **porto affrancato fino a . .**, carriage paid to . . .

affrontare *vb*, deal with, tackle; **vorrei affrontare il problema di . .**, I would like to tackle the problem of . . .

agenda *nf*, note-book; diary

agente *nm*, 1 agent; **agente di cambio** (fin) (stock)broker. 2 operator; **agente di trasporto**

misto, combined transport operator (CTO); **agente marittimo**, shipping agent; **agente esclusivo**, sole agent

agenzia nf, agency

aggeggio nm (unflattering), gadget

aggiornato(-a) adj, up to date; **essere aggiornato**, be up to date

aggiungere vb, add; **si prega di aggiungere al nostro ordine**, please add to our order

aggraffare vb (offce), staple

aggressivo(-a) adj (mktg, sales), aggressive

agricoltore nm, farmer

agricoltura nf, farming

aiutare vb, help; **il nostro agente milanese sarà in grado di aiutarvi**, our agent in Milan will be able to help you

aiuto nm, 1 (gen), help; **chiedere aiuto**, call for help. 2 (fin), aid; **aiuto finanziario**, financial aid

alimentare adj, food; **industria alimentare**, food industry

alimento nm, food

allargare vb, widen

allegare vb, enclose; include; **allego una copia del nostro opuscolo**, I enclose a copy of our brochure

allegato nm, enclosure

alleggerire vb (take some weight off), lighten

alleviare vb (give some comfort), lighten

alloggio nm, accommodation

alterare vb, alter, tamper with; **questi documenti sono stati alterati**, these documents have been tampered with

alternativa nf, alternative

altezza nf, height

alto(-a) adj, 1 (gen), high; **il prezzo è molto alto** the price is very high. 2 (big), tall; **è una donna molto alta**, she is a very tall woman. 3 (mktg, sales), buoyant; **il mercato è alto**, the market is buoyant

altro(-a) adj, other

alzare vb, lift, raise, put up; **alzare i prezzi** raise prices

amenità nfpl, (of a hotel), facilities; **tra le amenità offerte dal nostro albergo ci sono . .**, among the facilities offered by our hotel are . . .

ammenda nf (law), fine, penalty

ammettere vb, admit; **ammettere la verità**, admit the truth

amministrare vb, manage

amministrazione nf, administration, management

ammortizzare vb (acct, progressively) pay for itself, write down; **tra due anni la macchina sarà ammortizzata**, the machine will pay for itself in two years

ammortizzatore nm, shock absorber; **materiale per ammortizzatori**, shock-absorbent material

ammucchiare vb, 1 (gen), pile up. 2 (transp), stack; **merci ammucchiate**, stacked goods

ampio(-a) adj, wide; **un'ampia selezione**, a wide selection

ampliare vb, widen

analisi nf, analysis; **l'analisi è giusta**, the analysis is correct; **l'analisi delle cifre indica che . .**, the analysis of the figures indicates that . .; (fin) **analisi, (dei conti)** breakdown; **analisi dei bisogni**, needs analysis

analista nm/f, analyst

analizzare vb **i conti**, (figures), break down

analizzatore nm, scanner

ancoraggio *nm*, (naut), berth

ancorare *vb* (transp), berth

andare *vb*, go; **andare a prendere (qualcuno alla stazione, in albergo, etc)**, meet (someone at the station, etc); **andare in fretta**, speed; **andar bene**, (be the right size), fit; **le va bene il cappotto?**, does the coat fit you?; **andare in liquidazione**, go into liquidation; **andare in pensione**, retire; **andare su**, go up.

angolo *nm*, corner; **si prega di mettere la macchina in un angolo**, please put the machine in a corner

animato(-a) *adj*, heated; **discussione animata**, heated discussion

annata *nf*, year; **una buona annata lavorativa**, a good working year

anno *nm*, year **anno civile**, calendar year; **per anno**, p.a., per annum; **anno fiscale**, tax year; **un anno dopo l'altro**, year in year out

annuale *adj*, annual, yearly; **premio annuale**, annual bonus; **rapporto annuale**, annual report; **abbonamento annuale**, yearly subscription

annualmente *adv*, yearly

annullamento *nm*, cancellation

annullare *vb*, cancel

annuncio *nm*, **1** (gen), advertisement, ad. **2** (particular event), news; **l'annuncio della fusione**, the news of the merger

antiacustico(-a) *adj*, soundproof

anticipo *nm*, advance; **pagamento in anticipo**, advance payment; **in anticipo**, in advance; (before time) early

aperto(-a) *adj*, open; **mercato all'aperto**, open market; **conto aperto**, open account

apertura *nf*, opening, gap;

un'apertura nel mercato, an opening in the market; **apertura con scasso**, (law), break-in

appalto *nm*, contract, bid; **offerta d'appalto**, tender; **chiedere offerte d'appalto**, invite tenders

apparecchio *nm*, appliance, device; **apparecchio di controllo**, monitor

appartamento *nm*, flat

appellarsi *vb*, appeal

appello *nm*, appeal; **fare l'appello**, call the roll; **mancare all'appello**, be absent; **fare appello**, appeal, call on

appena *adv*, (barely), just; **appena abbastanza**, just enough; **appena in tempo**, just in time

appiattire *vb*, flatten

applicare *vb*, apply (something)

appoggiare *vb*, **1** (gen), support. **2** (give support), second; **appoggiare una proposta**, second a proposal

appoggio *nm*, support; **il progetto ha l'appoggio di . .**, the project has the support of . . .

apprezzare *vb*, appreciate, value

approssimativamente *adv*, roughly

approvare *vb*, **1** (gen), approve; **l'acquisto è stato approvato**, the purchase has been approved; **dettagliante approvato**, approved retailer; **fornitore approvato**, approved supplier. **2** (approve an idea), endorse

appuntamento *nm*, appointment, **fissare/prendere un appuntamento**, make an appointment

appunto *nm*, note, memo; **prendere appunti**, take notes

aprire *vb*, open; **aprire un programma**, open a programme; **aprire la posta**, open the mail; **aprire una filiale in . .**, open a branch in . .; **aperto tutta la settimana**, open 7 days a week; **conto aperto**, open account; **mercato aperto**, open market

arbitraggio *nm*, arbitration

arbitrato *nm* (law), arbitration

archivi *nmpl* (offce), records

archiviare *vb* (offce), file

archivista *nm*, filing clerk

area *nf*, area

argomento *nm*, argument, subject, topic

aria *nf* **condizionata**, air-conditioning

armadio *nm*, cupboard

arnese *nm*, 1 (gen). tool. 2 (small piece of equipment), gadget

arrampicarsi *vb*, climb

arretrato *nm*, arrears; **in arretrato**, in arrears; **pagamento in arretrato**, outstanding payment

arrivare *vb*, arrive; **arrivare in ritardo**, arrive late

arrivo *nm*, arrival; **l'arrivo della spedizione**, the arrival of the consignment; **posta in arrivo**, in-tray

arrugginire *vb*, rust

articolo *nm*, item, article; **articoli casalinghi**, household goods; **articoli di lusso**, luxury goods; **articoli di pelle**, leather goods; **articoli in sospeso**, outstanding items; **articolo di redazione**, advertorial

artificiale *adj*, man-made; artificial

artigianato *nm*, craft

ascensore *nm*, lift

ascolto *nm*, listening; **ore di grande ascolto**, prime time

assegno *nm*, cheque; **assegno al portatore**, cheque to bearer; **assegno circolare**, bank draft;

assegno in bianco, blank cheque; **libretto d'assegni**, cheque-book; **contrassegno**, cash on delivery; **emettere un assegno**, draw a cheque; **assegno postale**, giro cheque

assemblea *nf* (formal meeting), assembly; **Assemblea Generale**, Annual General Meeting

assenteismo *nm*, absenteeism

asserire *vb*, claim (to be true)

assessore *nm*, assessor

assicurare *vb* **(contro)**, insure (against); **essere assicurato contro . .**, be insured against; **'L'Assicurato'** 'The Insured'

assicuratore *nm*, insurer

assicurazione *nf*, insurance; **assicurazione sulla vita**, life insurance; **CIF (costo, assicurazione e nolo)**, CIF (cost, insurance, freight); **assicurazione casko**, comprehensive insurance; **assicurazione (a carico del datore di lavoro) contro gli infortuni sul lavoro**, employer's liability insurance; **assicurazione per danni contro terzi, furto e incendio**, third party fire and theft insurance

assistente *nm/f*, assistant; **assistente del direttore**, manager's assistant

assistenza *nf*, 1 (gen), assistance. 2 (comm), service. 3 (eng), maintenance; **assistenza su luogo**, site maintenance

assistere *vb*, assist

assomigliare *vb*, resemble, look like

assumere *vb* (pers), employ, take on

asta *nf*, auction

attaccare *vb*, 1 attack. 2 (label, stamp), attach

attacco *nm*, attack; **attacco di pazzia**, fit of madness; **attacco in massa**, mass attack

attendere *vb*, wait

atterrare *vb*, land

attesa *nf*, wait

attestare *vb*, certify

attestato(-a) *adj*, certified

attestato *nm*, certificate

attirare *vb*, **1** (gen), attract. **2** (be appealing), appeal; **attirare i clienti**, appeal to the customers

attività *nf*, activity; (of a company), operations; **attività commerciale**, business; **ho un'attività commerciale**, I am in business; **attività principale**, main activity

attivo *nm* (fin), (balance sheet), asset; **attivo immobilizzato**, fixed assets

atto *nm* (law), deed; **redigere un atto**, draw up a deed; **atto di vendita**, bill of sale

attraccare *vb* (transp), dock

attraente *adj*, **1** (gen), attractive; **colori attraenti**, attractive colours. **2** (mktg, sales), eye-catching

attraversare *vb*, cross; go through; **attraversare una crisi**, go through a crisis

attrezzatura *nf*, equipment; **attrezzatura essenziale**, basic equipment; **attrezzatura elettrica**, electrical equipment

attrezzo *nm*, tool

attualmente *adv*, currently

aumentare *vb*, **1** (gen), increase, rise; **il costo d'affitto è stato aumentato dell'8%**, the cost of hire has increased by 8%; **aumentare di velocità**, gather speed. **2** gain; **aumentare di peso**, gain in weight; **aumentare incessantemente**, soar; **costi che aumentano incessantemente**, soaring costs

aumento *nm*, **1** (gen), increase. **2** (fin), **aumento di salario**, wage increase; **aumento di valore**, appreciation; **aumento improvviso**, boom; **abbiamo notato un improvviso aumento delle vendite**, we have seen a boom in sales. **3** (increase) gain; **un aumento di peso**, a gain in weight; **aumento netto**, sharp rise; **aumento esorbitante**, steep rise; **essere in aumento**, be up

autenticare *vb* (law), certify

autenticato(-a) *adj* (law), certified; **copia autenticata**, certified copy

autista *nm/f*, driver; **autista di camion**, lorry driver

auto *nm*, car

autobus *nm*, bus; **stazione** *nf* **degli autobus**, bus station

autocarro *nm*, lorry

autocisterna *nf* (transp), tanker

auto-finanziamento *nm*, self-financing

automobile *nf*, car, motor; **salone dell'automobile**, motor show; **assicurazione automobilistica**, motor insurance; **ACI**, **Automobil Club Italiano**, Italian Automobile Association

automobilista *nm*, motorist

autorizzare *vb*, authorise; **autorizzare una licenza**, license

autorizzato(-a) *adj*, authorised; **non autorizzato**, unauthorised

auto-servizio *nm*, self-service

autostop *nm*, hitchhiking; **fare l'autostop**, hitchhike

autostrada *nf*, motorway

autostradale *adj* motorway; **nodo autostradale**, motorway junction

avallare *vb*, **1** (law), guarantee. **2** (fin), back

avallo *nm*, **1** (law), guarantee. **2** (fin), backing

avanguardia *nf*, van, vanguard;

all'avanguardia della moda, in the van of fashion; **la società è all'avanguardia nel campo della tecnologia**, the company is a leader in the field of technology

avanti *adv*, come in, go ahead

avanzamento *nm*, advance

avaria *nf*, **1** (gen), damage. **2** (ins), average; **liquidatore** *nm* **d'avaria**, loss adjuster. **3** (mech), failure

avariato(-a) *adj*, damaged; **non avariato**, undamaged

avere *vb*, have; **aver bisogno di**, need; **ha bisogno di un'analisi**, he needs an analysis; **aver cura di . .**, take care of . .; **avere lo scopo di . .**, aim to . .; **avere una perdita**, make a loss; **avere un colloquio con un candidato**, interview a candidate; **avere un guasto**, break down

aviazione *nf*, aviation

avvertimento *nm*, warning; **inviare una lettera di avvertimento**, send a warning letter

avvertire *vb*, warn; **preghiamo di avvertire il vostro autista che c'è uno sciopero al porto**, please warn your driver that there is a strike at the port

avviamento *nm* **(di una ditta)**, goodwill (of a firm)

avviso *nm*, **1** (gen), advice; **nota d'avviso**, advice note; **avviso di ricevuta**, advice of receipt **avviso di credito**, credit advice. **2** (on a wall), notice

avvitare *vb*, screw

avvocato *nm* (law), lawyer, barrister, legal adviser, attorney, advocate, counsel; solicitor

avvolgere *vb*, wrap

avvolto(-a) *adj*, wrapped

azienda *nf*, business, firm; **azienda individuale**, one-man business

azione *nf*, **1** (gen), action. **2** (fin), share; **azione ordinaria** (ordinary share) equity; **azione disonesta**, malpractice; **azioni**, stock. **3 azione di leva**, leverage. **4 azione legale** (law), proceedings

azionista *nm*, shareholder

B

bacchetta *nf*, (presentations), pointer

bagaglio *nm*, luggage

bagnato(-a) *adj*, wet

bagno *nm*, bath; **fare un bagno**, take a bath

balla *nf*, bale

bambino(-a) *nmf*, child; **bambini**, children

banca *nf*, bank; **Banca dei Saldi Internazionali**, Bank for International Settlements (BIS)

bancario(-a) *adj*, bank; **spese** *nfpl* **bancarie**, bank charges; **deposito** *nm* **bancario**, bank deposit **tratta** *nf* **bancaria**, bank draft; **tasso** *nm* **bancario**, bank rate; **assegno bancario**, cheque

banchina *nf*, 1 (railway) platform. 2 (transp), quay, wharf

banco *nm* (shop) counter

bancomat *nm*, cash dispenser

banconota *nf*, banknote, note

bando *nm*, ban; **il comunicato è stato messo al bando**, they have put a ban on the press release

bar *nm* (for drinks), bar

barattare *vb*, barter

baratto *nm*, barter

barattolo *nm*, can

barca *nf*, boat

barile *nm*, barrel

basato(-a) *adj* su . ., based on . .; **la valutazione è basata su . .**, the valuation is based on . . .

base *nf*, basis; **base dati**, database

basso(-a) *adj*, low; **voce bassa**, low voice; **mutuo a basso interesse**, low interest loan; **prezzi bassi**, low prices; **a basso prezzo**, cheap

battere *vb* **a macchina**, 1 (comp), key in. 2 (offce), keyboard

batteria *nf*, battery

bello(-a) *adj*, beautiful, fine

beneficiario *nm*, 1 (gen), beneficiary. 2 (fin), payee

benestare *nm*, approval; **abbiamo il benestare di . .**, we have the approval of . . .

beni *nmpl*, goods; **beni di capitale**, capital goods; **beni di consumo**, consumer goods; **beni di consumo corrente**, Fast-Moving Consumer Goods (FMCG)

benzina *nf*, petrol, fuel; **essere senza benzina**, run out of fuel

bevanda *nf*, drink; **bevanda analcolica**, soft drink; **bevanda alcolica**, strong drink

bianco(-a) *adj*, white

bibita *nf*, drink; **bibite analcoliche**, soft drinks; **bibite analcoliche frizzanti**, carbonated/fizzy soft drinks

biblioteca *nf*, library

bidone *nm*, 1 (metal container), can. 2 (imp/exp), drum

biglietto *nm*, note, ticket; **biglietto da visita**, business card; **biglietto omaggio**, complimentary ticket; **biglietto d'andata**, single fare/single ticket; **biglietto d'andata e ritorno**, return fare/return ticket

bilancio *nm*, balance; **bilancio d'esercizio**, balance sheet; **bilancio preventivo**, (fin), budget

biro *nf*, biro

bisogno *nm*, need; **pensiamo che ci sia un bisogno per . .**, we think there is a need for . .; **aver bisogno**, need

bivio *nm*, crossroad

bloccare *vb*, **1** (prices, rates), freeze; **prezzi bloccati**, frozen prices. **2** (mechanical), jam; **la macchina è bloccata**, the machine is jammed

blocco *nm* **note**, note-pad, pad, writing pad

bolletta *nf* (imp/exp), bill; **bolletta d'entrata**, bill of entry (B/E)

bordo *nm*, **1** edge, rim; **il bordo della strada**, the edge of the road; **il bordo della ruota**, wheel rim. **2 a bordo**, aboard; **franco a bordo**, free on board

borsa *nf* (gen), bag; **borsa della spesa**, shopping bag

Borsa *nf* **(valori)**, (fin), stock exchange; **essere introdotto in Borsa**, go public

borsetta *nf*, handbag

BOT *nmpl*, **Buoni Ordinari del Tesoro**, Treasury bonds

bozza *nf* (letters, reports), draft; **bozza di contratto**, draft contract

braca *nf*, sling

brevettare *vb*, patent; **brevettato (-a)** *adj*, patented

brevetto *nm*, patent; **contraffare un brevetto**, infringe a patent

bucatrice *nf* (offce), hole puncher

buco *nm*, hole

buono *nm*, voucher

buono(-a) *adj*, good; **a buon mercato**, cheap

busta *nf*, envelope; **busta affrancata con indirizzo**, SAE, stamped addressed envelope

cacciare *vb* **furtivamente**, poach

cacciatore *nm*, hunter; **cacciatore di teste**, headhunter

cadere *vb*, fall (down), drop, slip down

caduta *nf*, fall

calare *vb*, go down; **le vendite sono calate del 5%**, sales have gone down by 5%

calcolare *vb*, calculate, work out

calcolatore *nm*, calculator

calendario *nm*, calendar

calmo(-a) *adj* (mktg, sales), slack; **attualmente il mercato è molto calmo**, the market is very slack at present

calore *nm*, heat

cambiale *nf* (fin), bill of exchange

cambiamento *nm*, change, shift

cambiare *vb*, change, exchange; **cambiare un assegno**, cash a cheque

cambiavaluta *nm*, currency dealer

cambio *nm*, exchange; **tasso del cambio**, exchange rate

camera *nf*, room; **camera singola**, single room; **camera matrimoniale**, double room; **camera di commercio**, chamber of commerce

camicia *nf*, shirt; **camicia ampia**, loose shirt

camion *nm*, lorry; **camion semi rimorchio**, articulated lorry

camionetta *nf*, van

campagna *nf*, campaign; **fare una campagna**, campaign

campionatura *nf* (mktg, sales), sampling

campione *nm*, 1 (gen), sample, specimen; **campione gratuito**, free sample; **non conforme al campione**, not up to sample. 2 (scale model), model. 3 (sport), champion

campo *nm*, field; **indagine di campo**, field survey; **uno specialista nel campo di . .**, a specialist in the field of . . .

canale *nm*, 1 (gen, telec), channel. 2 (transp), canal

cancellare *vb*, cross out; **si prega di cancellare le sezioni non pertinenti**, please cross out the parts which do not apply

candidato *nm*, applicant

cantiere *nm*, building site, dockyard

capacità *nf*, capacity; **capacità di produzione**, production capacity; **capacità in eccesso**, overcapacity

capire *vb*, understand

capitale *nm* (fin), capital, money; **capitale di partecipazione**, venture capital; **capitale fisso**, capital assets; **capitale liquido**, working capital; **capitale sociale**, authorised capital/registered capital; **capitale versato**, paid-up capital; **beni di capitale**, capital goods; **giro del capitale liquido**, working capital turnover, **revoca di capitale**, call up capital

capitano *nm* (transp), captain

capo *nm*, 1 (leader), head; **capo dipartimento**, head of department; **capo funzionario**, senior executive. 2 **capo d'accusa**, (law), charge/specification of charge

capo-reparto *nm*, foreman

carattere *nm*, character

caratteristica *nf*, feature; **una caratteristica chiave**, a key feature

caricare *vb*, 1 (transp/comp) load; **caricare il programma**, (comp), boot up. 2 (gen), charge. 3 (transp), pick up

caricatore *nm*, 1 (gen), loader. 2 (transp), shipper

carico *nm*, 1 load. 2 (transp), cargo, shipment; **carico aereo**, air cargo; **carico del camion**, lorry load; **carico di ritorno**, back load; **carico, immagazzinamento e consegna**, loading, storage and delivery (LSD); **carico pagante**, (transp), payload; **carico-scarico**, roro, roll-on roll-off; **polizza di carico**, bill of lading; **polizza di carico senza clausola**, clean bill of lading; **si prega di ritirare il carico da . .**, please collect the load from . . .

carico(-a) *adj*, laden, loaded

caro(-a) *adj*, dear, expensive, costly

carrello *nm* **elevatore**, forklift (truck)

carriera *nf*, career

carrozza *nf*, coach

carta *nf*, paper, card; **carta geografica**, map; **carta intestata**, headed paper; **carta millimetrata**, graph paper

cartella *nf*, 1 (contains documents), folder. 2 (for documents, drawings, etc), portfolio

cartellino *nm*, tag

cartoleria *nf*, stationery

cartoncino *nm*, card

cartone *nm*, 1 (gen), cardboard. 2 (imp/exp), carton. 3 (for wine), case. 4 (pictures), cartoon

casa *nf*, house, home; **casa bi-familiare**, semi-detached house; **casa editrice**, publishing house

caso *nm*, case; **il caso del camion**

rubato, the case of the stolen lorry

casko (assicurazione) *nf*, comprehensive insurance

cassa *nf*, **1** (gen), case, box; **una cassa di vino**, a case of wine. **2** (fin), cash; **cassa malattie**, sickness fund; **fondo di cassa**, reserve fund; **pronta cassa**, by cash; **sconto cassa**, cash discount; **movimento di cassa**, cash flow; **avere denaro in cassa**, have money on hand; **pagare alla cassa**, pay at the cash desk; **tenere la cassa**, be in charge of the cash; **libro cassa**, cash book. **3** (imp/exp), crate. **4** (shops), counter

cassaforte *nf*, safe

cassetta *nf*, cassette, tape

cassiere *nm*, cashier

cassino *nm*, rubber

catalogo *nm*, catalogue; **il catalogo elenca tutti i punti di vendita**, the catalogue lists all the sales points

catena *nf*, chain; **catena di montaggio**, assembly line

cattivo(-a) *adj*, bad; **cattivo uso**, misuse; **di cattiva qualità**, cheap

causa *nf*, cause

causare *vb*, cause

cauzione *nf*, **1** (gen), bail; **libertà provvisoria su cauzione**, release on bail. **2** (guarantee), bond. **3** (fin), security

cavo *nm*, cable

CCT, Certificati *nmpl* **di Credito del Tesoro**, Treasury Credit Certificates

CD-ROM, CD-ROM

cedere *vb* (results, trends), sag

cellulare *nm*, cellular phone

centimetro *nm*, centimetre; **centimetro cubo**, cubic centimetre

centrale *adj*, central

centrale *nf* **elettrica**, electric power plant

centrale *nf* **idraulica**, water power plant

centrale *nf* **telefonica**, telephone exchange

centralinista *nm/f*, switchboard operator

centralino *nm* (offce), switchboard

centralizzare *vb*, centralise

centro *nm* **commerciale**, shopping centre

cerchio *nm*, circle

certificato *nm*, certificate; **certificato d'origine**, certificate of origin; **certificato di deposito**, dock warrant

certificazione *nf*, certification

cessare *vb*, **1** (stop) cease. **2** (interruption) discontinue; **cessare la produzione**, discontinue production

charter (volo) *nm*, charter

check in *nm*, check in

chiamare *vb*, call

chiamata *nf*, call; **chiamata a carico del destinatario**, reverse-charges call

chiaro(-a) *adj*, clear; **è chiaro che i prezzi sono bassi**, it is clear that the prices are low

chiatta *nf* (transp), barge

chiave *nf*, key; **una parte chiave**, a key part; **una caratteristica chiave**, a key feature; **un fattore chiave**, a key factor

chiavi *nf* **in mano**, **1** (contracts), turnkey. **2** (car purchase), on the road; **l'auto costa Lit 10.000.000 chiavi in mano**, the price of the car on the road is 10,000,000 Italian lire

chiedere *vb*, ask; **chiedere scusa**,

apologise; **chiedere il rimborso di un prestito**, call in a loan, **chiedere un aumento di salario**, claim a wage increase; **chiedere uno sciopero**, call for a strike

chilometraggio *nm* (distance in km), mileage

chimico *nm*, chemist

chimico(-a) *adj*, chemical, **prodotti chimici**, chemicals

chiudere *vb*, shut, close; **chiudere una ditta**, close down a firm; **chiudere in pareggio**, (fin) break even

chiuso(-a) *adj*, shut

chiusura *nf*, closing, shut-down; **data di chiusura**, closing date

cibo *nm*, food

ciclico(-a) *adj*, cyclical

ciclo *nm*, cycle

cifra *nf*, figure

cifrare *vb* (messages), code

circa *adv*, about, nearly, approximately, around; **il villaggio industriale è a circa 3 miglia dal centro città**, the industrial estate is about 3 miles from the town centre; **il prezzo è circa Lit 3000**, the price is around 3000 lire

circolante *adj* (fin), current; **attivo circolante**, current assets

circolare *adj*, round

circolazione *nf*, circulation; **mettere in circolazione**, circulate

circondare *vb*, **1** (surround), circle. **2** (make a ring around), ring

circostanze *nfpl*, circumstances

circuito *nm*, circuit; **circuito chiuso**, closed circuit

citare *vb* **a giudizio**, (law), sue

citare *vb* **in giudizio**, (law), summons

citazione *nf* (law), summons

città *nf*, town, city

classificare *vb*, **1** (gen), classify **2** (figures), break down

classificatore *nm* **ad anelli** (offce), ringbinder

clausola *nf*, clause; **clausola addizionale** (law), rider; **clausola condizionale** (law), proviso; **polizza di carico senza clausola**, clean bill of lading

client *nm*, **1** client, customer; **schede clienti**, client database; **fedeltà del cliente**, customer loyalty. **2** (hotel), guest

clone *nm*, clone

codice *nm*, code; **codice a sbarre**, bar code; **codice civile**, civil law; **codice di commercio**, mercantile law; **codice di onore**, code of honour; **codice di procedura penale**, code of criminal procedure; **codice marittimo**, navigation law; **codice penale**, penal code; **codice stradale**, highway code; **codice telefonico**, STD code

codificare *vb* (law), code

cogliere *vb*, pick, gather

coincidenza *nf*, **1** (gen), coincidence. **2** (travel), connection

coinvolgere *vb*, involve; **essere coinvolto(-a) in . . .**, be involved in . . .

colaggio *nm* (imp/exp), leakage

colazione *nf*, breakfast; **pensione con prima colazione**, bed and breakfast

colla *nf*, glue

collegamento *nm*, connection; **fare un collegamento**, make a connection

collegare *vb*, connect, link

collezione *nf*, collection; **fare una collezione**, collect

collocamento *nm*, placement

colonna *nf*, column (of figures, etc)

colonnina *nf* **di soccorso**, (on motorways), emergency phone

colpire *vb*, hit; **siamo stati colpiti dal fattore dell'alto prezzo del carburante**, we have been hit by the high price of fuel

colpo *nm*, blow, stroke; **colpo di genio**, brainstorm

coltivazione *nf*, farming

combinare *vb*, combine; **sforzi combinati**, combined efforts

combustione *nf*, combustion; **motore a combustione interna**, internal combustion engine

comitato *nm*, committee; **comitato esecutivo**, executive committee

commentare *vb*, comment

commerciale *adj*, commercial, trading, trade; **bilancio commerciale**, trade balance; **esercizio commerciale**, trading year; **fiera commerciale**, trade fair; **zona commerciale**, trading estate

commercialista *nm*, chartered accountant

commerciare *vb* **in**, deal in . ., trade in; **la società commercia in plastica**, the company trades in plastics

commercio *nm*, commerce; trade

commestibile *adj*, edible

commissione *nf*, commission, charge; **commissione d'inchiesta**, court of enquiry; **commissioni bancarie**, charges

compagnia *nf* (fin), company

compagno *nm*, mate

comparativo(-a) *adj*, comparative

compatto(-a) *adj*, compact, firm; **disco compatto**, compact disc, CD; **terreno compatto**, firm ground

compensare *vb*, **1** (gen), compensate. **2** (a loss), make up for

compenso *nm*, compensation

competenze *nfpl* (CV), skills

competitivo(-a) *adj*, competitive; **prezzi competitivi**, competitive prices

compilare *vb*, fill in, complete

compito *nm*, task

completare *vb*, complete, finalise; **completare un lavoro**, complete a job

completo(-a) *adj*, complete, full; **una serie completa di documenti**, a complete set of documents; **un contenitore completo**, a full container

complotto *nm*, plot

componente *nm*, component

comporre *vb*, compose, make up of; **composto di . . .** composed of . .; **essere composto da**, be made up of . . .

comprare *vb*, buy

compratore *nm*, **compratrice** *nf*, buyer, purchaser

comprensione *nf*, understanding; **sono grato della sua comprensione**, I am grateful for your understanding

comprensivo(-a) *adj*, **1** (gen) comprehensive, comprehending **2** sympathetic, understanding, compassionate

compreso(-a) *adj*, inclusive; **consegna compresa**, inclusive of delivery; **tutto compreso**, inclusive terms

compromesso *nm*, compromise

computer *nm*, computer; **operatore di computer**, computer operator; **computer portatile**, laptop

comunicare *vb*, communicate

comunicato *nm*, bulletin; **comunicato di guerra**, war bulletin

comunicazione *nf*, communication; **comunicazione della società**, corporate communication

concentrarsi *vb* **(su)** . ., focus (on) . . .

concessionario *nm*, (exclusive) dealer; concessionaire

concetto *nm* **assistito da computer**, computer-assisted design

concorrente *nm*, competitor, rival; **il concorrente principale è . .**, the main rival is . . .

concorrenza *nf*, competition

concorrere *vb*, compete; **concorrere per un contratto**, tender

condizione *nf*, condition; **condizioni lavorative**, working conditions; **condizione sociale**, status; **in buone condizioni**, undamaged; **le condizioni del mercato sono buone**, market conditions are good; **le nostre condizioni di vendita**, our conditions of sale; **la macchina è in ottime condizioni**, the machine is in very good condition

condizioni *nfpl* (mktg, sales), terms; **condizioni di pagamento**, terms of payment; **secondo le condizioni di . .**, under the terms of . . .

condurre *vb*, conduct; **condurre un'indagine**, conduct a survey

conduttura *nf* **principale**, (electr), mains electricity; **funziona sulla conduttura principale**, runs on mains electricity

conferenza *nf*, conference, talk; **sala** *nf* **conferenze**, conference hall; **fare una conferenza su . . .** give a talk on . . .

confermare *vb*, confirm

confermato(-a) *adj*, confirmed; **non confermato**, unconfirmed

confessare *vb*, (gen), confess, admit to

confidenziale *adj*, confidential; **un documento confidenziale**, a confidential document

Confindustria *nf*, Confederation of Italian Industry

confiscare *vb* (law), confiscate

conformarsi *vb* **a**, comply with

congedare *vb* dismiss (a person)

congedo *nm*, leave; **essere in congedo**, be on leave

congelare *vb*, freeze

congratularsi *vb* **con**, congratulate; **mi congratulo con lei**, I congratulate you

congratulazioni *nfpl*, congratulations

connesso(-a) *adj*, related; **spese** *nfpl* **connesse**, related charges

conoscenza *nf*, knowledge; **una buona conoscenza del mercato**, a good knowledge of the market; **conoscenze linguistiche**, (CV) languages spoken

consapevole *adj*, aware, conscious; **essere consapevole**, be aware of

consegna *nf*, **1** (gen), delivery; **termini di consegna**, delivery arrangements; **data di consegna**, delivery date; **data limite di consegna**, delivery deadline; **nota di consegna**, delivery note. **2** (one of a series of shipments), consignment

consegnare *vb*, **1** (gen), deliver; **consegnato(-a)**, delivered; **non consegnato**, undelivered; **consegnato franco dogana**, delivered duty paid; **consegnato alla frontiera**, (DAF), delivered at frontier. **2** (documents), surrender; hand over; **consegnare i documenti a . .**, surrender the documents to . . .

conserva *nf*, preserve; **mettere in conserva**, can

conservare *vb*, preserve, keep; **conservare degli alimenti**, preserve food; **si prega di conservare la ricevuta**, please keep the receipt

considerare *vb*, consider

considerevolmente *adv*, considerably; **considerevolmente più alto/più basso del . .**, considerably higher/lower than . .; **considerevolmente di più/di meno del . .**, considerably more/less than . . .

consigliare *vb*, advise

consigliere *nm* **delegato** (pers), managing director

consiglio *nm*, 1 advice. 2 (pers), **Consiglio d'Amministrazione**, Board of Directors

consociata *nf* **(società)**, subsidiary (company)

consolare *adj*, consular; **fattura consolare**, consular invoice

console *nm*, consul

consulente *nm/f*, consultant; **una ditta di consulenti**, a firm of consultants

consulenza *nf*, consultancy; **su una base di consulenza**, on a consultancy basis

consumatore *nm*, **consumatrice** *nf*, consumer; **protezione del consumatore**, consumer protection

consumo *nm*, consumption

contabile *nm/f*, bookkeeper, accountant, accounts clerk

contabilità *nf*, accounting

container *nm*, container; **carico incompleto del container**, less than container load (LCL)

contaminare *vb*, pollute

contaminazione *nf*, pollution

contanti *nmpl*, cash; **in contanti**, in cash; **abbiamo 500 mila lire in contanti**, we have 500 thousand lire in cash; **contanti alla consegna**, cash on delivery; **contanti all'ordine**, cash with order; **contanti prima della consegna**, CBD, cash before delivery; **vendita per contanti**, cash sale;

contare *vb*, count; **contare su**, count on, bank on

contattare *vb*, contact; **la prego di contattarmi a questo numero**, please contact me at this number; **contattate il nostro ufficio**, please contact our office

contatto *nm*, touch

contenere *vb*, hold; **il nostro deposito contiene scorte considerevoli di . .**, our warehouse holds considerable stocks of . . .

contenitore *nm*, (transp) container; **nave con contenitori**, container ship; **contenitore refrigerato**, refrigerated container; **contenitore sigillato**, sealed container; **contenitore completo**, full container

contenitorizzato(-a) *adj*, containerised

contingente *nf* (imp/exp), quota; **imporre una contingente**, impose a quota

continuare *vb*, continue; **continua . .**, to be continued . . .

continuo(-a) *adj*, continuous; **produzione continua**, continuous production; **carta continua**, continuous stationery

conto *nm*, 1 (fin), account; **versare del denaro su un conto**, pay money into an account; **conto acquisti**, accounts receivable to purchases; **conto di deposito**, deposit account 2 (to be paid), bill; **il conto, per favore**, the bill, please; **conto profitti**, (fin), trading account; **per conto di**, on behalf of, on account of; **conto pubblicità**, advertising account; **conto vendite**, accounts receivable to sales

contrabbandare *vb*, smuggle

contraente *nm/f*, contractor

contraffare *vb* **un brevetto**, infringe a patent

contrarre *vb* (fin), shrink

contrassegnare *vb*, countersign

contrattare *vb*, contract; **contrattato(-a)**, contracted

contrattempo *nm*, **1** mishap. **2** hitch

contratto *nm*, contract; **contratto a durata determinata**, fixed term contract; **contratto d'affitto**, lease; **cessione contratto d'affitto**, leaseback; **contratto d'impiego** (pers), contract of employment; **contratto di noleggio** (transp), charter-party

contravvenire *vb*, (law), contravene

contro *adv*, against; **contro tutti i rischi**, against all risks; **il Consiglio ha deliberato contro il progetto**, the Board has decided against the project; **essere contro corrente**, be against the trend

controbilanciare *vb*, offset

controllare *vb*, check, monitor; **controllare l'inflazione**, check inflation

controllo *nm*, control, check; **lista di controllo**, checklist

controstallia *nf* (transp), demurrage

conveniente *adj*, convenient, suitable; **essere conveniente**, be convenient; **quando sarebbe conveniente per una visita presso di noi?**, when would it be convenient to visit us?; **è un'ora conveniente?**, is this a suitable time?

convenuto(-a) *adj*, agreed

convocare *vb*, call (meetings); **convocare una riunione di comitato**, call a committee meeting

cooperazione *nf*, **1** (gen), cooperation. **2** networking (cooperation between companies)

coperchio *nm*, top (of a container)

copertura *nf*, cover; **nota di copertura**, cover note

copia *nf*, copy; **copia autenticata**, certified copy; **copia su carta**, (comp), hard copy; **copie multiple**, multiple copies; **copia firmata**, signed copy

copiare *vb*, copy

coprire *vb*, cover; **coperto(-a)**, covered; **essere coperto per 5 milioni di lire di rischi**, be covered for 5 million lire risks

corporativo(-a), *adj*, corporate

corredo *nm*, **1** outfit. **2** kit; **tipo di corredo**, kit form

corrente *nf*, **1** (gen), current; **corrente alterna**, alternating current; **corrente diretta**, direct current; **essere contro corrente**, be against the trend; **mettere al corrente**, brief, inform (on/about). **2** (electrical) power

corrente *adj*, **1** running, flowing; **acqua corrente**, running water. **2** current; **mese corrente**, current month; **opinione corrente**, current opinion; **prezzo corrente**, current price

corriera *nf*, coach

corrispondenza *nf*, (offce) mail; **ordinazione per corrispondenza**, mail order

corrispondere *vb* **a** (equivalent to), correspond to; **il campione corrisponde al nostro ordine**, the sample corresponds to our order

corso *nm*, course

corte *nf*, court

cortile *nm*, yard

corto(-a) *adj*, short; **abito corto**, short dress

coso *nm*, (colloquial), **1** (gen), thing. **2** (unflattering), gadget

costo *nm*, cost; **costo e nolo**, (imp/exp), cost and freight; **costo, assicurazione e nolo**, cost, insurance and freight (CIF); **indice del costo della vita**, cost of living index; **prezzo del costo**, cost price; **costo per migliaia**, cost per thousand (CPT); **costo supplementare**, additional charge

costoso(-a) *adj*, costly; valuable

costruire *vb*, build

costruzione *nf*, **1** (gen), construction. **2** (activity), building. **3** (ind), design; **motore di buona costruzione**, motor of good design. **4** **costruzione navale**, shipbuilding

creare *vb*, create, start; **creare una società**, start a company

creazione *nf*, creation

credito *nm*, credit; **credito appoggiato**, back to back credit; **credito permanente**, (fin), revolving credit; **a credito**, on credit; **carta di credito**, credit card; **nota di credito**, credit note; **termini di credito**, credit terms; **transferimento di credito**, credit transfer; **essere in credito** be in credit

creditore *nm*, creditor

crescere *vb*, grow

crescita *nf*, growth

crimine *nm*, (serious) crime

crisi *nf*, crisis

criticare *vb*, criticise

croce *nf*, cross; **fare una croce**, tick, put a cross

crollare *vb*, **1** (sales), collapse; **il prezzo è crollato**, the price has collapsed. **2** (mktg, sales), slump; **i profitti sono crollati**, profits have slumped

crudo(-a) *adj* (not cooked), raw; **carne cruda**, raw meat; **prosciutto crudo**, raw ham

cura *nf*, care; **con cura**, with care

curatore *nm*, **curatrice** *nf*, **1** (gen), trustee. **2** (law, fin), receiver; **nominare un curatore fallimentare**, call in the receiver

curriculum vitae *nm*, curriculum vitae, CV

curva *nf* (gen, fin), curve

curvarsi *vb* (shelves, materials), sag

D

danneggiato(-a) *adj*, damaged

danno *nm*, damage; **esaminare i danni**, (ins), survey damage

dare *vb*, give; **dare dei risultati migliori**, outperform; **dare istruzioni**, instruct; **dare la mancia**, tip; **dare le dimissioni**, give notice, resign; **dare una franchigia**, franchise; **darsi al . .**, take to . .; **si da al gioco**, he takes to gambling

darsena *nf*, marina

data *nf*, date; **data di nascita**, date of birth; **data interruzione**, cut-off date; **data limite di consegna**, deadline for delivery

datare *vb* (document), date

dati *nmpl*, (comm), details *npl*; **i dati del cliente**, customer details; **dati della società**, details of a company

datore *nm* **di lavoro**, employer

dattilografare *vb*, type

dattilografo(-a) *nm/f*, typist, keyboard operator; **dattilografo (-a) specializzato(-a)**, audiotypist, **sedia per dattilografo(-a)**, typist's chair

debito *nm*, debit, debt; **essere indebitato(-a)**, to be in debt

debitore *nm*, **debitrice** *nf*, debtor

debole *adj*, weak

decidere *vb*, decide

decidersi *vb*, make up one's mind

decisione *nf*, decision; **decisione collettiva**, joint decision

deciso(-a) *adj*, decisive, firm; **un carattere deciso**, a firm character

declinare *vb* (say no), decline

declino *nm*, decline

decollare *vb* (transp), (plane), take off

dedicarsi *vb* **(al proprio lavoro)**, apply oneself (to one's work)

defalcare *vb*, write off (a bad debt)

definitivamente *adv*, definitely

definito(-a) *adj*, definite, firm; **un ordine definito**, a firm order

defunto(-a) *adj*, late; **il defunto presidente**, the late president

delegare *vb*, delegate

delegato *nm*, representative

delineare *vb*, outline

denaro *nm* (coins, notes), money

depositare *vb*, 1 (gen), deposit. 2 (goods), store; **depositare in una banca**, bank

deposito *nm*, 1 (gen), deposit; **conto deposito**, deposit account; **certificato di deposito**, dock warrant. 2 (warehousing service) storage. 3 (for storage), store; **deposito (frigorifero)**, (cold) storage; **deposito rifiuti**, refuse tip

depresso(-a) *adj*, depressed, flat; **il mercato è depresso**, the market is flat; **mi sento un po' depresso**, I feel a bit depressed/flat

deputato *nm*, member of parliament

derivato *nm*, spin off, by-product; **un derivato di . .**, a by-product of . . .

derubare *vb*, rob

descrizione *nf*, description; **descrizione delle merci**, description of goods

desiderare *vb*, want

destinatario *nm*, 1 (gen), addressee. 2 (imp/exp), consignee

deteriorato(-a) *adj*, (slightly

damaged goods), shop-soiled

detraibile adj, deductible

detrarre vb, deduct; **si prega di detrarre il costo di . . . da . .**, please deduct the cost of . . . from . . .

detrazione nf, deduction

dettagliante nm, retailer

dettagliare vb, detail, itemise

dettagliato(-a) adj, detailed; **fattura dettagliata**, itemised invoice/bill

dettaglio nm, 1 (gen), detail. 2 (sales), retail; **commercio al dettaglio**, retail trade; **vendere al dettaglio**, retail; **prezzo al dettaglio**, retail price

dettare vb, dictate

dettatura nf, dictation

deviazione nf, deviation

diagramma nm, graph, diagram; **diagramma di Venn**, Venn diagram

diapositiva nf, slide

dibattere vb, debate

dibattito nm, debate

dichiarare vb, declare, state; **dichiarare fallimento**, go bust, file for bankruptcy

dichiarazione nf, declaration, statement; **dichiarazione dei redditi**, tax return

diesel nm, diesel; **motore diesel**, diesel engine

difendere vb **(contro)**, defend (against)

difesa nf (gen, law, etc), defence

difetto nm, defect, fault, flaw; **pensiamo che il problema sia dovuto a un difetto del sistema**, we believe the problem is due to a fault in the system

difettoso(-a) adj, defective, faulty

differenza nf, 1 (gen), difference; **la differenza tra . . . e . . . è**, the difference between . . . and. . . . is. 2 (eg differing), discrepancy

differimento nm, (postponement), shelving

differire vb **un progetto**, shelve a project

digitale adj, digital

dimensione nf, 1 (gen), dimension; **le dimensioni del carico sono 5 per 6**, the dimensions of the load are 5 by 6. 2 (transp) measurement, size; **quali sono le dimensioni del carico?**, what is the size of the load?

dimenticato(-a) adj, forgotten

dimettersi vb, resign

diminuire vb, 1 (gen), decrease. 2 (get worse), decline; **gli affari diminuiscono**, business is declining. 3 (rates, prices) ease; **i tassi sono diminuiti** rates have eased. 4 fall; **i prezzi sono diminuiti quest'anno**, prices have fallen this year. 5 (rates, trends), slacken

diminuzione nf, 1 (gen), decrease. 2 (sales), decline, 3 (slackening), fall off

dimissioni nfpl, notice; **dare le dimissioni**, give notice

dipendere vb **da**, depend on

diplomarsi vb, qualify

diretto(-a) adj, 1 (gen), direct; **corrente diretta**, direct current; **linea diretta**, direct line; **vendita diretta**, direct sales. 2 through; **treno diretto**, through train; **volo diretto**, through flight;

direttore nm, manager, director; executive; **vice direttore**, assistant manager; **direttore alle vendite**, sales manager; **direttore amministrativo**, finance director; **direttore del consiglio d'amministrazione**, board director; **direttore del**

marketing, marketing director; **direttore generale**, chief executive; **direttore di squadra**, shift manager; **direttore d'officina**, works manager

direzione *nf*, **1** (gen), direction. **2** (of a company), directorate, management

dirigente *nm*, executive

dirigere *vb*, **1** channel; **dirigere le vendite verso . .**, channel the sale towards . . . **2** manage, run; **dirigere una ditta**, manage a firm; **dirigere una sezione**, run a department

diritto *nm*, right; **avere il diritto di dire . .**, have the right to say . .; **avere diritto a . .**, be eligible for . . .

disapprovato(-a) *adj*, unapproved

disco *nm*, **1** (comp), disc. **2** (music), record

discussione *nf*, discussion; **discussione a ruota libera**, brainstorming session; **discussione animata**, heated discussion; **discussioni**, talks

discutere *vb*, discuss; debate

disegnare *vb*, **1** (gen), design. **2** (a plan), draft

disegno *nm*, **1** (gen), design. **2** (ornamentation), pattern. **3** (drawing), plan.

disfare *vb* (**le valigie**), unpack (bags)

disimballare *vb*, unpack

disoccupato *nm*, unemployed

disoccupazione *nf*, unemployment

disonesto(-a) *adj*, dishonest; **azione disonesta**, malpractice

dispari *adj*, odd; **numeri dispari**, odd numbers

disperso *nm*, missing person

disponibile *adj*, available; **non disponibile**, unavailable

dispositivo *nm* (small piece of equipment), gadget

disputa *nf* (law), argument; **avere una disputa**, have an argument

distanza *nf*, **1** (gen), distance. **2** (distance to travel) drive; **l'ufficio è a breve distanza dalla città**, the office is a short drive from the town

distinti saluti *nfpl*, yours faithfully, yours sincerely; **colgo/cogliamo l'occasione per porgere i miei/nostri più distinti saluti**, yours faithfully/yours sincerely; **mi/ci è gradita l'occasione per porgere i miei/nostri più distinti saluti**, yours faithfully/yours sincerely

distintivo *nm*, badge

distribuire *vb*, distribute

distributore *nm*, distributor; **distributore automatico**, vending machine, slot machine; **distributore automatico di banconote**, ATM, Automatic Teller Machine; **distributore esclusivo** (mktg, sales), sole distributor

distribuzione *nf*, distribution; **problemi di distribuzione**, distribution problems; **rete di distribuzione**, distribution network

ditta *nf*, firm, company

divergenza *nf* (difference of opinions), gap

diversificare *vb*, diversify

dividendo *nm*, dividend

dividere *vb*, divide, split (into); **dividere a metà**, halve; **lo dividiamo in quattro parti**, we split it into four parts

divisione *nf*, division

documento *nm*, **1** (gen), document; **documenti contro accettazione**, (imp/exp), documents against acceptance;

documenti contro pagamento, (imp/exp), documents against payment. **2** (mktg, sales), artwork. **3** (documents, forms), paperwork; **documenti d'imbarco**, shipping documents; **documento di trasporto misto**, combined transport document

dogana *nf*, customs; **franco dogana**, duty paid

doganale *adj*, customs; **bolletta** *nf* **doganale**, customs certificate; **magazzino** *nm* **doganale**, bonded warehouse; **visita** *nf* **doganale**, customs inspection

doganiere *nm*, customs officer

domanda *nf*, **1** (request for a job or loan) application; **domanda d'impiego**, job application form. **2** (gen), demand. **3** (information), enquiry

domandare *vb*, demand

dominante *adj*, dominant; **la società ha una posizione dominante nel mercato**, the company has a dominant position in the market

dominare *vb*, dominate; **dominare il mercato**, dominate the market

dopo *adv*, after; **ci metteremo in contatto con voi dopo che abbiamo provato i campioni**, we will contact you after we have tested the samples; **dopo la data**, after date; **90 giorni dopo la data**, 90 days after date; **dopo la vostra visita**, after your visit

dopo vendita *nf*, after sales; **il nostro servizio dopo vendita**, our after-sales service

dovere *vb* (be in debt), owe

dovuto(-a) *adj*, due

dozzina *nf*, dozen; **una dozzina di bottiglie**, a dozen bottles; **una dozzina di uova**, a dozen eggs; **a dozzine**, by the dozen; **mezza dozzina**, half-dozen

drogare *vb* **(un animale)**, tamper

(with animals)

duplicare *vb* (offce), duplicate

duplicato *nm* (offce), duplicate; **in duplicato**, in duplicate

durante *adv*, during, pending; **durante questo dibattito**, pending this debate

durata *nf*, duration

durevole *adj*, durable; **beni durevoli**, durables

duro(-a) *adj*, hard; **tempi duri**, hard times

E

eccedere *vb*, exceed

eccessivo(-a) *adj*, excessive

eccesso *nm*, excess

economia *nf*, **1** (subject, study), economics. **2** economy (of a country); **l'economia italiana e l'economia inglese**, the Italian and the English economy

economico(-a) *adj*, **1** (gen), economic. **2** (saves money), economical; **non economico**, uneconomical

economizzare *vb*, economise, save

economo(-a) *adj* (uses little), economical

editore *nm*, publisher

editrice *adj*, publishing; **casa editrice**, publishing house

edificio *nm*, building; premises; **fuori dall'edificio**, off the premises

effetto *nm*, effect; **avere un effetto su . .**, have an effect on . .; **effetto secondario**, side effect

effettuare *vb*, carry out, effettuare **una vendita**, (comm), make a sale; **effettuare il pagamento**, remit

efficace *adj*, effective

efficiente *adj*, efficient

efficienza *nf*, efficiency

eguagliare *vb*, equal

eleggibile *adj*, eligible; **essere eleggibile**, be eligible

elencare *vb*, list; **il catalogo elenca tutti i punti di vendita**, the catalogue lists all the sales points

elenco *nm*, list; **elenco di indirizzi**, mailing list; **elenco telefonico**, telephone directory

elettorale *adj*, electoral; **fare un giro elettorale**, canvass

elettrico(-a) *adj*, electrical; **attrezzatura elettrica**, electrical equipment

elettrodomestici *nmpl*, domestic appliances

elettronica *nf*, electronics

elettronico(-a) *adj*, electronic; **posta elettronica**, electronic mail; **sistema elettronico**, electronic system; **scambio dati elettronici**, electronic data interchange

eliminare *vb*, cut out

embargo *nm*, embargo; **togliere un embargo**, lift an embargo; **mettere un embargo su . .**, place an embargo on . . .

emettere *vb*, issue; **emettere una polizza di carico**, issue a bill of lading; **emettere un comunicato stampa**, issue a press release

emissione *nf* (fin), issue (of new shares); **emissione di diritti di sottoscrizione**, rights issue

energia *nf* (electr), power

enorme *adj*, huge

entrare *vb*, go in, come in, get in; **entrare dei dati**, (comp), input

entrata *nf*, **1** (gen), entrance, admittance; **entrata principale**, main entrance. **2** entry; **porto d'entrata**, POE, port of entry. **3** (fin), revenue

entrate *nfpl* (fin), incomings

equilibrare *vb*, balance

equipaggio *nm*, crew

ermetico(-a) *adj*, airtight

errore *nm*, mistake, error, fault; **salvo errori ed omissioni**, errors and omissions excepted; **fare un errore**, make a mistake; **nessun**

errore, zero fault

esami *nmpl* **di maturità**, A~levels, advanced level exams

esaminare *vb*, **1** (gen), examine. **2** (ins) survey; **esaminare i danni**, survey damage. **3** (property), view

esaurito(-a) *adj*, out of stock

esclusivo(-a) *adj*, **1** (gen), exclusive; **affare esclusivo**, exclusive deal; **diritti esclusivi**, exclusive rights. **2** (mktg, sales), sole; **agente esclusivo**, sole agent; **distributore esclusivo**, sole distributor

esecutivo(-a) *adj*, executive; **comitato esecutivo**, executive committee; **poteri esecutivi**, executive powers

eseguire *vb*, carry out, process; **eseguire un progetto**, carry out a project; **eseguire le istruzioni**, carry out instructions; **eseguire un ordine**, process an order

esercitare *vb* **una professione**, practise a profession

esercitarsi *vb*, practise

esercizio *nm*, **esercizio (finanziario)** business year; **esercizio commerciale**, trading year; **bilancio d'esercizio**, operating budget; **capitale d'esercizio** operating capital; **costi di'esercizio**, operating costs; **spese d'esercizio**, operating/running expenses

esibire *vb*, **1** (mktg, sales), exhibit. **2** (a product) demonstrate

esibizione *nf*, **1** (gen), exhibition, show. **2** (of product), demonstration

esigente *adj*, demanding

esiliato *nm*, outcast

esorbitante *adj* (fin), steep; **un aumento esorbitante**, a steep rise

espansione *nf*, expansion; **in espansione**, expanding; **società in espansione**, expanding company; **mercato in espansione**, expanding market

esperienza *nf*, **1** (gen), experience; **acquistare esperienza nel marketing**, gain experience in marketing. **2** (pers), track record; **avere una buona esperienza**, have a good track record; **esperienza professionale**, (CV), employment history

esperimento *nm*, experiment

esperto *nm*, expert

esperto(-a) *adj*, experienced; **cerchiamo un direttore esperto**, we are looking for an experienced manager

esplorare *vb*, **1** (gen), explore. **2** (mktg, sales), prospect

esplosione *nf*, outburst

esporre *vb*, **1** (new model), bring out. **2** (product), display

esportare *vb*, export

esportatore *nm*, exporter

esportazione *nf*, export; **direttore all'esportazione**, export manager

espositore *nm*, exhibitor

esposizione *nf*, exhibition; **centro esposizione**, exhibition centre

espresso *nm*, (train), express; **consegna per espresso**, express delivery

espresso(-a) *adj*, express; **per espresso**, (by) express

esprimere *vb* **a parole**, word

essenziale *adj*, essential, basic; **attrezzatura essenziale**, basic equipment

essere *vb*, be; **essere conforme a . .**, correspond to . . .

esterno(-a) *adj*, external, outside; **per uso esterno**, for outside use

estero(-a) *adj*, foreign; **commercio**

estero, foreign trade

estero *nm*, foreign countries; **andare all'estero**, go abroad

estraneo *nm*, outsider

estraneo(-a) *adj*, foreign; **estraneo alla legge**, outside the law; **un corpo estraneo**, a foreign body

estrudere *vb*, extrude

estrusione *nf*, extrusion; **in estrusione**, extruded

etichetta *nf*, 1 label; **etichetta autodesiva**, sticky label. 2 code of conduct; **etichetta professionale**, professional code

etichettare *vb*, label

evento *nm*, event

eventuale *adj* (possible), eventual

eventualmente *adv*, possibly, eventually

evidenza *nf*, evidence; **mettere in evidenza**, emphasise

evidenziatore *nm* (offce), highlighter

evitare *vb*, avoid

ex molo, ex-quay

ex nave, ex-ship

ex stabilimento, ex-works

F

fabbrica *nf*, plant; **la società ha una nuova fabbrica a Bologna**, the company has a new plant in Bologna; **dalla fabbrica**, ex-mill; **marchio di fabbrica**, trade mark

fabbricante *nm*, maker, manufacturer

fabbricare *vb*, make, manufacture

fabbricato(-a) *adj* in . ., (imp/exp), made in . . .

facile *adj*, easy

facilitare *vb*, ease

facilitazioni *nfpl*, facilities; **una gamma completa di facilitazioni**, a comprehensive range of facilities

facoltativo(-a) *adj*, optional

fallimento *nm*, bankruptcy, failure; **andare in fallimento**, go bankrupt, go bust; **curatore fallimentare** (fin), receiver

fallire *vb*, 1 fail, miss; **tutti i nostri piani fallirono**, all our plans failed; **fallire il bersaglio**, miss the target. 2 fall through; **le trattative sono fallite a causa di . .**, the negotiations fell through because of . . .

falsificare *vb*, falsify; fabricate

falsificazione *nf*, fabrication

falso(-a) *adj*, false; untrue

fare *vb*, do, make

fare affidamento su, rely on

fare i bagagli, pack

fare il grafico, chart

fare il pieno, fill up

fare innovazioni, innovate

fare la fila, queue

fare la media, average

fare la messa a punto, debug

fare la somma, add up

fare progressi, go ahead

fare scalo, stop

fare una conferenza su . ., give a talk on . . .

fare una domanda d'impiego, make an application

fare un bagno, take a bath

fare un cerchio, circle

fare un'inchiesta, make an inquiry

fare un'inserzione per un posto, advertise

fare un'offerta, make an offer

fare uno studio del mercato, survey the market

fare un rapporto su, report on

fare un sondaggio, sample opinion

far fare, (oblige) make

far fronte ai propri impegni, meet one's commitments

far funzionare, operate

far pagare, charge for

far pratica, practise

far visita a, pay a visit to

farmaceutico(-a) *adj*, pharmaceutical; **industria farmaceutica**, pharmaceutical industry

farmacista *nm/f*, (dispensing) chemist

fase *nf*, phase; **la prima fase del progetto**, the first phase of the project; **fase di raffreddamento**, cooling-off period

fattibile *adj*, feasible

fatto(-a) *adj*, made; **fatto di**, made of; **fatto su misura**, made

to measure

fattore *nm*, **1** factor; **è un fattore determinante**, it is a deciding factor; **uno dei fattori principali nella decisione è stato quello di . .**, a major factor in the decision was . . . **2** farmer

fattura *nf*, invoice, bill; **valore** *nm* **della fattura**, invoice value; **fattura proforma**, proforma invoice; **fattura quietanzata**, receipted invoice

fatturare *vb*, invoice

fatturazione *nf*, invoicing

fax *nm*, fax

fedeltà *nf*, loyalty; **fedeltà alla marca**, brand loyalty

Federazione dei Sindacati Britannici *nf*, Trades Union Congress, (TUC)

femminile *adj*, female

ferie *nfpl*, holidays; **il signor Sellitri è in ferie**, Mr Sellitri is on holiday

fermare *vb*, stop, switch off; **fermare il motore**, turn off the engine

fermarsi *vb*, stay; **fermarsi a . .**, call at . . .

ferramenta *nm*, hardware, ironware; **negoziante di ferramenta**, ironmonger

ferro *nm*, iron

ferrovia *nf*, railway; **trasportare un rimorchio per ferrovia**, (transp) piggyback; **per ferrovia**, by rail; **FS, Ferrovie dello Stato**, Italian State Railways

ferroviario(-a) *adj*, railway; **trasporto ferroviario**, rail transport; **nolo ferroviario**, rail freight

fiato *nm*, breath; **senza fiato**, out of breath

fiducia *nf*, confidence, goodwill, trust;

avere fiducia in . ., have confidence in . ., trust

fiera *nf*, fair

figli *nmpl* (forms), children

fila *nf*, row; **in fila**, in a row

filiale *nf* (part of group of companies), branch

finale *adj*, final

finalizzare *vb*, finalise

finalmente *adv*, finally

finanza *nf*, finance

finanziamento *nm*, financing; **auto-finanziamento**, self-financing

finanziare *vb*, finance

finanziario(-a) *adj*, financial; **le disposizioni finanziarie**, the financial arrangements; **direttore finanziario**, financial manager; **esercizio finanziario**, accounting period, business year

finanziatore *nm*, **1** (somebody who can finance someone), financer. **2** financial backer

finanziere *nm*, financier

fine *adj*, fine

finire *vb*, **1** (gen), finish. **2** come to an end; **prodotti finiti**, finished goods/products

finitura *nf*, finish

firma *nf*, signature; **firma autorizzata**, authorised signature

firmare *vb*, sign; **copia firmata**, signed copy

fisco *nm*, Inland Revenue

fissare *vb*, fix

fisso(-a) *adj*, fixed; **tasso fisso**, fixed rate

flessibile *adj*, flexible

flusso *nm*, flow; **flusso di capitali**, flow of capital

fluttuante *adj*, floating; **tassi fluttuanti**, floating rates

fluttuare *vb*, fluctuate

fluttuazioni *nfpl*, fluctuations; **il cambio dei prezzi è dovuto alle fluttuazioni nel tasso di interesse**, the change in prices is due to fluctuations in the interest rates

foglio *nm*, sheet, leaf; **foglio d'informazioni**, newsletter; **foglio di via** (imp/exp), waybill

fondare *vb*, establish, found; **questa società è stata fondata nel 1945**, this company was established in 1945; **la cooperativa è stata fondata nel 1900**, the cooperative was founded in 1900

fondere *vb*, merge; **fondere con . .**, merge with . . .

fondo *nm* fund; **fondo comune**, pool; **mettere in un fondo comune**, pool

formalità *nf*, formality; **senza formalità**, informal; **una discussione senza formalità**, an informal discussion

fornire *vb*, supply

fornitore *nm*, supplier; **fornitore di cibo e bevande**, caterer

fornitura *nf*, supply; **problemi di fornitura**, supply problems; **una fornitura di . .**, a supply of . . .

forte *adj*, strong

fotocopia *nf*, photocopy, copy

fotocopiare *vb*, photocopy

fotocopiatrice *nf*, photocopier

fra *prep*, between

franchigia *nf*, franchise; **dare una franchigia**, franchise

franco(-a) *adj* (imp/exp), free; **franco a bordo**, FOB, free on board; **franco avaria comune**, free of general average; **franco avaria particolare**, FPA, free of particular average; **franco banchina**, FAQ, free alongside quay, (imp/exp), ex-wharf; **franco dogana**, duty paid;

franco lungo la nave, free alongside ship; **franco trasportatore**, FRC, free carrier; **franco vagone**, FOR, FOT, free on rail, free on truck

francobollo *nm*, stamp

fratellastro *nm*, half-brother

fratello *nm*, brother; **fratelli**, bros, brothers

frenare *vb*, brake

frequente *adj*, frequent

frequenza *nf*, frequency

frigorifero *nm*, fridge

fronte *nm*, forehead, face; **essere di fronte a**, face; **sono di fronte all'edificio**, I am facing the building

FS, Ferrovie *nfpl* **dello Stato**, Italian State Railways

funzionamento *nm*, operating; **istruzioni di funzionamento**, operating instructions; **sistema di funzionamento**, operating system

funzionare *vb* (machines, method of operation), work; **la dimostrazione illustrerà come la macchina funziona**, the demonstration will show how the machine works

funzionario *nm*, executive; **capo funzionario**, senior executive

fuoco *nm*, fire

fuori *adv*, out, outside; **fuori servizio**, off-duty

fuorilegge *nm*, outlaw

furgone *nm*, van

furterello *nm*, pilfering

furto *nm*, theft; **furto con scasso**, burglary; **commettere un furto con scasso**, burgle

fusione *nf*, merger

fusto *nm* (oil), barrel

futuro *nm*, future; **nel futuro**, in the future

futuro(-a) *adj*, future; **è possibile che i futuri sviluppi includano . .**, future developments may include . . .

G

galleria *nf* (mktg, sales), arcade; **galleria di negozi**, shopping arcade

gamma *nf*, range (of goods)

garantire *vb*, guarantee, warrant; **possiamo garantire che . .**, we can guarantee that . .; **consegna garantita**, guaranteed delivery

garanzia *nf*, **1** (gen), guarantee, warranty; **il prodotto ha due anni di garanzia**, the product comes with a 2-year guarantee; **garanzia addizionale**, collateral. **2** (fin), security

gas *nm*, gas; **gas di petrolio liquefatto**, LPG, liquified petroleum gas

gelare *vb* (weather), freeze

generale *adj*, general; **tariffe generali di carico**, general cargo rates; **direttore generale**, general manager

gentile *adj*, kind; **persona gentile**, kind person

gestione *nf* (fin), management, handling; **la gestione quotidiana**, day-to-day management; **le spese di gestione**, handling charges

gettare *vb*, throw, cast; **gettare la palla**, throw the ball; **gettare uno sguardo a qualcuno**, cast a glance at someone

getto *nm* (eng), casting

giardino *nm* garden

giocare *vb*, **1** (gen), play. **2** (fin), gamble on; **gioca in Borsa**, he gambles on the Stock Exchange;

giocare d'azzardo, gamble

gioco *nm* game; **gioco d'azzardo**, gamble

giornale *nm*, newspaper

giornata *nf* (length of time), day; **una giornata stanchevole**, a tiring day; **una giornata di riunioni**, a day of meetings

giorno *nm*, day; **a novanta giorni dalla data**, 90 days after date; **il primo giorno del mese**, the first day of the month; **giorno lavorativo**, working day

giovane *adj*, young; (younger), junior; **impiegato giovane**, junior employee

girare *vb*, **1** (gen), turn. **2** (a cheque), endorse

giro *nm*, tour; **un giro dello stabilimento**, a tour of the plant; **giro d'affari**, (comm), turnover

giudicare *vb*, judge

giudice *nm* (law), judge

giudizio *nm* (law), judgment, trial

giuoco *nm*, play, game; **è in giuoco la mia carriera**, my career is at stake

giuria *nf* (law), jury

giurista *nm* (law), lawyer

giustificare *vb*, justify

giustizia *nf*, justice

giusto *adv*, just; **giusto in tempo**, JIT, just in time

giusto(-a) *adj*, right, fair

gomma *nf*, rubber

gradevole *adj*, pleasant; **una personalità gradevole**, a pleasant personality

grado *nm*, grade

graffa *nf*, staple

graffetta *nf*, **1** paper clip. **2** staple

graffettatrice *nf*, stapler

grafico *nm*, chart, graph; **grafico a sbarre**, bar chart; **grafico a settori**, pie chart; **grafico da muro**, wall chart; **fare il grafico** (results), chart

grande *adj*, big, large

gratifica *nf*, bonus, benefit; **gratifiche extra**, fringe benefits

gratuito(-a) *adj*, free; **entrata gratuita**, free admission

greggio *nm*, crude oil

greggio(-a) *adj*, raw, crude

grossa *nf* (12×12), gross

grossista *nm*, **1** (gen), wholesaler. **2** (mktg, sales), stockist

gru *nf* (transp) crane

guadagnare *vb*, **1** (gen), earn. **2** (fin), gain; **guadagnare terreno**, gain ground

guadagno *nm*, gain

guasto *nm*, breakdown

guasto(-a) *adj*, out of order

guidare *vb*, drive

guidatore *nm*, driver

gustare *vb*, taste; **vorremmo gustare parecchie bottiglie prima di acquistare**, we will want to taste several bottles before buying

gusto *nm*, taste; **un nuovo gusto**, a new taste

H

hangar *nm*, hangar, shed

hertz *nmpl* (electr), hertz

hovercraft *nm*, hovercraft

hurrà *interjection*, hurray

I

iarda *nf* (measurement), yard

ignorare *vb*, ignore

illegale *adj*, illegal; unlawful

illeggibile *adj*, illegible; **la seconda pagina del fax è illeggibile**, the second page of the fax is illegible

illuminare *vb*, light

illuminazione *nf*, lighting

imballare *vb*, **1** (gen), wrap. **2** (transp), pack; **imballato nei trucioli di legno**, wrapped in wood wool; **la macchina è stata imballata**, the machine has been packed

imballato(-a) *adj*, packed

imbarcare *vb*, embark

imbottito(-a) *adj*, (imp/exp), padded

imbottitura *nf*, padding

imbucare *vb* (a letter), post

imbullonare *vb*, (eng) bolt; **imbullonato(-a)**, bolted

importanza *nf*, importance

importare *vb*, import; **merci importate**, imported goods

imposta *nf*, tax; **imposta sulle società**, corporation tax; **imposta sul reddito**, income tax

impresa *nf*, undertaking, enterprise; **Piccola o Media Impresa**, SME, Small or Medium-Sized Enterprise

imprevisto(-a) *adj*, unexpected, unforeseen

improbabile *adj*, unlikely

inadatto(-a) *adj*, unsuitable

inattivo(-a) *adj*, inactive; **essere inattivo**, stagnate

incassare *vb*, cash

incendio *nm*, fire

incentivo *nm*, incentive

inchiesta *nf*, inquiry; **fare un'inchiesta**, carry out an inquiry/poll (after elections)

incidente *nm*, accident; **egli ha avuto un incidente**, he has had an accident

includere *vb*, include; **il contratto include una clausola su . .**, the contract includes a clause on . . .

inclusione *nf*, inclusion

incollare *vb*, **1** (gen), stick, glue. **2** (comp), paste

incondizionato(-a) *adj*, unconditional

incontrare *vb*, encounter; **incontrare degli ostacoli**, encounter problems; **incontrarsi con un cliente**, meet a customer

inconveniente *nm* (disadvantage), drawback

incorretto(-a) *adj*, (imp/exp), wrong; **prezzo incorretto**, wrong price

incremento *nm*, increase, upturn

indebolire *vb*, weaken

indennità *nf*, **1** (gen), indemnity, allowance. **2** (extra payment), bonus. **3** (ins), no claims bonus

indennizzare *vb*, compensate; **vorremmo indennizzarvi per . . .** we would like to compensate you for . . .

indennizzo *nm*, **1** (gen), compensation. **2** (law), damages

indicare *vb*, indicate

indicatore *nm* (sign), pointer

indicazione *nf*, indication

indice *nm* **d'ascolto**, (TV, radio), ratings

indipendente *adj*, independent

indipendenza *nf*, independence

indirizzo *nm*, address; **indirizzo privato**, private address; **elenco indirizzi**, mailing list

indispensabile *adj*, indispensable

industria *nf*, industry; **industria alimentare**, food industry; **industria dell'acciaio**, steel industry; **industria farmaceutica**, pharmaceutical industry; **industria manufatturiera**, manufacturing industries; **industria nazionale**, domestic industry; **industrie del settore servizi**, the service industries

industriale *adj*, industrial; **zona industriale**, industrial estate; **disputa industriale**, industrial dispute; **relazioni industriali**, industrial relations

industriale *nm*, industrialist

inesatto(-a) *adj*, untrue

inferiore *adj*, inferior; (quality), poor

inflazione *nf*, inflation

influenza *nf*, influence; **avere un'influenza su . .**, have influence on . .; **essere influenzato(-a) da . .**, be influenced by . . .

informare *vb*, inform

informatica *nf*, computing

informazione *nf*, information; **delle informazioni su . .**, some information about . .; **foglio d'informazioni**, newsletter

infrangere *vb*, break; **infrangere la legge**, break the law

infrarosso(-a) *adj*, infra-red; **comando a raggi infrarossi**, infra-red control

ingannare *vb*, **1** deceive. **2** mislead, divert

ingannevole *adj*, misleading

ingiunzione *nf* (law), summons

ingiusto(-a) *adj*, unfair

ingorgo *nm* (traffic), hold-up, jam; **ingorgo stradale**, traffic jam

ingresso *nm*, admittance; **vietato l'ingresso**, no admittance

ingrosso, all'ingrosso *adv*, by the gross (12×12), by wholesale, in bulk; **prezzo all'ingrosso**, wholesale price; **acquisti all'ingrosso**, bulk buying

iniziale *adj*, initial

iniziare *vb*, start; **iniziare una campagna**, start a campaign

iniziativa *nf*, drive, enterprise; **avere molta iniziativa**, have plenty of drive; **è una buona iniziativa**, it is a good enterprise

inizio *nm*, start

innovare *vb*, innovate

innovativo(-a) *adj*, innovative

inoltrare *vb*, forward; **si prega inoltrare la lettera all'indirizzo sopra indicato**, please forward the letter to the above address

inopportuno(-a) *adj*, unadvisable

inquinamento *nm*, pollution

inquinare *vb*, pollute

insegna *nf*, badge, sign; **insegna al neon**, neon sign

insegnamento *nm*, teaching; education

inserire *vb*, insert; **inserire un annuncio sul . .**, insert an ad in . .; **inserire la corrente**, (comp), plug in

inserzione *nf*, **1** (mktg, sales), insert. **2** (publicity), advertisement; **fare un'inserzione**, advertise; **mettere un'inserzione**, place an advertisement; **rispondere ad un'inserzione**, reply to an advertisement

inserzionista *nm/f*, advertiser

insistere *vb*, **1** (gen), insist. **2** (stress),

point out

insolito(-a) *adj*, unusual, novel

installare *vb*, install

installazione *nf*, installation

insuccesso *nm*, failure, setback

insufficiente *adj*, insufficient, short

intangibile *adj*, intangible; **attività intangibile**, intangible assets

intensificare *vb* (campaign), step up

intentare *vb* **un processo contro**, (law), take legal action against

interessare *vb*, interest; **essere interessato in**, be interested in

interesse *nm*, (return on capital), interest

interessi *nmpl*, 1 (money paid for capital on a % basis), interest. 2 (CV), interests. 3 (gen), interests; **interessi comuni**, joint interests

interfacciare *vb* (comp), interface

intermediario *nm*, go-between

interno(-a) *adj*, internal, interior, inner, in-house; **una rivista interna**, an in-house magazine

interrompere *vb*, interrupt; **interrompere il lavoro**, (pers), stop work; **interrompere la produzione**, cease production

interruttore *nm* (electricity) switch

interruzione *nf*, 1 (gen), interruption. 2 (fin), cut-off; **data d'interruzione**, cut-off date. 3 (pers), **interruzione (del lavoro)**, stoppage (of work)

intervallo *nm*, gap

intervenire *vb*, intervene

intervento *nm*, intervention

intervista *nf*, interview

intervistare *vb*, interview

intestare *vb*, 1 (eg a chapter head); **carta intestata**, headed paper. 2 (accounts, property) enter,

register; **l'edificio è intestato a me**, the building is registered under my name; **questo denaro va intestato al direttore**, this money must be entered in the director's account

intraprendente *adj*, go-ahead; **una donna d'affari intraprendente**, a go-ahead business woman

intrigo *nm*, plot

introdurre *vb*, introduce; **introdurre a tappe**, phase in; **introdurre sul mercato un nuovo prodotto**, introduce a new product; **introdurre una nuova idea**, introduce a new idea

introduttivo(-a) *adj*, introductory; **prezzo introduttivo**, introductory price

inutile *adj*, useless

inutilizzabile *adj*, unserviceable; **l'attrezzatura adesso è inutilizzabile**, the equipment is now unserviceable

invendibile *adj*, unsaleable

invenduto(-a) *adj*, unsold

inventare *vb*, fabricate

inventario *nm*, inventory, stocktaking; **fare un inventario**, make an inventory

invenzione *nf*, fabrication

invertire *vb*, reverse

investigare *vb*, investigate

investimento *nm*, 1 (gen), investment. 2 (fin) interest

investire *vb*, 1 (fin), invest. 2 (eg capital), tie up

inviare *vb*, send, address; **inviare il cv all'attenzione di . .**, address your CV for the attention of . . .

invitare *vb*, invite

invitato *nm* (invited for meal or stay), guest

invito *nm*, invitation

ipermercato *nm*, hypermarket, superstore

ipoteca *nf*, mortgage; **mutuo ipotecario**, mortgage loan

ipotecare *vb*, mortgage

ipotesi *nf*, supposition, guess

irregolare *adj*, uneven

irrevocabile *adj*, irrevocable; **lettera di credito irrevocabile**, irrevocable letter of credit

irritante *adj*, irritating

iscriversi *vb* (educ), register, enrol; **iscriversi ad un corso di lingue**, register for a language course

iscrizione *nf*, registration; **modulo d'iscrizione**, registration form

isolare *vb*, insulate

isolato(-a) *adj* (electr), insulated

isolazione *nf*, insulation

ispezionare *vb*, inspect

ispezione *nf*, inspection

istruzione *nf*, instruction, direction; **dare istruzioni**, instruct/give instructions; **le istruzioni d'uso**, the instructions for use; **manuale d'istruzioni**, operator's manual; **istruzioni d'imbarco**, (transp), shipping instructions

itinerario *nm*, itinerary, route

IVA, Imposta *nf* **sul Valore Aggiunto**, VAT, Value Added Tax

L

lacuna *nf*, gap

lagnanza *nf*, grievance

lamentarsi *vb*, complain

laminare *vb*, laminate

lana *nf*, wool; **di lana**, woollen

lanciare *vb* (comm), launch; **lanciare una società**, (fin), float a company; **lanciare un prodotto**, launch a product; **lanciare un prodotto sul mercato**, market a product

lancio *nm*, launch; **prezzo di lancio**, launch price; **il lancio del prodotto avverrà in settembre**, the product launch will be in September

larghezza *nf*, width

largo(-a) *adj*, wide

lasciare *vb*, leave; **si prega di lasciare una copia del rapporto in ufficio**, please leave a copy of the report at the office

latta *nf* (container), tin

laurearsi *vb*, take a degree

laureato *nm*, graduate, Bachelor of Arts

lavagna *nf*, blackboard; **lavagna luminosa**, overhead projector, OHP; **lavagna a fogli volanti**, flip chart

lavastoviglie *nf*, dishwasher

lavorare *vb*, work; **lavorare sotto la direzione di . . .** work for . . .

lavorativo(-a) *adj*, working; **giorno lavorativo**, working day

lavorazione *nf*, processing;

lavorazione degli scarti, waste processing

lavoro *nm*, work, job; **lavoro in corso**, work in progress; **lavoro a contratto**, contract work; **è un lavoro molto difficile**, it is a very difficult job; **lavoro amministrativo**, paperwork

leasing *nm*, leasing

legale *adj*, legal; **consigliere** *nm* **legale**, legal adviser

legge *nf*, law

leggere *vb*, read

leggermente *adv*, **1** (gen), lightly. **2** (fin), slightly; **risultati leggermente più alti/più bassi dell'anno scorso**, slightly higher/lower results than last year

leggero(-a) *adj*, **1** (gen), light; **un pranzo leggero**, a light meal. **2** (small), slight; **una leggera diminuzione di profitti**, a slight fall in profits

legname *nm* **da costruzione**, timber

legno *nm*, wood; **di legno**, wooden

lento(-a) *adj*, **1** (gen), slow. **2** (sales), sluggish

lettera *nf*, letter; **lettera di accompagnamento**, (imp/exp), packing note; **lettera di credito**, LC, L/C, Letter of Credit; **lettera di credito rinnovabile**, revolving letter of credit; **lettera di sollecito**, reminder letter; **lettera di trasporto aereo**, (imp/exp), AWB, air waybill; **lettera di vettura**, (imp/exp), waybill

letteratura *nf*, literature

lettore *nm*, reader; **numero di lettori**, readership

libero(-a) *adj*, free, loose; **una camera libera**, a free room; **una traduzione libera**, a loose translation

libertà *nf*, freedom; **libertà**

provvisoria, (law), bail

libro *nm*, book; **libro mastro**, (offce), ledger; **libro paga**, (fin), payroll

licenza *nf*, licence; **accordare una licenza**, license

licenziamento *nm* (too many employees), redundancy; **licenziamenti** *nmpl*, (pers), layoffs

licenziare *vb*, (pers), sack, lay off; (too many employees), make redundant

limitare *vb*, limit

limite *nm*, limit, bound; **entro i limiti**, within bounds; **arrivare al limite massimo**, go through the ceiling

linea *nf*, line; **linea diretta**, direct line; **linea di produzione**, production line; **linea dei prodotti**, product line; **linea di condotta**, policy

lingua *nf*, language; **lingua straniera**, foreign language; **conoscenza di lingue straniere**, (CV) languages spoken

liquefatto(-a) *adj*, liquified; **gas di petrolio liquefatto**, LPG, Liquified Petroleum Gas

liquidare *vb* **lo stock**, clear stocks, sell off surplus stock

liquidazione *nf*, clearance, liquidation; **vendita di liquidazione**, (mktg, sales), clearance sale; **andare in liquidazione**, go into liquidation

liquidità *nf*, liquidity; **problemi di liquidità**, liquidity problems

liquido(-a) *adj*, liquid, available; **capitale liquido**, working capital

lista *nf*, list

lite *nf* (law), litigation

livello *nm*, level

locale *adj*, local; **rete locale**, (comp), LAN network; **radio locale**, local

radio

locatario *nm*, lessee

locatore *nm*, lessor

lordo(-a) *adj*, gross; **reddito lordo**, gross earnings; **prodotto nazionale lordo**, gross national product; **profitto lordo**, gross profit; **entrata lorda**, gross revenue; **peso lordo**, gross weight

lottare *vb*, fight

lotto *nm*, batch, item; **trattamento in lotto**, batch processing; **lotto no 3**, item no 3

lucido *nm*, OHP transparency

lunghezza *nf*, length

lungo(-a) *adj*, long; **a lunga distanza**, long distance; **mutuo a lunga scadenza**, long-term loan

luogo *nm*, site; **luogo di riunione**, venue

lusso *nm*, luxury; **rivista di lusso**, glossy magazine, **articoli di lusso**, luxury goods

macchiato(-a) *adj*, stained, soiled

macchina *nf*, machine, car; **macchina utensile**, machine tool; **macchina da scrivere**, typewriter; **macchina fotografica**, camera

macchinario *nm*, machinery

magazzinaggio *nm*, warehousing

magazzino *nm*, store, warehouse; **magazzino con succursali**, chain store; **tenere a magazzino**, stock

magistrato *nm*, magistrate

maggioranza *nf*, majority

maggiore *adj*, major; **la maggior parte della nostra produzione è venduta all'estero**, the major part of our production is sold abroad

maiuscola *nf*, capital (letter)

malato *nm*, patient

malato(-a) *adj*, sick

mancanza *nf*, lack, shortage; **una mancanza di . .**, a lack of . . .

mancare *vb*, lack, miss; **la relazione manca di dettagli**, the report lacks detail; **ci manca il sole**, we miss the sun

mancia *nf* tip, gratuity; **dare la mancia**, tip

mandare *vb*, send, forward, dispatch; **mandare per posta**, mail

mandato *nm*, writ

maneggiare *vb*, handle

manifesto *nm* (transp), manifest

mano *nf* d'opera, I labour; **il**

mercato della mano d'opera, labour market; **costo della mano d'opera,** labour costs; **mano d'opera specializzata,** skilled labour. **2** manpower

manomettere vb (eg with goods), tamper; **le scatole sono state manomesse,** the boxes have been tampered with

mansione nf, job; **descrizione delle mansioni,** job description

mantenere vb, keep, maintain; **ha due famiglie da mantenere,** he has two families to keep; **mantenere una promessa,** keep a promise; **mantenersi calmo (-a),** keep cool; **mantenere in buone condizioni,** service

manuale nm, handbook, manual; **manuale del consumatore,** user manual; **manuale d'istruzioni,** operator's manual

manuale adj, manual; **controllo manuale,** manual control

manufatturiero(-a), adj, manufacturing; **industrie manufatturiere,** manufacturing industries

manutenzione nf, **1** (gen), handling; **carrello di manutenzione,** handling truck; **costi di manutenzione,** handling costs. **2** (eng), servicing; **una manutenzione regolare è essenziale,** regular servicing is essential

marca nf, **1** brand, make; **concetto di marca,** brand image; **fedeltà alla marca,** brand loyalty; **marca del distributore,** own brand. **2** label; **venduto sotto la marca Olivetti,** sold under the Olivetti label

marcare vb, label, mark; **si prega di marcare le scatole in modo chiaro,** please label the boxes clearly

marchio nm, mark; **marchio di fabbrica,** trade mark; **senza**

marchio, unbranded

mare nm, sea

marea nf, tide

marginale adj, marginal; **profitto marginale,** marginal profit

margine nm, margin; **tasso di margine,** margin ratio; **margine di profitto,** profit margin

marketing nm, marketing; **marketing diretto,** direct marketing; **servizio marketing,** marketing department; **marketing per telefono,** telemarketing

marino(-a) adj, marine; **acqua marina,** marine water; **aria marina,** sea air

marittimo(-a), adj, marine; **assicurazione marittima,** marine insurance; **stazione marittima,** marine station; **per via marittima,** by sea

massa nf, mass; **memoria di massa,** (comp), mass memory; **attacco in massa,** mass attack

massimizzare vb, maximise

massimo nm, maximum; **raggiungere il massimo,** peak

massimo(-a) adj, maximum

mass media nmpl the media

materiale nm (cloth), material; **materiali grezzi,** raw materials, **materiale da pacco,** wrapping

materie nfpl **prime,** raw materials

matita nf, pencil

mattino nm, morning; **le 5 del mattino,** 5 a.m.

maturare vb, mature

maturità nf, **esami di maturità,** ~ A levels, advanced level exams

maturo(-a) adj (personal quality) mature

meccanico(-a) adj, mechanical

meccanismo nm, mechanism

media *nmpl*, the media

mediatore *nm*, mediator, agent; **mediatore immobiliare**, estate agent

medicina *nf*, medicine; **studente in medicina**, medical student

medico *nm*, doctor; **medico generico**, GP, General Practitioner

medico(-a) *adj*, medical; **corpo medico**, medical board

membro *nm*, member; **membro del consiglio d'amministrazione**, member of the board of directors

memorandum *nm*, memo, memorandum; **inviare un memorandum**, send a memo

memoria *nf* (gen, comp), memory; **tenere in memoria**, (comp), save

meno *adv*, less, minus; **è meno di quanto pensassi**, it is less than I thought; **in men che non si dica**, in less than no time

mensile *adj*, monthly; **consegne mensili**, monthly deliveries; **pagamenti mensili**, monthly payments

menu *nm*, menu

menzognero(-a) *adj*, misleading; **pubblicità menzognera**, misleading advertising

mercanteggiare *vb* deal, trade; **mercanteggiare sul prezzo**, haggle over the price

mercantile *adj*, merchant; **nave mercantile**, merchant ship

mercato *nm*, market; **c'è un enorme mercato per . .**, there is a big market for . .; **analisi di mercato**, market analysis; **domanda di mercato**, market demand; **parte di mercato**, market share; **penetrazione di mercato**, market penetration; **prezzo di mercato**, market price; **ricerca di mercato**, market research; **settore di mercato**, market sector; **tendenza di mercato**, market trend; **valore di mercato**, market value; **mercato all'aperto**, open market; **essere nel mercato per . .**, be in the market for . .; **fare uno studio del mercato**, survey the market; **mercato di merci vendute con consegna a termine**, (fin), futures market; **mercato nazionale**, home market

merce *nf*, goods; **merce in prova**, goods on approval; **vagone merci**, goods wagon; **merci lavorate**, manufactured goods; **merci importate**, imported goods; **merci di lusso**, luxury goods

mese *nm*, month; **a . . . mesi dalla data**, at . . . months after date

messa *nf* (religious), mass

messaggio *nm*, message; **inviare un messaggio**, send a message; **ricevere un messaggio**, receive a message; **messaggio registrato**, recorded message

mestiere *nm*, occupation, job

metà *nf*, half; **metà del lavoro**, half of the work; **metà prezzo**, half price

metodo *nm*, method; **metodo di pagamento**, methods of payment; **metodo di produzione**, method of production

metro *nm*, metre

mettere *vb*, put; **mettere a fuoco**, focus; **mettere a frutto**, invest; **mettere a posto**, (transp), stow; **mettere a repentaglio** jeopardise; **mettere al corrente**, brief; **mettere da parte**, dismiss; **mettere il veto**, veto; **mettere in circolazione**, (document), circulate; **mettere in evidenza**, feature; **mettere in liquidazione (una società)**, wind up (a company); **mettere in marcia**, switch on; **mettere in memoria**, store; **mettere in ordine**, tidy up; **mettere in pericolo**, jeopardise; **mettere in rete** (comp), network,

mettere in un fondo comune, pool; **mettere sul mercato,** market

mezzo nm, **1** (gen), means, way. **2** (eng), device

mezzo(-a) adj, half; **mezzo stipendio,** half pay; **mezze misure,** half measures; **mezza dozzina,** half-dozen; **mezzo stupido,** half-witted

miglio nm, mile; **distanza in miglia,** mileage

migliorare vb, improve, upgrade

minaccia nf, threat

minacciare vb, threaten

mini computer nm, mini computer

minimizzare vb, minimise

minimo nm, minimum

minimo(-a) adj, minimal, minimum; **i costi di manutenzione sono minimi,** maintenance costs are minimal; **l'altitudine minima è 1000 metri,** the minimum altitude is 1000 metres.

Ministero nm **dell' Industria e Commercio,** DTI, Department of Trade and Industry

minoranza nf, minority; **essere in minoranza,** be in a minority

minore adj, minor

miscellaneo(-a) adj, miscellaneous

misto(-a) adj, mixed, miscellaneous

misura nf, **1** (gen), measure. **2** (dimensions), measurement; **fatto(-a) su misura,** tailor-made, made to measure

mittente nm, sender

mobile adj, mobile, sliding; **una scala mobile,** a sliding scale

modello nm, **1** (gen), model; **l'ultimo modello è più potente,** the latest model is more powerful. **2** (mktg, sales), design

modifica nf, modification; **apportare**

una modifica a . ., make a modification to . . .

modificare vb, modify, alter, vary

modo nm **di trasporto,** (imp/exp, transp), mode of transport

modulare adj, modular

modulazione nf **di frequenza,** FM, frequency modulation

modulo nm, form, module; **modulo di prenotazione,** booking form; **modulo di richiesta,** application form; **riempire un modulo,** fill in a form

molo nm, wharf

moltiplicare vb, multiply

mondiale adj, worldwide

moneta nf, coin

montaggio nm, assembly; **catena di montaggio,** assembly line

montare vb, **1** (gen), (kits), assemble; **facile da montare,** easy to assemble; **la macchina è stata montata,** the machine has been assembled. **2.** fit, fix on. **3** go up; **stanno montando le scale,** they are going up the stairs

montatore nm, assembler

morto(-a) adj, dead

mostra nf, display, exhibition, show

mostrare vb, show; **le cifre mostrano che la recessione ha avuto un efffetto sulle vendite,** the figures show that the recession has affected sales; **il nostro agente sarà lieto di mostrarvi il nuovo modello,** our agent will be happy to show you the new model; **mostrare sullo schermo,** (comp), display

motivare vb, motivate

motivazione nf, motivation

motivo nm, **1** (gen), reason. **2** (design), pattern

motore nm, engine; **motore a**

combustione interna, internal combustion engine

motto *nm* **pubblicitario**, slogan

mouse *nm* (comp), mouse

movimento *nm*, movement; **movimento di cassa**, (fin) cashflow; **difficoltà nei movimenti di cassa**, cashflow problems; **previsioni di movimenti di cassa**, cashflow projection

mucchio *nm*, 1 (gen), pile. 2 (transp), stack

multa *nf*, fine, penalty; **pagare una multa**, pay a fine

multare *vb*, fine

multiplo(-a) *adj*, multiple; **copie multiple**, multiple copies

mutuo *nm*, loan; **mutuo ipotecario**, mortgage loan; **mutuo a lunga scadenza**, long-term loan

nafta *nf*, diesel

nascere *vb*, be born; **nata il 28 luglio 1944**, born 28 July 1944; **nato a Milano**, born in Milan

navale *adj*, naval

nave *nf*, ship, vessel

navetta *nf*, shuttle

nazionale *adj*, national, home; **mercato nazionale**, home market; **reputazione nazionale**, national reputation

nazionalità *nf* (CV) nationality

nazionalizzare *vb*, nationalise

nazionalizzato(-a) *adj*, nationalised

negare *vb*, deny; **non posso negarlo**, I cannot deny it

negoziabile *adj*, negotiable

negoziante *nm*, shopkeeper, dealer; **negoziante di ferramenta**, ironmonger

negoziare *vb*, bargain

negozio *nm*, shop

netto(-a) *adj*, net; **aumento netto**, sharp rise; **contribuzione netta**, (fin), net contribution; **peso netto** (imp/exp), net weight; **reddito netto** (fin), net income; **risultato netto**, net result; **valore netto**, net worth

nicchia *nf*, niche

nodo *nm* **autostradale**, motorway junction

noleggiare *vb*, 1 (gen), hire. 2 (transp), charter

noleggio *nm*, I (gen), hire; **noleggio auto**, car hire. **2** (transp), charter; **contratto di noleggio**, charter-party

nolo *nm*, I (transp), charter, chartering; **nolo a tempo**, time charter. **2** (imp/exp), freight; **costo e nolo**, CF, cost and freight; **nolo veloce**, fast freight; **nolo pagato fino a . .**, freight paid to . .; **nolo vuoto per pieno**, dead freight; **nolo pagato**, freight paid; **nolo pagabile a destinazione**, FPAD, freight payable at destination; **nolo per tutti i generi di merci**, FAK, freight of all kinds; **nolo più spese di carico e scarico**, FIO, free in and out

nome *nm*, name

nomina *nf*, appointment; **nomina di presidente**, appointment as chairman

nominare *vb*, appoint, call; **è stato nominato presidente**, he has been appointed chairman; **nominare un curatore fallimentare**, call in the receiver

norma *nf*, rule, norm; **la norma britannica per l'assicurazione qualità**, BS 5750 (British Standard)

nota *nf*, note; **nota interna**, internal memo; **blocco note**, note-pad; **nota d'imbarco**, (imp/exp), shipping note

notare *vb*, note

notevole *adj* (quality) outstanding

notifica *nf*, notification; **ricevere una notifica**, receive a notification

notificare *vb*, notify

notizia *nf*, news; **notizia pubblicitaria**, (mktg, sales), blurb

novità *nf*, novelty

numerare *vb*, number; **abbiamo numerato le scatole da I a I0**, we have numbered the boxes I to I0

numerico(-a) *adj*, numerical; **in ordine numerico**, in numerical order

numerizzato(-a) *adj* (comp), digitised

numero *nm*, I (gen), number, figure; **numero verde**, (mktg, sales), freephone number; **il nostro numero di fax è . .**, our fax number is . .; **il numero del prodotto è . .**, the product number is . .; **numeri dispari**, odd numbers; **numero di serie**, serial number. **2** (magazine), issue. **3** (of journal or newspaper), copy. **4** (of shoes), size

nuovo(-a) *adj*, new, novel

O

obbligare *vb*, oblige

obbligatorio(-a) *adj*, obligatory, binding; **un contratto obbligatorio**, a binding agreement

obbligazione *nf*, (fin), (stock market) bond

obbligo *nm*, obligation, duty, liability

obiettare *vb*, object

obiettivo *nm*, **1** (gen), objective; **il reparto vendite ha raggiunto il suo obiettivo**, the sales team reached their objective. **2** (mktg, sales), target; **raggiungere l'obiettivo**, be on target; **obiettivo vendite**, sales target; **prezzo d'obiettivo**, target price

obiezione *nf*, objection

occasione *nf*, **1** bargain; **è una buona occasione**, it is a good bargain. **2** opportunity

occupare *vb*, (premises), occupy

occuparsi *vb* **di . .**, handle, deal with . .; **il rapporto si occupa di . .**, the report deals with . .; **si occupa della parte commerciale**, he deals with the commercial side; **me ne occupo io**, I'll handle it; **occuparsi di qualcosa**, see to something

occupato(-a) *adj*, **1** (telec), engaged; **la linea è occupata**, the line is engaged. **2** **non sono libero, sono molto occupato**, I am not available, I am very busy

offerta *nf*, **1** (gen), offer; **fare un'offerta**, make an offer; **ricevere un'offerta**, receive an offer; **rifiutare un'offerta**, refuse an offer; **offerta d'appalto**, tender. **2** (fin) bid

officina *nf*, workshop; **direttore d'officina**, works manager

offrire *vb*, offer; **offrire un prezzo per . .**, bid for . .; **offrire a un prezzo minore**, (sales) undercut; **offrire a un prezzo minore di quello della concorrenza**, undercut the competition; **offrire di riprendere indietro la merce**, offer to take back the goods; **offrire lo stesso prezzo**, match the price; **offrire uno sconto del 10%**, offer a 10% discount

oggettivo *adj*, objective; **caso oggettivo**, objective case

oggetto *nm*, object

olio *nm*, oil

omaggio *nm* **(biglietto)**, complimentary ticket

ombra *nf*, shade; **un'ombra di dubbio**, a shadow of doubt

omissione *nf*, omission; **salvo errori ed omissioni**, errors and omissions excepted

ondata *nf*, (mktg, sales), surge; **un'ondata di importazioni**, a surge in imports

onesto(-a) *adj*, honest

onorario *nm*, fee; **l'onorario di un medico**, a doctor's fee

onore *nm*, honour; **far onore alla scadenza**, meet the target

operare *vb*, operate

operatore *nm*, (of machines, computers), operator

opportunità *nf*, opportunity; **afferrare un'opportunità**, seize an opportunity

optimum *nm*, optimum

opuscolo *nm*, brochure; **opuscoli pubblicitari**, publicity literature

opzione *nf*, option

ora *nf*, hour; (telec, mktg, sales), **ore di grande ascolto**, prime time; **ora di punta**, rush hour; **ora zero**, zero hour

orario *nm*, timetable, hours; **l'orario di lavoro**, the working hours; **l'orario del corso**, the course timetable

orario(-a) *adj*, hourly; **tariffa oraria**, hourly rate; **voli orari**, hourly flights

ordinare *vb*, order

ordinario(-a) *adj*, ordinary

ordinazione *nf*, order; **ordinazione per corrispondenza**, mail order; **articolo fatto su ordinazione**, customised item

ordine *nm*, **1** (gen), order; **eseguire un ordine**, process an order; **non conforme all'ordine**, not as ordered; **ordine per telefono/per fax**, telephone/fax order; **ottenere un ordine**, secure an order; **passare un ordine**, place an order. **2 in ordine numerico**, in numerical order; **mettere in ordine**, tidy up. **3 all'ordine di . . .** (fin) draw to . ., o/o, order of . . . **4 ordine del giorno**, (meetings) agenda; **all'ordine del giorno**, on the agenda. **5** (comp), command

organico(-a) *adj*, organic; **prodotti organici**, organic products

organigramma *nm*, organisation chart (of a company structure)

organizzare *vb*, organise; **organizzare picchetti**, (pers), picket; **organizzare picchetti a una fabbrica**, picket a factory

organizzazione *nf*, organisation

originale *adj*, original; **attrezzatura originale**, original equipment; **scrittore originale**, original writer

origine *nf*, origin, source; **l'origine della parola**, the origin of the word; **trattenute all'origine**, deduction at source

ormeggiare *vb* (transp), moor

ormeggio *nm*, mooring

orologio *nm* **(da muro)**, clock

orologio *nm* **(da polso)**, watch

orto *nm*, kitchen garden; market garden

ospedale *nm*, hospital

ospitalità *nf*, hospitality

ospitare *vb* (hotels, etc), accommodate

ospite *nm*, guest

ossatura *nf*, frame, structure, shell

osservare *vb*, note, notice

ostacolato(-a) *adj*, hampered; **essere ostacolato da . .**, be hampered by . . .

ostacolo *nm*, obstacle

ottenere *vb*, obtain, get, gain; **diploma ottenuto nel . .**, (CV), qualification obtained in . . .

ottimista *nm*, optimist; **essere ottimista**, be an optimist

P

pacchetto nm (mktg, sales), packet, parcel

pacco nm, 1 (mktg, sales), pack; **un pacco da 10 kg**, a 10 kg pack. 2 (transp) package. 3 (offce, transp) parcel; **materiale da pacco**, wrapping

paese nm, 1 (nation), country; **paese d'origine**, country of origin. 2 small town, village

paga nf, pay, wage

pagabile adj, payable; **pagabile alla fine di maggio**, payable at the end of May

pagamento nm, payment; **pagamento alla consegna**, (mktg, sales), POD, payment on delivery; **pagamento a rate**, payment in instalments; **pagamento contro documenti**, (fin), payment against documents; **pagamento eccessivo**, overpayment; **pagamento in arretrato**, outstanding payment; **pagamento parziale**, part payment; **nessun pagamento**, non payment

pagare vb, pay; **pagare in contanti**, pay cash; **pagare il conto e lasciare l'albergo**, check out; **non pagare una cambiale**, dishonour a bill; **pagato alla consegna**, paid on delivery; **pagato(-a) in anticipo**, paid in advance

pagina nf (of book), page

pallet nm (transp), pallet

panfilo nm, yacht

panna nf, 1 double cream. 2 (transp),

breakdown

pannello nm **pubblicitario**, (mktg, sales), billboard

paragonare vb, compare

paragone nm, comparison; **in paragone a . .**, in comparison with . . .

parcheggiare vb, park

parcheggio nm **auto**, car parking

parco nm, park; **parco divertimenti**, leisure park

pareggiare vb (acct), balance

pareggio nm, **pareggio dei conti**, (acct), break even; **pareggio delle entrate e le uscite**, break-even point

pari nf (comm), par; **alla pari**, at par; **sopra la pari**, above par; **sotto la pari**, below par

parlare vb, talk, speak; **parlare di . .**, give a talk on . . .

parola nf, word; **parola d'ordine** (comp), password; **parola d'uso comune**, household word

parte nf, 1 (component) part. 2 **da parte di . .**, on behalf of . . .

partecipare vb, 1 (gen), participate, share. 2 (comm), join; **partecipare ad un'impresa**, join in a enterprise

partecipazione nf, 1 (gen), participation, sharing. 2 (shares) interest; **una partecipazione del 10%**, a 10% interest. 3 stake; **avere una partecipazione nella società**, have a stake in the company

partenza nf, departure

particolare adj, particular; **avaria particolare**, (ins), particular average

partire vb, leave; **il camion è partito**, the lorry has left

parziale adj, part; **carico parziale**, part load; **consegna parziale**, part delivery; **pagamento parziale**, part payment

passagio *nm* **(pedonale)**, walkway

passare *vb* (tests), pass; **passare il tempo**, spend time; **passare un esame**, pass an exam; **passare un ordine**, place an order

passatempo *nm*, pastime, hobby, leisure

passatempi *nmpl* (CV), hobbies

passato *nm*, past

passato(-a) *adj*, past

passeggero *nm*, passenger

passività *nfpl* (acct), liabilities

patente *nf* **(di guida)**, driving licence

patrocinare *vb*, sponsor

patrocinato *nm*, sponsoring

patrocinatore *nm* (mktg, sales), sponsor

patto *nm*, agreement, understanding

pavimento *nm*, floor

PC *nm*, PC, personal computer

pedaggio *nm* (on road), toll

pelle *nf*, **I** (gen), skin; **la sua pelle è molto morbida**, his/her skin is very soft. **2** (goods) leather; **articoli di pelle**, leather goods

pellicola *nf*, film

penalizzare *vb*, penalise

penna *nf*, pen; **penna evidenziatrice**, marker

pensare *vb*, think; (opinion) feel; **considerando quanto dite, pensiamo che . .**, in view of what you say, we feel that . . .

pensionamento *nm*, retirement

pensione *nf*, **I** lodging; **pensione con prima colazione**, B + B, Bed and Breakfast. **2** (pers), pension; **andare in pensione**, retire; **pagare una pensione**, pay a pension; **ricevere una pensione**, receive a pension

per *prep*, **I** (gen), for; **caffè per tutti**, coffee for everybody. **2** per **per anno**, per year; **per trimestre**, per quarter

percentuale *nf*, percentage; **un'alta percentuale**, a high percentage; **una piccola percentuale**, a small percentage

perdere *vb*, lose; **perdere al gioco**, gamble away; **perdere il treno**, miss the train; **perdere il volo**, miss the flight

perdita *nf*, loss; **avere una perdita**, make a loss; **vendere in perdita**, dump, sell at a loss; **perdita di liquido**, (imp/exp), leakage; **perdita totale**, (ins), write-off; **il veicolo è una perdita totale**, the vehicle is a write-off

perduto(-a) *adj*, lost

pericolo *nm*, danger; **mettere in pericolo**, jeopardise

pericoloso(-a) *adj*, dangerous

periferia *nf*, suburb

periferici *nmpl* (comp), peripherals

periodico *nm*, magazine; **periodici**, periodicals

periodo *nm*, period; **periodo di prova**, (pers), period of probation/(mktg, sales), trial period

permanente *adj*, permanent

permesso *nm*, permit, permission, licence; **permesso di caccia**, shooting licence; **ottenere il permesso**, obtain permission; **rilasciare un permesso**, grant a permit

permettere *vb*, permit, allow

persona *nf*, person; **persona irritante/persona dispettosa**, teaser

personale *nm*, **I** staff, personnel; **personale lavorativo**, workforce; **direttore del personale**, personnel manager; **riunione del personale**, staff meeting; **spese**

del personale, (acct), labour costs. 2 (transp.), crew

personale *adj*, personal; **assistente personale**, personal assistant; **computer personale**, PC, personal computer; **informazioni personali**, (forms, CV), personal details; **proprietà personale**, personal property; **segretaria personale**, personal secretary

personalizzare *vb* (mktg, sales), personalise

personalizzato(-a) *adj* (appearance of product), customised

pertinente *adj*, relevant, applicable; **non pertinente**, (forms), NA, N/A, not applicable

pesante *adj*, heavy

pesare *vb*, weigh

peso *nm*, weight

pessimistico(-a) *adj*, (financial outlook), gloomy

petroliera *nf*, (naut) oil tanker

petrolio *nm*, crude oil

pezzo *nm* **di ricambio**, spare part

piano *nm*, 1 floor; **l'ufficio è al primo piano**, the office is on the first floor. 2 plan; **un piano strategico**, a strategic plan

piano *adv*, slowly, softly

piano(-a) *adj*, flat; **terreno piano**, flat ground

pianterreno *nm*, ground floor

piattaforma *nf*, platform

piatto *nm*, 1 (gen), dish, plate. 2 (in restaurant), course

piatto(-a) *adj*, flat

picchetto *nm*, picket; **picchetto di scioperanti**, strike picket; **organizzare picchetti a una fabbrica**, picket a factory

piccolo(-a) *adj*, small; **una piccola quantità di . .**, a small quantity of . .; **piccoli annunci**, small ads;

Piccola o Media Impresa, SME, Small or Medium Sized Enterprise

piede *nm*, foot; **piede cubo**, cu ft, cubic foot

piegare *vb*, fold

pieno(-a) *adj*, full; **un posto a tempo pieno**, a full-time job

pila *nf*, (small) battery

piscina *nf*, swimming pool, pool

più *adv*, more; **si prega di inviare più copie**, please send more copies; **più attraente**, more attractive; **più caro(-a)**, more expensive; **più economico(-a)**, more economical; **questo prodotto è più attraente che utile**, this product is more attractive than useful; **per favore, più latte che caffè**, more milk than coffee, please; **la presentazione è più interessante di quanto pensassimo**, the presentation is more interesting than we thought; **è più utile di quanto si possa dimostrare**, it is more useful than one could possibly demonstrate; **il modello A è più efficace del modello B**, model A is more effective than model B

placcare *vb*, plate (silver, etc)

plastica *nf*, plastic

plastico(-a) *adj*, plastic

pneumatico *nm*, tyre

polizia *nf*, police

polizza *nf*, policy; **polizza d'assicurazione casko**, all risks insurance policy; (imp/exp) **polizza di carico**, B/L, bill of lading; **polizza di carico diretta**, through bill of lading; **polizza di carico senza clausola**, clean bill of lading; **polizza di carico di trasporto misto**, FBL, FIATA combined transport bill of lading

poltrona, *nf*, armchair

pompa *nf*, pump

pompare *vb* (transp), pump

ponte *nm*, **1** (gen), bridge. **2** (transp), deck *n*; **ponte da carico**, cargo deck

popolazione *nf*, population

porre *vb*, put; **porre dei quesiti**, query

porta *nf*, **a porta**, (comm), door to door; **vendita porta a porta**, door-to-door sales; **venditore porta a porta**, door-to-door salesman

portare *vb*, bring; **portare in tribunale**, take to court

portatile *adj*, portable; **computer portatile**, laptop

portatore *nm*, bearer; **titoli al portatore**, (fin) bearer securities

portavoce *nm/f*, spokesman

porto *nm*, **1** (gen), port; **porto d'imbarco**, (imp/exp), POE, port of embarcation; **porto d'entrata**, POE, port of entry; **tasse portuali**, (transp), port charges. **2** (transp), carriage; **porto assegnato**, (imp/exp), carriage forward; **franco di porto**, carriage free; **porto affrancato fino a . .**, carriage paid to . .; **porto pagato inclusa assicurazione fino a . .**, CIP, carriage, freight and insurance paid to . . .

posizione *nf*, position, location; **il luogo è in una posizione ideale**, the site is in an ideal position; **è una buona posizione per l'edificio**, it is a good location for the building

posporre *vb*, postpone

possedere *vb*, own; **possedere i requisiti per . .**, qualify for . . .

possibile *adj*, possible, feasible

possibilità *nf*, possibility, feasibility; **è una possibilità**, it is a possibility; **uno studio di possibilità**, a feasibility study

posta *nf*, post, mail; **posta in arrivo** (offce), in-tray; **posta in partenza**, out-tray; **mandare per posta**, mail; **posta normale**, surface mail

postale *adj*, postal; **codice postale**, post code; **servizio postale**, postal service; **tariffa postale**, postage; **timbro postale**, postmark; **società di servizi postali**, mailing company **ufficio postale**, post office

postino *nm*, postman

posto *nm*, **1** job, position, post; **posto vacante**, vacancy. **2** (place) spot; **sul posto** on the spot

potente *adj*, powerful, strong

potenza *nf*, power; **potenza in cavalli**, HP, hp, horse power, **potenza sviluppata**, (electr), output

potenziale *nm*, potential; **il prodotto ha un gran potenziale**, the product has great potential

potenziale *adj*, potential; **c'è un mercato potenziale di 3 milioni di unità**, there is a potential market of 3 million units

potere *vb*, be able to; **possiamo consegnare**, we are able to deliver

potere *nm*, power; **potere esecutivo**, executive power

povero(-a) *adj*, poor

pratica *nf* **(illecita)**, (mal)practice; **essere colpevole di pratiche illecite**, be guilty of malpractice

preavviso *nm*, (warning of future action), notice

precedente *nm*, precedent

precedenza *nf*, priority; **un ordine di precedenza**, a priority order; **vi saremmo grati se voleste dare precedenza a . .**, we would be grateful if you would give priority to . . .

precipitare *vb* (fin) (figures, rates), plunge

precisione *nf*, precision

preciso(-a) *adj*, precise, definite, accurate; **essere preciso su . .**, be definite about . .; **persona precisa**, accurate person; **è un concetto preciso**, it is a precise concept

preconcetto *nm*, prejudice; **non avere preconcetti**, have an open mind

predisporre *vb*, arrange for . .; **abbiamo predisposto la consegna delle merci per domani**, we have arranged for the goods to reach you tomorrow

preferenza *nf*, preference; **c'è una preferenza per . .**, there is a preference for . . .

preferire *vb*, prefer; **i nostri clienti preferiscono merci di marca alle merci non di marca**, our customers prefer branded goods to unbranded goods

pre-imballato(-a) *adj*, prepacked

prelevare *vb*, 1 (gen), pick up, collect. 2 (money), withdraw

prelievo *nm*, collection, pick-up; **prelievo automatico**, (bank), direct debit; **prelievo e consegna**, (imp/exp), P+D, pick-up and delivery

premio *nm*, 1 (ins), bonus, premium. 2 (of a lottery, etc), prize; **estrazione del premio**, prize draw

prendere *vb*, take; **prendere appunti**, take notes; **prendere a prestito**, borrow; **prendere cura**, take care; **prendere di mira**, (mktg, sales), target; **prendere in affitto**, lease; **prendere in considerazione**, take into account; **prendere nota**, note; **prendere provvedimenti**, take steps; **prendere un appuntamento**, make an appointment; **prendere un treno/un aeroplano**, catch a train/an aeroplane; **prendersela con comodo**, take it easy

prenotare *vb*, book, reserve; **prenotare una camera**, reserve/book a room; **prenotare un posto**, book/reserve a seat

prenotazione *nf*, reservation, booking; **annullare una prenotazione**, cancel a reservation; **avere una prenotazione**, have a reservation; **fare una prenotazione**, make a booking

preparativi *nmpl*, arrangements

prepensionamento *nm*, early retirement

presentare *vb*, 1 (gen), present; **presentare una fattura all'accettazione**, present a bill for acceptance; **presentare un reclamo contro . .**, lodge a complaint against . . . 2 (mktg, sales), feature; **l'articolo presenterà la nostra società**, the article will feature our company. 3 introduce; **la presenterò alla signora Sellitri Rita, il nostro nuovo direttore**, I will introduce you to our new director, Mrs Rita Sellitri

presentazione *nf*, presentation; **fare una presentazione**, (give a talk), give a presentation

presidente *nm*, chairman, president; **Presidente del Consiglio**, PM, Prime Minister; **Presidente Direttore Generale**, CEO, Chief Executive Officer

presiedere *vb* **un'assemblea**, chair a meeting

pressione *nf*, pressure, stress; **la pressione del sangue è molto alta**, the blood pressure is very high; **il direttore è sotto pressione**, the director is under stress

prestare *vb*, lend

prestatore *nm*, lender

prestito *nm* (fin), loan, borrowing

presto *adv*, early

pretese *nfpl* (admin), career objective

prevedere *vb* (fin), forecast

preventivare *vb*, estimate; **costo preventivato**, estimated cost

preventivo *nm*, estimate

previsione *nf*, **I** (fin), forecast. **2** prospection; **previsioni di movimenti di cassa**, (fin), cashflow projection

prezioso(-a) *adj*, valuable

prezzo *nm*, price, charge; **prezzo d'acquisto**, purchase price; **prezzo raccomandato**, recommended price; **prezzo tutto compreso**, all-in price; **il prezzo è molto alto/basso**, the price is very high/low; **aumento dei prezzi**, price increase; **blocco dei prezzi**, price freeze; **listino prezzi**, price list; **politica dei prezzi**, pricing policy; **ribasso (dei prezzi)**, price cut

prima *adv*, before; **prima del 5 maggio**, before 5 May; **prima di ordinare**, before ordering

primato *nm*, record; **risultati da primato**, record results

primo(-a) *adj*, **I** first; **la prima volta**, the first time; **essere il primo**, to be ahead/to have a lead. **2** prime; **Primo Ministro**, Prime Minister

principale *adj*, main; **attività principale**, main activity; **conduttura principale**, mains (electricity)

privare *vb*, deprive; **privare della nazionalità**, denationalise

privatizzare *vb*, privatise

privato(-a) *adj*, private

procedimento *nm*, **I** (gen), procedure; **si prega di seguire il procedimento giusto per . .**, please follow the correct procedure for . .; **il procedimento per le ordinazioni è spiegato nel retro del catalogo**, the procedure for

ordering is set out at the back of the catalogue. **2** (manufacturing), process

processo *nm* (law), proceedings; **intentare un processo contro . .**, institute proceedings against . .; **2** trial; **essere sotto processo**, be on trial

procurarsi *vb*, (fin), raise; **procurarsi un prestito**, raise a loan

prodotto *nm*, **I** product; **è un prodotto di prima qualità**, it is a first-class product; **lanciare un prodotto**, market a product; **prodotti alimentari**, food products; **prodotti farmaceutici**, pharmaceutical products; **prodotti petroliferi**, petroleum products; **prodotto di sostituzione**, (materials) substitute; **Prodotto Interno Lordo, PIL**, GDP, Gross Domestic Product; **Prodotto Nazionale Lordo, PNL**, GNP, Gross National Product. **2** produce; **prodotti agricoli**, farm produce; **prodotto locale**, home produce

produrre *vb*, produce, yield

produttore *nm*, producer

produzione *nf*, **I** production; **produzione in serie**, mass production; **catena di produzione**, production line; **costo di produzione**, production cost; **direttore alla produzione**, production manager. **2** (pers), productivity; **premio di produzione**, productivity bonus

professionale *adj*, professional; **esperienza professionale**, professional experience

professione *nf*, **I** (gen), profession **2** (pers), occupation

professionista *nm*, professional (man/woman)

profilo *nm*, profile; **alto/basso profilo**, high/low profile

profittare *vb*, . . . benefit from . . .

profitto *nm*, profit; **profitto lordo/netto**, gross/net profit; **un alto livello di profitti**, a high level of profits; **realizzare profitti record**, make record profits

profondo(-a) *adj*, deep, thorough

pro forma *adj* pro forma; **fattura** *nf* **pro forma**, pro forma invoice

progettare *vb*, **1** (gen), plan; **progettiamo di fare publicità nelle riviste dei commercianti**, we plan to advertise in the trade journals. **2** (drawings, plans), design, draw

progettazione *nf*, planning

progettista *nm*, planner

progetto *nm*, **1** project; **è un progetto interessante**, it is an interesting project. **2** plan; **il nostro progetto è quello di . . .**, our plan is to . . .

programma *nm*, programme, schedule; **programma televisivo**, television programme; **programma utilitario** (comp), utility; **la visita è in programma**, the visit is on schedule

programmare *vb*, program, schedule

programmatore *nm* (comp), programmer

progresso *nm*, progress; **fare progressi**, make progress

proibire *vb*, forbid, prevent, ban

proibitivo(-a) *adj*, prohibitive; **il costo del trasporto aereo delle merci è proibitivo**, the cost of airfreighting goods is prohibitive

proiettare *vb* (fin), project

proiettore *nm* **diapositive**, slide projector, carousel

promemoria *nm*, reminder

promettere *vb*, promise, undertake

promotore *nm* (start businesses), promoter

promozione *nf*, (mktg, sales), promotion

promuovere *vb*, promote; **è stato promosso al posto di direttore**, he has been promoted to the post of manager

pronto(-a) *adj*, ready, quick, early; **sono pronta**, I am ready; **quel ragazzo è pronto**, that boy is quick; **possiamo garantire una consegna pronta**, we can guarantee early delivery; **l'ordine è pronto**, the order is ready; **pronto per l'uso**, ready for use

proporre *vb*, propose; **vorrei proporre una soluzione**, I would like to propose a solution

proposta *nf*, **1** proposal; **abbiamo studiato la vostra proposta e . .**, we have studied your proposal and . .; **fare una proposta** make a proposal. **2** proposition; **è una buona proposta**, it is a good proposition

proprietà *nf*, property; **proprietà privata**, private property; **proprietà fondiaria**, (acct), land

proprietario *nm*, owner; **a rischio del proprietario**, (ins), OR, owner's risk

prospero(-a) *adj*, thriving

prospettiva *nf*, outlook; **la prospettiva è buona**, the outlook is good

prospetto *nm* **di vendita**, (comm), lead

prossimo(-a) *adj*, near; **in un prossimo futuro**, in the near future

proteggere *vb*, protect; **proteggere con i diritti d'autore** (law), copyright

protetto(-a) *adj* **dai diritti d'autore**, copyright

prova *nf*, test

provare *vb*, try, test; **vuole provare l'abito?**, would you like to try the dress on?; **il meccanico ha provato la macchina**, the engineer has tested the machine

provvedere *vb*, **I** (gen), provide. **2** cater (food)

provvedimento *nm*, provision; **prendere provvedimenti per i debiti insolvibili**, make provision for bad debts

provvigione *nf*, (fin), commission

provvisorio(-a) *adj*, **I** (gen), provisional. **2** (agreement), tentative

pubblicità *nf*, (mktg, sales), advertising; **direttore alla pubblicità**, advertising manager **pubblicità commerciale**, commercial; **pubblicità sul luogo di vendita**, POS advertising

pubblicitario(-a) *adj*, advertising; **agente pubblicitario**, advertising agent; **opuscoli pubblicitari**, literature

pubblico(-a) *adj*, public; **giardini pubblici**, public gardens; **lavori pubblici**, public works; **pubblico ministero** (law), public prosecutor; **relazioni pubbliche**, public relations; **scandalo pubblico**, open scandal; **trasporto pubblico**, public transport

pulito(-a) *adj*, clean

pulmann *nm*, coach; **stazione pulmann**, coach station

punta *nf* (end of something), tip

punteggio *nm*, (in competitions), draw

punto *nm*, **I** point; **punto essenziale**, basic point; **fare un punto**, make a point; **un punto principale**, a major point; **punto di vendita**, point of sale. **2** (grammar) full stop; **punto e virgola**, semicolon

quadrato *nm*, square

quadrato(-a) *adj*, square; **la stanza è quadrata**, the room is square

quadratura *nf*, squaring

quadricromia *nf* (mktg, sales), four-colour process

qualifica *nf*, qualification

qualità *nf*, **1** (gen), quality; **questo è un prodotto di qualità**, this is a quality product. **2** (role), capacity; **agisce in qualità di . .**, he is acting in the capacity of . . .

quantità *nf*, quantity; **una piccola/una grande quantità**, a small/large quantity; **in grande quantità**, (transp), in bulk

quartiere *nm*, quarter, district (of town)

quarto *nm* (maths), quarter

quasi *adv*, almost, nearly; **il vostro ordine è quasi pronto**, your order is almost ready; **l'inflazione ha raggiunto quasi il 15%**, inflation has reached nearly 15%

querela *nf*, complaint; (law), **sporgere/presentare una querela**, lodge a complaint

quesito *nm*, query; **avere un quesito su . .**, have a query about . ., **porre dei quesiti**, query

questionario *nm*, questionnaire; **riempire il questionario**, fill in a questionnaire

questione *nf*, **1** (subject of discussion), issue; **dobbiamo discutere la questione della manutenzione**, we must discuss the issue of maintenance. **2** item (of an agenda); **questioni all'ordine del giorno**, items on the agenda

quietanza *nf*, receipt; **fattura quietanzata**, receipted invoice

quota *nf*, share, quota, instalment

quotare *vb*, quote; **quotare un prezzo**, quote a price; **quotato (-a) in borsa**, quoted on the stock exchange

quotazione *nf*, quotation, quote; **inviare una quotazione**, send a quotation

quotidiano(-a) *adj*, daily

quotidiano *nm*, the daily newspaper

quoziente *nm*, quotient, ratio; **quoziente d'intelligenza**, IQ, intelligence quotient

R

raccogliere vb, gather, pick up; **raccogliere informazioni**, gather information; **raccogliere voti**, poll

raccoglitore nm, (office), file

raccolta nf, collection

raccomandare vb, recommend; **prezzo raccomandato**, (fin) recommended price

raccordo nm, 1 (electr), cable. 2 (transp), junction. 3 (eng), connection

raddoppiare vb, double

radio nf, radio; **diramare/contattare per radio**, radio

raffinare vb, refine

raffreddamento nm, cool; **fase di raffreddamento**, cooling-off period

ragazza nf, girl

ragazzi nmpl, children

ragazzo nm, boy

raggio nm, 1 (gen), ray; **raggio infrarosso**, infra-red ray; **raggio luminoso**, ray of light. 2 (geog, med, eng) radius; **entro un raggio di 20 chilometri**, within a radius of 20 km; **raggio di curvatura**, radius of curvature. 3 range (of vehicle or machine). 4 spoke (of a wheel)

raggiungere vb, 1 (gen), reach; **raggiungere un accordo**, reach an agreement; **raggiungere un pareggio di conti**, (fin) reach break even. 2 (fig) approach; **il tasso raggiunge il 3%**, the rate is approaching the 3% mark; **raggiungere il massimo**, peak; **riteniamo che la domanda ha raggiunto il massimo**, we believe that demand has peaked

raggiungimento nm, achievement

ragioniere nm, accountant

rallentamento nm, slow-down

rallentare vb, slow down

rammentare vb, remind; **devo rammentargli di . .**, I must remind him to . . .

rapido(-a) adj, rapid; **consegna rapida**, (transp), rapid delivery

rapporto nm, 1 (gen), relationship. 2 report; **scrivere un rapporto**, write a report; **fare un rapporto su . .**, report on . . . 3 (maths), ratio. 4 (fin), **rapporto di liquidità immediata**, acid test ratio

rappresentazioni nfpl **grafiche**, graphics

raro(-a) adj, rare, scarce

rata nf, 1 (of club), fee; **la rata annuale di associazione include . .**, the annual membership fee includes . . . 2 (part payment of a loan), instalment; **la prima rata dovrà essere pagata il primo maggio**, the first instalment is due to be paid on 1 May

razionalizzare vb, 1 (gen), rationalise. 2 (production, a company), streamline

razionalizzazione nf, (pers), rationalisation

razionare vb, ration

razione nf, ration

recentemente adv, recently, lately

recessione nf, recession

reciproco(-a) adj, reciprocal; **un accordo reciproco**, a reciprocal agreement

reclamare vb, claim (a right)

reclamo *nm*, 1 (ins), claim; **sezione reclami**, claims department. 2 (mktg, sales), complaint; **fare un reclamo**, make a complaint; **presentare un reclamo contro . . ./sporgere querela contro . .**, lodge a complaint against . . .

reclutamento *nm*, (soldiers), recruitment

reclutare *vb* (soldiers), recruit

redattore *nm*, editor (of a newspaper); **redattore pubblicitario**, (mktg, sales), copywriter

reddito *nm*, 1 (gen), income; **reddito regolare**, regular income; **imposta sul reddito**, income tax. 2 (fin), yield

redigere *vb*, 1 (gen), draw up; **redigere un contratto**, draw up a contract. 2 (write), draft; **redigere un patto**, draw an agreement

referenze *nfpl* (CV), references

refrigerare *vb*, refrigerate; **refrigerato(-a)** *adj*, refrigerated; **contenitore refrigerato**, (imp/exp), refrigerated container

regalo *nm*, 1 (gen), present, gift. 2 (mktg, sales), giveaway; **regalo pubblicitario**, (mktg, sales), freebie

regionale *adj*, regional

regione *nf*, region

registrare *vb*, 1 register, record; **registrare una società**, register a company; **registrare un messaggio**, (ansaphone) record a message; **registrare un ordine**, book an order; **registrare i bagagli**, check in (luggage); **registrare (su nastro)**, (record sound), tape. 2 enter (a figure); **registrare (sui libri contabili)**, (acct), enter figures in the accounts. 3 adjust; **registrare le valvore**, adjust the valves.

registratore *nm*, tape recorder; **registratore per video**, VCR,

video cassette recorder; **registratore (di cassa)**, cash-register

registrazione *nf*, 1 (gen), registration; **numero di registrazione**, registration number. 2 (written), record

registro *nm*, register

Regno Unito *nm*, UK, United Kingdom

regola *nf*, rule

regolamento *nm*, 1 (gen), regulation. 2 (fin), adjustment; **regolamento dei conti**, adjustment of the accounts

regolare *vb*, 1 (fin, mech), adjust. 2 (adjust and assemble), fit

regolare *adj*, regular; **volo regolare**, scheduled flight

regolazione *nf* (of machine), adjustment

relazione *nf*, relationship

rendere *vb* (fin), yield; **rendere noto** declare (a result); **rendersi conto**, appreciate; **ci rendiamo conto della vostra situazione**, we appreciate your situation

rendimento *nm* (factory), output

reparto *nm*, department; **direttore di reparto**, departmental manager

repentaglio *nm*, risk, danger; **mettere a repentaglio**, jeopardise

reputazione *nf*, reputation; **avere una buona reputazione**, have a good reputation

resistente *adj*, durable; (materials), strong

resistenza *nf*, strength

respingere *vb*, turn down; **respingere una proposta/un'offerta**, turn down a proposal/an offer

responsabile *nm*, 1 (pers) head, **responsabile del Marketing**,

Head of Marketing; **responsabile di magazzino**, warehouse manager. **2** executive; **responsabile alle vendite**, sales executive

responsabile *adj*, **1** (gen), responsible. **2** (law), liable; **essere responsabile di . .**, be liable to . . .

responsabilità *nf*, **1** (gen), responsibility. **2** (law), liability; **SRL, Società a responsabilità limitata**, Ltd, limited company

restituire *vb*, return, give back; **da non restituire**, non-returnable

resto *nm*, change

rete *nf* (comp), network; **rete locale**, LAN network; **mettere in rete**, network; **sistema di rete**, networked system; **rete ad anello a gettone**, token ring network

retromarcia *nf*, reverse (gear); **innestare la retromarcia**, reverse

revisione *nf*, **1** (gen), revision. **2** (fin), audit

revisore *nm* **(di conti)**, (fin), auditor

riaddestramento *nm*, retraining

rialzare *vb* **i prezzi**, raise/mark up prices

rialzista *nm* (comm), (stock market), bull

rialzo *nm*, increase in price, mark up

riapprovvigionare *vb*, restock

riassumere *vb*, summarise

riattivare *vb* **un contatto**, (mktg, sales), follow up a lead

ribassista *nm*, (stock market) bear

ribasso *nm*, fall, drop; **mercato con tendenza al ribasso**, (stock market), bear market; **giocare al ribasso**, (stock market), bear; **tendenza al ribasso**, (gen, fin), downward trend; **essere in ribasso**, (gen), be down; **un ribasso rapido nei prezzi**, a rapid fall in prices

ricaricare *vb* (electr), (batteries), recharge

ricavo *nm* (acct), proceeds

ricerca *nf*, research; **ricerca di mercato**, market research; **fare ricerche**, research; **ricerca di persone**, (telec) paging; **Ricerca e Sviluppo**, R + D, R and D, Research and Development

ricercato(-a) *adj*, popular

ricetta *nf*, **1** (med), prescription. **2** recipe

ricevere *vb*, receive; **ricevere la notifica di . .**, receive notification of . ., **ricevere una pensione**, receive a pension

ricevimento *nm*, **1** (of goods), receipt; **pagamento al ricevimento merci**, payment on receipt of goods. **2** (drinks, snacks), reception; **dare un ricevimento**, hold a reception

ricevitore *nm* **(tascabile)**, (radio) pager

ricevuta *nf* (document), receipt; **emettere una ricevuta**, make out a receipt; **ricevuta di bordo**, (imp/exp), mate's receipt

ricezione *nf*, reception (desk); **zona di ricezione**, reception area

richiamare *vb* **(al telefono)**, (telec) call back

richiedere *vb*, call for; **richiedere dei cambiamenti**, call for changes; demand changes

richiesta *nf*, **1** (gen), request, demand. **2** (for job, loan), application; **modulo di richiesta**, application form. **3** (of a right), claim. **4** (request for information), inquiry; **vi ringraziamo per la vostra richiesta d'informazioni**, thank you for your inquiry

riciclare *vb*, recycle

riciclo *nm*, recycling; **un impianto di riciclo**, a recycling plant

ricompensare *vb*, compensate

riconoscere *vb*, recognise, admit; **riconoscere qualcuno**, recognise somebody; **riconoscere un errore**, admit a mistake

riconoscimento *nm*, recognition

ricontattare *vb*, follow up

ricorrere *vb* **alla legge**, go to/resort to law

ridurre *vb*, **1** (gen). reduce. **2** (prices, costs, production) cut, mark down; **ridurre i prezzi in modo drastico**, slash prices

riduzione *nf*, reduction, cutback, rebate; **riduzione dei prezzi**, reduction in prices; **una riduzione nella produzione**, a cutback in production; **concedere una riduzione**, give a rebate

riempire *vb*, **1** (a form), fill in. **2** (with liquids), fill up

riferire *vb* (inform someone of an event), report

riferirsi *vb*, apply; **questo si riferisce a noi**, this does apply to us; **riferirsi a . .**, refer to . . .

rifiutare *vb* (gen), refuse, deny, reject; **in teoria rifiuto l'idea**, I reject the idea in principle; **è stata rifiutata l'entrata**, entry was denied; **il cliente ha rifiutato le merci**, the customer has rejected the goods

rifiuto *nm*, denial

rifornire *vb* **di carburante**, (ship, a plane), refuel

rigido(-a) *adj*, strict

rigore *nm* (sport), penalty

riguadagnare *vb* **il tempo perduto**, make up for lost time

riguardare *vb*, affect; **la questione riguarda solo me**, the matter affects only me

rilasciare *vb*, issue, release; **rilasciare una ricevuta**, issue a receipt; **rilasciare le merci**, release the goods

rilevante *adj*, significant; **un'offerta rilevante**, a significant offer

rilevare *vb*, buy out, take over; **abbiamo rilevato la società . .**, we bought out the company . .; **la società X è stata rilevata dalla . .**, X have been taken over by . . .

rilievo *nm* takeover (of company); **offerta di rilievo**, takeover bid; **fare/ricevere un'offerta di rilievo**, make/receive a takeover bid

rimandare *vb*, defer; **rimandare una decisione**, defer a decision; **rimandato(-a)**, deferred

rimanere *vb*, remain

rimborsare *vb*, reimburse, refund

rimborso *nm* (money back), rebate

rimessa *nf* (fin), remittance

rimettere *vb* (fin), (send money), remit

rimorchiare *vb*, tow

rimorchio *nm*, **1** tow. **2** trailer; **trasportare un rimorchio per ferrovia**, (transp), piggyback

rimostranza *nf*, complaint, protest; **fare le rimostranze**, complain

rimpiangere *vb*, regret

rinforzare *vb*, reinforce, strengthen; **rinforzato(-a) con . .**, reinforced with . .; **rinforzato (-a)**, (imp/exp), strengthened

ringraziare *vb*, thank

rinnovare *vb*, renew

rinomato(-a) *adj* **per . .**, noted for . . .

rinuncia *nf* (ins), waiver

rinunciare *vb* **(a un diritto)**, (ins), waive (a right)

rinviare *vb*, put off (a meeting); **la riunione è stata rinviata fino al mese prossimo**, the meeting has been put off until next month

riorganizzare *vb*, reorganise

riorganizzazione *nf*, reorganisation

ripagare *vb* **nello stesso modo**, repay in kind

riparare *vb*, mend, repair

riparazione *nf* (make good), repair

riparo *nm* (place of repair), repair

ripiano *nm*, shelf

riportare *vb*, carry forward

riporto *nm* (fin, acct), bf, b/f, brought forward, cf, carried forward

riprendere *vb*, take back; **siamo disposti a riprendere le merci non soddisfacenti**, we are willing to take back the unsatisfactory goods; **riprendere forza**, gather strength

riprendersi *vb*, pick up; **le vendite si sono riprese nel secondo trimestre**, sales picked up in the second quarter

ripresa *nf*, (fin), revival, upturn; **una ripresa nelle vendite**, a revival/an upturn in sales

riproduzione *nf* **vietata**, copyright

riprogrammare *vb* (fin), reschedule (repayments)

risarcimento *nm*, smart money

riscaldamento *nm*, heating; **riscaldamento centrale**, central heating

riscatto *nm*, 1 (gen), ransom. 2 (fin), surrender; **valore di riscatto**, surrender value

rischiare *vb*, risk

rischio *nm*, risk; **a rischio del proprietario**, (ins), OR, owner's risk; **tutti i rischi**, all risks

riserva *nf* **di materiali**, stockpile

riservare *vb*, book; **riservare uno stand**, book a stand

risolvere *vb*, solve; **risolvere un problema**, solve a problem

risorsa *nf* (fin), asset; **la sua risorsa principale è . .**, his main asset is . .; **risorse umane**, human resources

rispettabile *adj*, reputable

rispettare *vb* **la data limite** meet/keep to a deadline

rispondere *vb*, answer, reply; **rispondere ad una domanda**, answer a question; **rispondere ad un'inserzione**, reply to an advertisement

risposta *nf*, answer, reply; **nessuna risposta**, no answer; **cedola di risposta**, reply coupon; **la nostra lettera di reclamo è rimasta senza risposta**, our letter of complaint has remained unanswered

ristagnare *vb*, stagnate

ristagno *nm* (fin), slump

ristrutturare *vb*, restructure

ristrutturazione *nf* (pers), restructuring

risultato *nm*, 1 (gen), result, outcome. 2 (fin), achievement. 3 (of a company), performance; **salario in relazione al risultato**, (pers), performance-related pay; **dare dei risultati migliori**, outperform; **la società ha dei buoni risultati**, the company has a very successful track record

ritagliare *vb* **il tagliando**, (mktg, sales), clip the coupon

ritardare *vb*, delay

ritardo *nm*, 1 (gen), delay; **in ritardo**, delayed/late, overdue. 2 (in production), hold up; **essere in ritardo**, be late

ritirare *vb* (fin), withdraw (money)

ritirarsi *vb* **dagli affari**, retire from business/cease trading

ritmo *nm* (regular amount/time), rate

ritornare *vb*, return; **ritorneremo a Milano fra breve**, we will return to Milano shortly; **le merci sono state ritornate**, goods have been returned

ritorno *nm* (gen, fin), return; **ritorno sull'investimento**, return on investment; **biglietto di andata e ritorno**, return ticket

riunione *nf*, meeting; **riunione d'informazione/di preparazione**, briefing

riunire *vb*, **1** (unite again), re-unite. **2** (put together), gather

riuscire *vb* **fare qualcosa**, manage to do something/succeed in doing something

rivalutare *vb*, reassess

rivalutazione *nf*, reassessment; **fare una rivalutazione di . .**, make a reassessment of . . .

rivedere *vb*, **1** (gen), revise; **rivedere i termini di pagamento** revise, terms of payment. **2 rivedere (i conti)**, (fin), audit

rivenditore *nm*, dealer

rivista *nf*, magazine

robot *nm*, robot; **montaggio a mezzo di robot**, robot assembly

ROM (comp), ROM

rompere *vb*, (gen), break; **rotto(-a)**, broken; **rompere un contratto**, be in breach of contract

rosso(-a) *adj*, red; **essere in rosso**, (fin), be in the red

rotazione *nf* **(scorte)**, (inventory) turnover

rotolare *vb*, roll

rotonda *nf* (transp) roundabout

rotondo(-a) *adj*, round

rottame *nm*, scrap; **rottame di ferro**, scrap iron

rottura *nf*, breach; **rottura di un**

contratto, breach of a contract

rovesciare *vb*, spill; **il nostro camion si è rovesciato con il carico**, our lorry has shed its load

rovescio *nm* (fin), setback, reverse; **avere un rovescio finanziario**, have a financial setback

rovina *nf*, fall, collapse; **andare in rovina**, go to the dogs

rovinare *vb*, (affect quality), spoil; **le merci sono state rovinate dall'umido**, the goods have been spoiled by the damp

rubare *vb*, steal

ruggine *nf*, rust; **ci sono delle macchie di ruggine sulla superficie del prodotto**, there are patches of rust on the surface of the product

rullino *nm* (photos), film

ruota *nf*, wheel

ruvido(-a) *adj* (gen), rough (finish on goods)

S

sacchetto *nm*, bag

sacco *nm* (imp/exp), sack

sala *nf*, hall, chamber, (large) room; **sala d'attesa**, waiting room

salario *nm*, pay, wage

salone *nm*, hall, reception room

saldare *vb*, 1 (fin), pay; **saldato(-a)**, paid; **non saldato(-a)**, unpaid; **saldare una fattura** (fin), settle a bill. 2 (eng), weld; **la catena è stata saldata**, the chain has been welded

saldo *nm*, 1 (fin), balance; **il saldo dell'ordine sara spedito in breve tempo**, the balance of the order will be sent shortly; **saldo da pagare**, balance due; **saldo a nuovo**, balance brought down. 2 (autumn sale), sale. 3 (fin), settlement; **Banca dei Saldi Internazionali**, BIS, Bank for International Settlements; **il saldo della fattura**, the settlement of the invoice

salire *vb* (fin), go up; **i prezzi sono saliti del 5%**, prices have gone up by 5%

salpare *vb* (naut), (leave port), sail

salutare *vb*, greet

saluti, distinti saluti, yours faithfully, yours sincerely

salvaguardare *vb*, 1 (gen), safeguard. 2 (comp), back up

salvare *vb*, save; **salvare le apparenze**, keep up appearances

sapore *nm*, taste; **avere un sapore**, taste; **ha un sapore molto dolce**,
it tastes very sweet

satellite *nm*, satellite; **TV a mezzo satellite**, satellite TV

saturato(-a) *adj*, saturated

saturazione *nf*, saturation

sbagliato(-a) *adj*, wrong; **hanno inviato le merci sbagliate**, they sent the wrong goods

sbaglio *nm*, fault, mistake

sbalzo *nm* **dei prezzi**, upswing of prices

sbarcare *vb* (naut), land

sbarco *nm*, landing; **spese di sbarco**, landing charges

sbarrare *vb* **un assegno**, cross a cheque

scadente *adj*, poor; **qualità scadente**, poor quality; **risultati scadenti**, poor results

scadenza *nf* (fin), expiry, due date; **venire a scadenza**, fall due; **il pagamento viene a scadenza in giugno**, payment falls due in June

scadere *vb* (fin), mature

scaffalatura *nf*, shelving

scala *nf* (set charges, rates, etc), scale; **scala mobile**, sliding scale; **disegno in scala**, scale drawing

scalo *nm* (transp), stopover; **fare scalo**, stop

scambiare *vb*, exchange

scandalo *nm* **(pubblico)**, (open) scandal

scandire *vb*, spell out

scaricare *vb*, 1 (transp), discharge, unload. 2 (cargo), land; **scaricare un carico** (transp), shed a load

scarico *nm*, discharge, unloading

scarso(-a) *adj*, 1 (gen), scarce, poor. 2 (fin), tight; **il denaro è scarso**, money is tight

scartare *vb*, 1 (an idea or argument), dismiss. 2 (a plan, a product), scrap

scarto nm, 1 (gen), waste. 2 (goods), reject. 3 (rubbish), scrap; **pradotti di scarto**, waste products

scatola nf, box

scegliere vb, choose, pick

scendere vb, 1 (rates, prices), go down. 2 (a bus, train, car), get off

scheda nf, file card

schedario nm, card index, filing cabinet

schema nm, scheme

schermo nm (gen, comp), screen

scialbo(-a) adj, flat

sciolto(-a) adj, loose; **merci sciolte**, loose goods

scioperante adj, strike

scioperante nm, striker

scioperare vb, strike, walk-out

sciopero nm, strike, walk-out; **sciopero bianco**, sit-down strike; **gli operai sono in sciopero**, the workers are on strike

scivolare vb, slide, slip

scontato(-a) adj (fin), discounted

sconto nm, discount, reduction, cut

scontrare vb, collide; **scontrare violentemente**, crash

scontrino nm, ticket, till receipt

scontro nm **violento**, crash; **il camion che trasportava la vostra merce ha avuto uno scontro violento**, the lorry carrying your goods has had a crash

scoperta nf, discovery

scoperto nm, overdraft

scoperto(-a) adj (fin), OD, O/D, overdrawn; **essere scoperto (in banca)**, be overdrawn

scopo nm, aim, purpose; **lo scopo principale è quello di . .**, the main aim is to . .; **lo scopo della visita è . .**, the purpose of the visit is . . .

scorie nfpl, waste; **scorie tossiche**, toxic waste

scorta nf (mktg, sales), supply, provision, stock; **rotazione scorte**, inventory turnover

scotch nm (offce), sellotape

scrivania nf, desk

scrivere vb, write; **scrivere un rapporto**, write a report; **scrivere a qualcuno**, write to someone

scrupoloso(-a) adj, dedicated

scusa nf, apology, excuse; **vi preghiamo di accettare le nostre scuse**, please accept our apologies; **è una scusa**, it is an excuse

scusarsi vb (corr), apologise, **ci scusiamo per il ritardo**, we apologise for the delay

sdoganamento nm, clearance

sdoganare vb (imp/exp), clear customs; **sdoganato(-a) senza ispezione preliminare**, CWE, cleared without examination

secco(-a) adj, dry

secondo adv, according to; **secondo me**, according to me; **secondo il valore**, (fin), ad val, ad valorem

secondo(-a) adj, second; **il secondo punto è . .**, the second point is . .; **in secondo luogo**, secondly

secondo prep **le condizioni di . .**, under the terms of . . .

sede nf **(di una ditta)**, head office; **sede sociale**, (registered office), headquarters

segmentazione nf, segmentation

segmento nm, segment; **segmento di mercato**, market segment

segno nm, sign

segretario(-a) nm/f, secretary; **segretaria di direzione**, director's secretary

segreteria nf **telefonica**,

ansaphone/answerphone

segreto *nm*, secret

segreto(-a) *adj*, secret

seguire *vb*, follow

selezionare *vb*, **I** (gen), select.
2 (quality of goods), grade.
3 (comp), sort

selezione *nf*, selection; **fare una selezione**, make a selection; **il procedimento di selezione** (pers), the selection procedure

self-service *nm*, self-service

semaforo *nm*, traffic light

semestralmente *adv*, half-yearly

semestre *nm*, half year; **i risultati del semestre**, the half-year results

sensibile *adj*, **I** (gen), sensitive; **essere sensibile a . .**, be sensitive to . . . **2** (sales, acct), tangible; **ce' stato un sensibile aumento**, there has been a tangible increase

sensibilità *nf*, sensitivity

sensibilizzare *vb*, make aware of; **sensibilizzare i clienti su . .**, make customers aware of . . .

sentenza *nf*, (law), sentence

sentire *vb*, hear, listen; **sentir dire**, understand; **abbiamo sentito dire che voi al momento state trattando con un agente di Roma**, we understand that you are currently dealing with an agent in Rome

senza *prep*, without; **senza fiato**, out of breath

separare *vb*, separate

sequestrare *vb* (imp/exp), impound

serbatoio *nm* (imp/exp), tank

serie *nf*, series, set; **una serie completa di documenti**, a complete set of documents; **numero di serie**, serial number

serrare *vb*, tighten up

servizio *nm*, service; **servizio postale**, postal service

settimana *nf*, week

settimanale *adj*, weekly

settimanalmente *adv*, weekly

settore *nm* (mktg, sales), sector; **settore del bruno**, brown goods

settoriale *adj*, sectorial

severo(-a) *adj*, **I** (discipline), strict. **2** (law), tight

sezione *nf*, department; **la sezione lingue straniere**, the foreign language department; **direttore di sezione**, departmental manager

sfavorevole *adj*, unfavourable; **i risultati sono sfavorevoli**, the results are unfavourable; **la prospettiva è sfavorevole**, the outlook is unfavourable

sfida *nf*, challenge

sfumatura *nf* (colour), shade; **mi piace la sfumatura del verde**, I like the green shade

shock *nm*, shock; **a prova di shock**, shock-proof

sicurezza *nf*, safety, security; **norme di sicurezza**, safety standards

sicuro(-a) *adj*, safe; **un investimento sicuro**, a safe investment

sigillare *vb* (imp/exp), seal; **sigillato sottovuoto**, vacuum sealed

sigillo *nm* (imp/exp, law), seal

sigla *nf*, acronym

significativo(-a) *adj*, significant; **un aumento significativo**, a significant increase; **un fatto significativo**, a significant fact

simbolo *nm*, logo

singolo(-a) *adj*, single; **camera singola**, single room

sinistra *nf*, left

sinistro *nm* (mishap), accident;

assicurazione contro i sinistri, insurance against damage

sinistro(-a) *adj* (direction), left

sintetico(-a) *adj* (fabrics), man-made, synthetic

sistema *nm*, system; **sistema di rete**, (comp), networked system

sistemare *vb* **una disputa**, settle a dispute

situare *vb*, locate, base; **la macchina è situata in un angolo**, the machine is located in a corner; **la società è situata in . .**, the company is based in . . .

situazione *nf*, **1** situation; **la situazione economica**, the economic situation. **2** status; **la situazione finanziaria**, the financial status

sleale *adj*, unfair; **concorrenza sleale**, unfair competition

slittamento *nm*, slippage

slogan *nm*, slogan

smontare *vb*, take down; **lo stand deve essere smontato entro 24 ore**, the stand must be taken down within 24 hours

sociale *adj*, **1** (gen), social. **2** (fin), registered, of the company; **capitale sociale**, registered capital; **sede sociale**, registered office; **condizione sociale**, status

società *nf*, **1** (Plc, Ltd, etc), company; **società anonima**, Plc, plc, public limited company; **società a responsabilità limitata**, LTD, limited company; **società consociata**, subsidiary; **società d'investimento**, unit trust; **società finanziaria**, holding company; **società di servizi postali**, mailing company; **società interamente controllata**, wholly-owned subsidiary; **società madre**, parent company; **società per azioni**, joint stock company. **2** partnership; **i due fratelli sono in società**, the two brothers have

entered into a partnership

socio *nm*, partner; **socio dirigente**, senior partner; **socio accomodante**, sleeping partner

soddisfare *vb*, satisfy; **soddisfatto (-a)**, satisfied; **soddisfare le richieste/le condizioni**, meet the requirements/the conditions

soffitto *nm*, ceiling

soffrire *vb*, suffer

software *nm* (comp), software

soggetto *nm*, subject

soggiornare *vb* (spend some time in a place), stay

soggiorno *nm* (period of residence), stay

soglia *nf*, threshold; **raggiungere la soglia del 10%**, reach the 10% threshold

solido(-a) *adj* (strong construction), heavy duty

sollecitare *vb* (mktg, sales), canvass

sollevare *vb*, lift

solvibilità *nf*, liquidity

somma *nf*, sum; **somma globale pagata con un versamento unico**, lump sum

sommario *nm*, summary; **per fare un sommario del rapporto**, make a summary of the report

sondaggio *nm*, survey, public opinion poll; **fare un sondaggio**, sample opinion

sopportare *vb*, stand; **la cassa può sopportare temperature fino a 100 gradi c**, the case can stand temperatures of up to 100° C

sopra *prep*, **1** above; **sopra l'entrata principale**, above the main entrance; **l'indirizzo sopra indicato**, the above address. **2** over; **al di sopra del 5%**, over 5%; **al di sopra dell'obbiettivo**, over target

sorellastra *nf*, half sister

sorpassare *vb*, **1** (fin), outbid; **la ditta Bibi ha sorpassato la ditta Didi**, Bibi outbid Didi. **2** overtake; **sorpassare a grande velocità**, overtake at high speed

sospendere *vb*, suspend; **sospendere i pagamenti**, suspend payments; **sospendere l'attività**, shut down (company)

sospeso, in sospeso *adv* (fin), pending; **sistemare una questione in sospeso**, settle a matter pending

sostegno *nm*, backing

sostenere *vb*, **1** back; **sosteniamo il vostro progetto**, we back your project. **2 sostenere un esame**, take an exam

sostituire *vb* (gen, ins), replace, substitute

sostituzione *nf*, substitution; **prodotto di sostituzione**, (materials), substitute

sotto *prep*, below, under; **sotto il letto**, below/under the bed; **al di sotto del 10%**, below/under 10%

sottomettere *vb* **un prezzo**, tender/offer a price

sottopassaggio *nm*, subway

sottoprodotto *nm*, by-product

sottoscrivere *vb*, underwrite, undersign; **il sottoscritto . . . dichiara . .**, I, the undersigned, . . . declare

sottosviluppato(-a) *adj*, underdeveloped; **paesi sottosviluppati**, developing countries

sottovalutare *vb*, underestimate, undervalue

sottovuoto(-a) *adj*, vacuum; **sigillato sottovuoto**, vacuum sealed

sovraccaricare *vb*, overcharge, overload

sovraccarico *nm*, surcharge; **sovraccarico di deposito combustibile**, (imp/exp), BAF, bunker adjustment factor; **sovraccarico monetario**, (fin, imp/exp), CAC, currency adjustment charge/CAF, currency adjustment factor

sovrapprezzo *nm*, overprice; **dare in sovrapprezzo**, overprice

sovrintendente *nm* (pers), supervisor

sovvenzionare *vb*, subsidise

sovvenzione *nf*, subsidy

spalmare *vb*, spread

spartire *vb* (fin), share; **spartire il costo della riparazione**, share the cost of repair

spaziare *vb*, space out

spazio *nm*, **1** (gen), space. **2** (mktg, sales), slot; **spazio pubblicitario**, advertising slot

speciale *adj*, special; **offerta speciale**, special offer; **condizioni speciali**, special conditions

specialista *nm/f*, specialist; **è uno specialista nel campo di . .**, he is a specialist in the field of . . .

specialità *nf*, speciality

specializzarsi *vb*, specialise, qualify

specializzato(-a) *adj*, specialised, skilled; **rivista specializzata**, specialised magazine; **mano d'opera specializzata**, skilled labour

specie *nf*, kind; **è una buona specie di materiale**, it is a good kind of material

specificare *vb*, specify

specificazione *nf*, specification; **specificazioni tecniche**, technical specifications

speculare *vb*, speculate

spedire *vb*, **1** (gen), send; **spedire a nolo aereo**, (transp) send by airfreight. **2** (imp/exp), despatch, forward. **3** (naut), ship

spedizione *nf*, (transp), consignment, shipment

spedizioniere *nm*, carrier, forwarding agent, (transp); **spedizioniere di grandi quantità**, bulk carrier; **spedizioniere marittimo**, shipper

spegnere *vb*, **1** switch off. **2** (car), shut down

spendere *vb*, spend

sperare *vb*, hope, expect; **si spera che ci sia bel tempo domani**, we hope the weather is going to be fine tomorrow; **speriamo di firmare un contratto con . .**, we expect to sign a contract with . . .

spesa *nf*, **1** (gen), expenditure. **2** (initial capital spent), outlay

spese *nfpl*, **1** (gen), expenses; **spese d'esercizio**, running/operating expenses; **spese generali**, overheads; **spese straordinarie**, exceptional items. **2** (fin), charges; **spese connesse**, related charges; **spese da pagare**, charges payable; **spese di viaggio**, travelling expenses; **spese dovute**, (imp/exp), cc, charges collect. **3** (recurring expenses), cost; **spese del personale**, labour costs; **spese d'impianto**, start-up costs

spettacolare *adj*, spectacular

spola *nf*, shuttle

sporco(-a) *adj*, **1** (gen), dirty. **2** (goods), soiled

sport *nm*, sport

sportello *nm*, counter

sportivo(-a) *adj*, sports; **centro sportivo**, sports centre; **equipaggiamento sportivo**, sports equipment

sposato(-a) *adj*, married

spreadsheet *nm*, spreadsheet

sprecare *vb*, waste

spreco *nm*, waste

spremere *vb*, squeeze

spruzzare *vb*, spray

squadra *nf*, team

stabile *adj*, stable; steady

stabilimento *nm*, **1** factory; **prezzo all'uscita stabilimento**, factory gate price; **produzione dello stabilimento**, factory production. **2** plant; **la società ha uno stabilimento a Pavia**, the company has a plant in Pavia. **3** works; **dallo Stabilimento**, (imp/exp), EXW, ex-works

stabilire *vb*, establish, appoint, fix; **la causa è stata stabilita**, the cause has been established; **sul luogo stabilito**, on the appointed place; **stabilire un piano**, fix a plan

stabilizzare *vb*, stabilise; **stabilizzare i prezzi**, (mktg, sales), peg prices; **stabilizzarsi**, (gen, fin), level out

stadio *nm*, **1** (of a project), stage. **2** sports ground

stagionale *adj*, seasonal; **impiego stagionale**, seasonal employment

stagione *nf*, season; **la stagione morta**, the quiet season; **la stagione piena**, the busy season

stallie *nfpl* (transp), lay days

stampa *nf*, print, printing; **fuori stampa**, out of print

stampante *nf* (comp), printer

stampare *vb* (comp), print (off/out)

stampato *nm* (comp), printout

stampatore *nm* printer

stand *nm*, stand; **responsabile dello stand**, stand manager

stanziamento *nm* **(di una somma)**, (balance sheet), appropriation

stanziare *vb* **una somma**, budget; **abbiamo stanziato una somma**

per l'aumento delle spese, we have budgeted for an increase in overheads

stare *vb* **al passo con**, keep up with

statale *adj*, state; **aiuto statale**, state aid; **controllo statale**, state controlled

statistica *nf* (science), statistics

statistiche *nfpl*, statistics

Stati Uniti *nmpl* **(d'America)**, USA, United States (of America)

stato *nm*, state; **lo Stato**, the State

statutario(-a) *adj*, statutory

stazionario(-a) *adj*, stationary

stazione *nf*, station; **stazione ferroviaria**, railway station

stelle *nfpl*, stars; **i prezzi sono arrivati alle stelle**, (mktg, sales), prices are extremely high

stenodattilografo(-a) *nm/f*, shorthand typist

stenografia *nf*, shorthand; **note in stenografia**, shorthand notes; **stenografia e dattilografia**, (pers), shorthand and typing

stenografo(-a) *nm/f*, shorthand writer, stenographer

sterlina *nf* (currency), sterling, pound

stilista *nm/f*, designer

stilografica *nf* **(penna)**, fountain pen

stimolante *adj*, challenging; **un posto stimolante**, a challenging job

stipendiare *vb*, salary

stipendiato *nm*, salaried worker

stipendiato(-a) *adj*, salaried

stipendio *nm*, salary

stipulare *vb*, stipulate

stiva *nf* (naut), hold

stivare *vb* (transp), stow

stock *nm*, stock; **rotazione dello stock**, stock turnover

strada *nf* **d'accesso**, slip road

straniero *nm*, foreigner

straniero(-a) *adj*, foreign; **questo è un motore straniero**, this is a foreign engine

straordinari *nmpl*, overtime; **fare degli straordinari**, to work overtime

strappare *vb* (materials), tear

strategia *nf*, strategy

stretto(-a) *adj*, narrow, tight

struttura *nf*, structure

strutturale *adj*, structural

stile *nm*, style

studi *nmpl*, (section in CV), education

studiare *vb*, study

studio *nm*, study, survey; **studio di mercato**, market survey; **fare uno studio del mercato**, survey the market

stuzzichino *nm* (sales), teaser

su *prep*, up; **andar su**, go up; **i prezzi sono andati su**, prices have gone up

subappaltare *vb*, subcontract, contract work out; **la società ha intenzione di subappaltare il lavoro di assemblaggio**, the company intends to contract out assembly work

subappaltatore *nm*, subcontractor

subappalto *nm*, subcontract, (pers), subcontracting

successo *nm*, success, hit; **è un prodotto di successo**, it is a successful product

succursale *nf* (part of retail chain), branch

suono *nm*, sound

superare *vb* (beat), top; **quest'anno i profitti superano i 10 milioni**, this year profits top 10 millions

supermercato *nm*, supermarket

supplementare *adj*, additional, supplementary; **premio supplementare**, additional premium; **spesa supplementare**, supplementary charge

supplemento *nm*, **1** (gen), supplement. **2** (fin), extra charge

supporre *vb*, guess

supposizione *nf*, guess

sussidio *nm* (fin), aid

svaligiare *vb*, burgle

svalutazione *nf*, depreciation

svantaggio *nm*, disadvantage

svendita *nf* sale (eg autumn sale)

sviare *vb*, mislead

sviluppare *vb*, develop

sviluppo *nm* (mktg, sales, fin), growth, development; **in pieno sviluppo**, booming; **le vendite sono in pieno sviluppo**, sales are booming; **Ricerca e Sviluppo**, R + D, Research and Development; **paesi in via di sviluppo**, developing countries

T

tabella *nf* (mktg, sales), table; **la tabella mostra le cifre di vendita per questo mese**, the table shows the sales figures for this month

tabellone *nm* **pubblicitario** (mktg, sales), boarding

taccuino *nm*, note-pad

tacito(-a) *adj*, tacit; **abbiamo l'accordo tacito del fabbricante**, we have the tacit agreement of the manufacturer

tagliando *nm*, coupon; **ritagliare il tagliando**, clip the coupon; **tagliando per ristorante**, LV, luncheon voucher

tagliare *vb*, cut

tangibile *adj*, tangible

targa *nf*, number plate

tariffa *nf*, **1** fare; **la tariffa per Londra è 15 sterline**, the fare to London is £15; **mezza tariffa**, half fare; **tariffa di un biglietto andata e ritorno**, return fare; **tariffa di un biglietto in seconda classe**, second class fare; **tariffa singola**, single fare. **2 tariffa postale**, postage

tariffe *nfpl*, rates; **tariffe a scalare**, tapering rates; **tariffe generali di carico** (transp), GCR, general cargo rates

tassa *nf*, tax, charge; **tasse portuali**, port charges; **esente da tasse**, tax free

tassabile *adj*, taxable

tasso *nm* (fin), rate; **tasso del**

cambio, exchange rate; **tasso uniforme**, flat rate; **tasso di base**, base rate; **tasso d'interesse**, interest rate; **tasso di solvibilità** (acct), owner's equity to debts; **tasso fisso**, fixed rate; **tasso giornaliero**, daily rate; **tasso in vigore**, CR, current rate

tastiera nf, keyboard

tasto nm (comp), key

tattica nf, tactic; **la loro tattica abituale è di . .**, their usual tactic is to . .; **una tattica di trattativa**, a negotiating tactic

tavola nf, **tavolo** nm, (furniture), table

tecnica nf, technique

tecnico nm, technician

tecnico(-a) adj, technical

tecnologia nf, technology; **la tecnologia più avanzata**, the latest technology

telecomando nm, remote control

telefonare vb, telephone, dial; **telefonare clienti eventuali**, cold calling (by phone)

telefonata nf, telephone call; **ricevere una telefonata da . .**, receive a telephone call from . . .

telefonico(-a) adj, phone; **carta telefonica**, phone card; **codice telefonico**, STD code; **numero telefonico**, phone number; **segreteria telefonica**, answering machine

telefonino nm, portable/cellular phone

telefonista nm/f, (telephone) operator

telefono nm, telephone, phone; **marketing per telefono**, telemarketing; **telefono portatile**, mobile phone; **telefono pubblico**, payphone; **telefono senza fili**, cordless telephone; **vendita per telefono**, telephone sales

telegiornale nm, TV news programme

telegrafico(-a) adj, telegraphic; **indirizzo telegrafico**, telegraphic address; **trasferimento telegrafico**, telegraphic transfer

telescrivente nf, telewriter

telestampante nf, teleprinter

televisione nf, television; **alla televisione**/(colloquial) **alla tivù**, on the TV; **programma televisivo**, television programme

telex nm, telex; **inviare un telex a una ditta**, telex a company; **numero di telex**, telex number

telone nm **impermeabile**, tarpaulin

temperamatite nm, pencil sharpener

tempo nm, time; **tempo passivo**, down time

temporaneo(-a) adj, temporary; **indirizzo temporaneo**, temporary address; **impiego temporaneo**, temporary employment

tendenza nf, trend, tendency; **tendenza al ribasso**, downward trend; **tendenza al rialzo**, upward trend; **ha una tendenza a . .**, he has a tendency to . .; **avere tendenza a . .**, tend to . . .

tendere vb, tend to

tenere vb, keep; **tener conto di**, allow for, cater for; **tenere a magazzino** stock; **tenere in memoria** (comp), save; **tenere la contabilità**, keep the books; **tenere lo stesso livello di**, keep up with (prices, etc); **tenersi in testa a . .**, keep ahead of

tensione nf (gen), tension; **sotto tensione**, (electr), live

tentare vb, try; **tenteremo di trovare il modello che voi desiderate**, we will try to find the model you want

terminare vb, terminate; **terminare un contratto**, terminate a contract

termini nmpl **di credito**, credit terms

terra nf, land

territorio nm (mktg, sales), territory

terzo(-a) adj, third; **un terzo**, a third; **in terzo luogo**, thirdly

teso(-a) adj, tight; **corda tesa**, tightrope

tessuto nm, fabric; **tessuti per arredamento**, soft furnishings

testa nf, head; **essere in testa**, be ahead, come top

testimone nm, witness; **testimone oculare**, eye witness; **agire da testimone**, (law), act as a witness

testimoniare vb, witness

testo nm, text, wording; **il testo di questo libro**, the text of this book; **secondo il testo del contratto**, according to the wording of the contract; **trattamento del testo**, wordprocessing

timbro nm **(postale)**, postmark

tipo nm, type; **un nuovo tipo di macchina**, a new type of machine

tiratura nf, (print run), circulation; **grande tiratura di giornali**, large circulation of newspapers

tiro nm **a sorte**, prize draw

titolo nm, 1 (in newspaper) headline. 2 (fin) share; **titolo azionario**, share certificate. 3 (CV), qualification; **titoli di studio**, academic qualifications. 4 title; **titolo di proprietà**, title deed

tolleranza nf, tolerance

tollerare vb, tolerate

tonnellaggio nm, tonnage

tonnellata nf, ton

torto nm, wrong; **avere torto**, be wrong

totale adj, total; **gestione di qualità totale**, total quality management

totale nm, total; **un totale di 50 milioni**, a total of 50 millions

totalizzare vb, total

tra prep, between

tracciare vb **il grafico**, graph

tradurre vb, translate

traduzione nf, translation

traente nm (fin), drawer

traffico nm, traffic; **traffico stradale**, road traffic

traghetto nm, ferry

tralasciare vb, neglect

trama nf (of a film, opera, etc), plot

transito nm, transit; **in transito**, in transit; **merci danneggiate o smarrite in transito**, goods damaged or lost in transit

trapanare vb, drill

trasbordo nm, (transp), transhipment

trascorrere vb (time), spend

trascurare vb, overlook, forget

trasferibile adj, (fin), transferable

transferimento nm, transfer; **trasferimento fondi a mezzo via aerea**, (fin), AMT, Air Mail Transfer; **trasferimento telegrafico**, TT, telegraphic transfer

trasferire vb, shift, transfer; **il carico è stato trasferito**, the load has been shifted; **il conto è stato trasferito**, the account has been transferred

trasferirsi vb (offices, house), move

trasmettere vb, transmit; **trasmettere per radio/televisione**, broadcast (on radio/TV)

trasmissione nf, 1 (gen), transmission; **trasmissione dati**, data transmission. 2 (propulsion), transmission

trasportare *vb*, carry, transport;
trasportare un carico a . ., take
a load to . . .

trasportatore *nm*, carrier; (transp)
haulier, transporter;
trasportatore multimodale,
MTO, multimodal transport
operator

trasporto *nm*, **1** transport, carriage;
lettera di trasporto aereo,
(imp/exp), air waybill;
**Nolo/Trasporto pagato fino
a . .**, (imp/exp), DCP,
Freight/Transport paid to . . .
2 (transp) haulage; **trasporto
misto** (imp/exp), CT, combined
transport

tratta *nf*, **1** draft; **tratta bancaria**,
B/D, bank draft; **tratta a vista**,
sight draft. **2** (negotiable), bill

trattamento *nm* processing;
trattamento in lotto, batch
processing; **trattamento dati**,
data processing; **trattamento del
testo** (comp), wordprocessing

trattare *vb*, **1** deal with (a customer),
negotiate. **2** process (goods);
trattare i minerali, process
minerals

trattario *nm*, drawee

trattativa *nf*, negotiation, deal, talk;
avere trattative con . ., have
talks with . . .

treno *nm*, train; (transp), **treno
diretto**, through train; **treno
merci**, goods train; **treno
viaggiatori**, passenger train

tribunale *nm*, court; **portare in
tribunale**, take to court

trimestrale *adj*, quarterly

triplicare *vb*, triple, treble

trovare *vb*, find, locate

trucioli *nmpl*, wood wool;
**imballato(-a) nei trucioli di
legno**, wrapped in wood wool

turismo *nm*, tourism

turista *nm/f*, tourist

turno *nm*, shift; **turno di notte**,
night shift

U

ufficiale *nm*, official; **ufficiale fiscale**, (law), bailiff

ufficiale *adj*, official, formal; **una visita non ufficiale**, an informal visit

ufficio *nm*, office; **ufficio postale**, post office; **attrezzatura d'ufficio**, office equipment; **immobile con uffici**, office block; **impiegato d'ufficio**, clerical assistant; **indirizzo dell'ufficio**, business address; **mobili d'ufficio**, office furniture

ufficioso(-a) *adj*, unofficial

uguagliare *vb*, equal

uguale *adj*, equal; **essere uguale a**, be equal to

ultimamente *adv*, lately

ultimatum *nm*, ultimatum

ultimo(-a) *adj*, last, latest, final

umidità *nf*, damp; **imballaggio a prova di umidità**, damp-proof packing; **le merci hanno sofferto l'umidità**, the goods have been spoilt by damp

umido(-a) *adj*, damp

unanime *adj*, unanimous

unanimemente *adv*, unanimously

unico *adj*, unique; **una caratteristica unica**, a unique feature; **strada a senso unico**, one-way street

uniforme *adj*, uniform

unione *nf*, union; **Unione Europea**, EU, European Union

unire *vb*, unite, combine, join; **unire due cavi**, join two cables; **unire due colori differenti**, combine two different colours; **unire due persone**, bring two people together

unità *nf*, unit; **unità centrale di trattamento**, (comp), CPM, central processing unit

unitario(-a) *adj*, unit; **prezzo unitario**, unit price; **costo unitario**, unit cost

urbano(-a) *adj*, urban

usare *vb*, use

usato(-a) *adj*, used; **non usato**, unused

uscire *vb*, go out, come out; **il nuovo modello uscirà il mese prossimo**, the new model will come out next month

uscite *nfpl* (fin), outgoings

uso *nm*, 1 (gen), use. 2 (use of a product), application; **il nostro nuovo prodotto ha molti usi**, our new product has many applications

usuale *adj*, usual

utente *nm*, user

utile *nm*, profit, earnings; **utile per azione**, profit/earnings per share; **premio di partecipazione agli utili**, profit-related pay; **partecipazione agli utili**, (pers), profit sharing

utilizzazione *nf*, use; **di facile utilizzazione**, user-friendly

V

vacanza *nf*, holiday

vagone *nm* (transp), (rail)carriage; **vagone letto**, sleeping-car

valere *vb*, be worth; **valere la pena**, be worthwhile; **non vale la pena di andare adesso**, it is not worthwhile going now

validità *nf*, validity

valido(-a) *adj*, valid; **questo biglietto è valido dal 10 al 20 di maggio**, this ticket is valid from 10 to 20 May

valore *nm*, 1 value; **valore contabile**, book value; **valore nominale**, (fin) face value; **senza valore**, no commercial value. 2 worth; **senza valore**, worthless; **valore di primo ordine**, blue-chip

valuta *nf*, currency; **valuta straniera**, foreign currency

valutare *vb*, value, estimate, price at; **valutare il costo**, (calculate expenditure), cost; **il costo del progetto è stato valutato a Lit. 200.000**, the project has been costed at 200.000 lire

valutazione *nf*, 1 assessment; **la valutazione è basata su . .**, the assessment is based on . . . 2 estimate; **è una valutazione sommaria**, it is a rough estimate

vantaggio *nm* (mktg, sales), advantage, benefit; perk; **il vantaggio è enorme**, the advantage is huge; **uno dei vantaggi del nostro servizio è . .**, one of the benefits of our service is . .; **ricevere dei vantaggi**, receive perks;

vantaggio unico del prodotto, USP, Unique Selling Proposition

vantaggioso(-a) *adj*, profitable

vapore *nm*, steam; **nave a vapore**, (imp/exp, transp), steamship

variabile *adj*, variable; **la domanda è molto variabile**, the demand is very variable; **la qualità delle merci è variabile**, the quality of the goods is variable

variare *vb*, vary; **il prezzo varia secondo la stagione**, the price varies according to the season

variazione *nf*, variation

vasto(-a) *adj*, wide

vedere *vb*, 1 (gen), see. 2 (a property), view

veicolo *nm*, vehicle; **veicolo per transporti ingombranti** = LGV, Large Goods Vehicle; **veicolo per trasporti pensanti** = HGV, Heavy Goods Vehicle;

vela *nf*, sail; **fare la vela**, sail

veloce *adj*, fast, quick; **consegna veloce**, fast delivery; **risposta veloce**, quick reply

velocemente *adv*, fast, quickly; **lavora velocemente**, he works fast; **parla velocemente**, she speaks quickly

velocità *nf*, speed

vendere *vb*, sell; **vendere a prezzo superiore**, outsell; **vendere al dettaglio**, retail; **vendere all'ingrosso**, sell by wholesale; **vendere in quantità superiore**, outsell

vendita *nf*, sale **vendita di liquidazione**, clearance sale; **vendita per appalto**, sale by tender; **vendita per contanti**, cash sale; **vendita per telefono**, (mktg, sales), telesale

venditore *nm*, seller, vendor

verbale *adj*, verbal

verde *adj*, green; **carta verde**, (ins), green card

verificare *vb*, check, verify

vero(-a) *adj*, true

veto *nm*, veto; **mettere il veto**, veto

vettore *nm* (transp) carrier

via *adv*, via; **via Milano e Bologna**, via Milan and Bologna

via *nf*, street

viaggiare *vb*, travel

viaggiatore *nm*, traveller; **viaggiatore d'affari**, business traveller

viaggio *nm*, travel, trip; **viaggio d'affari**, business travel; **agenzia di viaggio**, travel agency; **assicurazione di viaggio**, travel insurance; **essere in viaggio per Venezia**, be on a trip to Venice; **spese di viaggio**, travel expenses;

vice *adj* (pers), deputy, vice; **vice direttore**, deputy manager; **vice presidente**, vice chairman/vice president

vicino(-a) *adj*, near; **vicino all'aeroporto**, near the airport

video *nm*, video; **video promozionale**, promotional video; **fare un video**, video

villetta *nf*, detached house

vincere *vb*, win

violare *vb* **la legge**, be in breach of the law

virus *nm*, virus; **protezione da virus**, virus protection

visita *nf*, call, visit; **fare una visita a . .**, call on . . .

visitare *vb*, visit; **visitare clienti senza appuntamento**, cold calling

visitatore *nm*, visitor

vista *nf*, sight, view; (fin), **tratta a vista**, sight draft; **pagabile a vista**, payable at sight; **una camera con una bella vista**, a room with a nice

view; **in vista del costo delle materie prime . .**, in view of the cost of raw materials . . .

vivere *vb*, live; **vivere in campagna**, live in the country

vivo(-a) *adj*, live

viziare *vb*, spoil; **persona viziata**, spoilt person

vocabolo *nm*, word

voce *nf*, **1** (gen), word. **2** (fin), item; **questa voce non appare nei libri contabili**, this item does not appear in the books

voga *nf*, (fashion), vogue, fashion; **in voga**, popular, fashionable; **moda in voga**, popular fashion; **questo tipo di indumento è molto in voga**, this type of garment is very popular

volantino *nm*, folder, leaflet

volare *vb*, fly

volere *vb*, want

volo *nm* (transp), flight; **volo charter**, chartered flight; **volo regolare**, scheduled flight; **volo diretto**, through flight

volontario(-a) *adj*, voluntary

votare *vb*, vote

votazione *nf*, poll

voto *nm*, vote

vuoto(-a) *adj*, empty

Z

zero *nm*, zero, nil; **sotto/sopra zero**, below/above zero; **ora zero**, zero hour

zona *nf*, zone, area; **zona da costruzione**, building site; **zona commerciale**, trading estate

ENGLISH — ITALIAN

A

aar, against all risks (ins), contro tutti i rischi

able, be able to *vb* (ability), potere; **we are able to deliver . .,** possiamo consegnare. . .

aboard *adv*, a bordo

about *adv/prep* **1** (approximately), circa; **the industrial estate is about 3 miles from the town centre,** il villaggio industriale è a circa 3 miglia dal centro città. **2** (on subject of), su; **the meeting will be about the new product launch,** la riunione sara sul lancio del nuovo prodotto

above *adv/prep* **1** (gen), sopra; **above the main entrance,** sopra l'entrata principale. **2** (in forms), sopra; **the above address,** l'indirizzo sopra indicato. **3** (fin), oltre; **above 5%,** oltre il 5%

abroad *adv*, all'estero; **go abroad,** andare all'estero

absenteeism *n* (pers), assenteismo *nm*

abuse *n,* **1** (gen), abuso *nm*; **abuse of confidence,** abuso *nm* di fiducia. **2** (misuse), cattivo uso *nm*

A/C, account/current (fin), conto *nm* corrente (c/c)

A/C, a/c, AC, alternating current (electr), corrente *nf* alterna

acc, acct, account, conto *nm*

accelerate *vb,* accelerare

accept *vb,* accettare

acceptable *adj,* accettabile
   acceptable conditions, condizioni accettabili

acceptance *n,* accettazione *nf*

access *vb* (comp), avere l'accesso a; **access the network,** avere l'accesso alla rete

accessories *npl,* accessori *nmpl*; **car accessories,** accessori auto

accident *n* (pers), incidente *nm*; **he has had an accident,** egli ha avuto un incidente

accommodate *vb,* **1** (hotels, etc), ospitare. **2** (available space, machines, etc), contenere

accommodation *n* (hotel, flat), alloggio *nm*

accompany *vb,* accompagnare; **accompanied by,** accompagnato (-a) da; **our manager will be accompanied by . .,** il nostro direttore sarà accompagnato da . . .

according to *adv,* secondo, conformemente a; **according to me,** secondo me; **according to the law,** conformemente alla legge

account *n* (fin), conto *nm*; **advertising account** (mktg, sales), conto pubblicità; **accounts receivable to purchases** (fin, acct), **accounts receivable to sales** conto acquisti (fin), conto vendite; **buy on account,** comprare in acconto; **on account** (financial statements), in conto

accountant *n,* ragioniere *nm*; **chartered accountant,** commercialista *nm/f*

accounting *n,* contabilità *nf*; **accounting period,** esercizio *nm* finanziario

accounts clerk *n,* contabile *nm*

accurate *adj,* **1** preciso(-a); **accurate person,** persona precisa. **2** esatto (-a), **accurate accounts,** conti esatti

accuse *vb* **(of),** accusare (di)

achieve *vb* (fin results), ottenere

achievement n, raggiungimento nm; (fin result), risultato

acid test ratio n (fin), rapporto nm di liquidità immediata

acknowledge vb **receipt (of . . .)** accusare ricevuta (di)

acronym n, sigla nf

ad n, (mktg, sales), annuncio nm

a/d, after date (fin), dalla data nf; **90 days after date**, a novanta giorni dalla data

adapt vb, adattare; **adapt to our needs**, adattare ai nostri bisogni

add vb **(to)**, aggiungere (a); **please add to our order**, si prega di aggiungere al nostro ordine

add up vb (fin, offce), fare la somma

additional charge n, costo nm supplementare

additional premium n (ins), premio nm supplementare

address vb, **1** (letters), inviare; **address your CV for the attention of . .**, inviare il cv all'attenzione di. **2** (deal with), **address a problem, a task**, affrontare un problema, un compito

addressee n, destinatario nm

adjust vb, **1** (gen) adattare; **adjust to the situation**, adattare alla situazione. **2** (eng), regolare; **adjust a machine**, regolare una machina. **3 adjust accounts**, pareggiare i conti

adjustment n, **1** (fin), regolamento nm. **2** (adjustment of the figures) pareggio nm. **3** (of machine), regolazione nf

administration n, amministrazione nf

admit vb, **1** ammettere; **admit the truth**, ammettere la verità. **2** riconoscere; **admit a mistake**, riconoscere un errore

admittance n, **1** (gen), entrata nf. **2** ingresso nm; **no admittance** vietato l'ingresso

ad valorem (imp/exp), secondo il valore

advance n, **1** (pers, move forward), avanzamento nm. **2** (move forward), movimento nm in avanti. **3** (law), provvigione nf. **4** (part payment in advance), anticipo nm; pagamento nm in anticipo

advantage n (mktg, sales), vantaggio nm

advertise vb, **1** (a post), fare un'inserzione per un posto. **2** (a product), fare pubblicità ad un prodotto; **we plan to advertise in the trade journals**, progettiamo di fare pubblicità nelle riviste dei commercianti

advertisement n, inserzione nf; **place an advertisement**, mettere un'inserzione; **reply to an advertisement**, rispondere ad un'inserzione

advertiser n (mktg, sales), inserzionista nm

advertising n, pubblicità nf; **advertising agent**, agente nm pubblicitario; **advertising campaign**, campagna nf pubblicitaria; **advertising manager**, direttore nm pubblicitario

advertorial n (mktg, sales), articolo nm di redazione

advice n, **1** (piece of advice), consiglio nm. **2** (corr), avviso nm; **advice note**, nota d'avviso; **advice of . .**, avviso di . .; **advice of payment**, avviso di pagamento; **advice of receipt** (imp/exp), avviso di ricevuta

advise vb, **1** (give advice), consigliare. **2** (formal, letters etc), dare notizia di; **please advise us of the date of delivery**, preghiamo di darci notizia della data di consegna

advocate n (law), avvocato nm

affect vb, **1** (gen), riguardare; **the**

matter affects only me, la questione riguarda solo me. **2** (have an effect on), avere un effetto su . .; **the sun affects the product**, il sole ha un effetto sul prodotto

affected *adj* **by**, affetto(-a) da

after *adv* (gen), dopo; **after date** (fin), dalla data; **90 days after date**, 90 giorni dalla data; **after sight** (fin), dalla vista; **30 days after sight**, 30 giorni dalla vista; **we will contact you after we have tested the samples**, ci metteremo in contatto con voi dopo che abbiamo provata i campioni

after-sales *adj*, dopo vendita; **our after-sales service**, il nostro servizio dopo vendita

against *adv* (opposed to, opposite direction), contro; **the board has decided against the project**, il Consiglio ha deliberato contro il progetto; **be against the trend**, essere contro corrente

agency *n*, agenzia *nf*

agenda *n*, ordine *nm* del giorno; **on the agenda**, all'ordine del giorno

agent *n*, agente *nm*

aggressive *adj* (mktg, sales), aggressivo(-a)

AGM, Annual General Meeting *n*, Assemblea *nf* Generale

agree *vb*, **I** (be in agreement), essere d'accordo; **I agree with you**, sono d'accordo con lei. **2** (reach agreement), mettersi d'accordo; **at the meeting we agreed to . .**, alla riunione ci siamo messi d'accordo di . . .

agree to *vb*, **I** (gen), accettare di fare qualcosa. **2** (law), accettare; **we agree to the terms of the contract**, accettiamo i termini del contratto

agree with *vb*, essere d'accordo con; **we agree with your assessment of the situation**, siamo d'accordo con la vostra valutazione della situazione

agreed *adj*, convenuto(-a); **agreed price**, prezzo *nm* convenuto

agreement *n*, accordo *nm*; **reach an agreement**, arrivare ad un accordo

agt, agent, agente *nm/f*

aid *n*, **I** (gen), aiuto *nm*. **2** (fin grant), sussidio *nm*

aim *n*, scopo *nm*

aim to *vb*, avere lo scopo di

air *n*, **by air** (transp), per via *nf* aerea; **air cargo** (transp), carico *nm* aereo; **air-conditioned**, con aria *nf* condizionata; **air-conditioned bedrooms**, camere *nfpl* con aria condizionata; **air consignment note** (imp/exp), nota *nf* di trasporto aereo; **Air Mail Transfer, AMT** (fin), trasferimento *nm* per via aerea; **air waybill** *n* (imp/exp), lettera *nf* di trasporto aereo

airfreight *n* (transp), nolo *nm* aereo; **send by airfreight** (transp), spedire a nolo aereo; **airfreight collect** (imp/exp), porto *nm* aereo

airport *n*, aeroporto *nm*; **airport terminal**, stazione *nf* aerea

airtight *adj*, ermetico(-a)

A levels, advanced level (exams) *npl*, = (esami di), maturità *nf*

all-in price *n*, **I** (fin), prezzo *nm* tutto compreso. **2** (mktg, sales), prezzo *nm* forfettario

allow for *vb* (fin), tener conto di

all risks *adj* (fin, ins), tutti i rischi; **all risks insurance policy**, polizza *nf* d'assicurazione casko

almost *adv* (nearly), quasi; **inflation has reached almost 9%**, l'inflazione ha raggiunto circa il 9%; **your order is almost ready**, il vostro ordine è quasi pronto

alter *vb*, modificare

alternating current n (electr), corrente nf alterna

alternative n (arrangement), alternativa nf

a.m., ante meridian del mattino; **5 a.m.,** 5 del mattino

amount n (fin), importo nm; **the amount of the invoice is £321,** l'importo della fattura è di £321

AMT, Air Mail Transfer (fin), trasferimento fondi a mezzo via aerea

analyse vb, analizzare

analysis n, (of figures, results), analisi nf; **an analysis of the figures indicates that . .,** l'analisi delle cifre indica che . . .

analyst n, analista nm

annual adj, annuale; **annual bonus** (pers), premio nm annuale; **Annual General Meeting,** Assemblea nf Generale; **annual report** (fin), rapporto nm annuale

ansaphone/answerphone n, segreteria nf telefonica

answer n, risposta nf; **in answer to your letter,** in risposta alla vostra lettera

answer vb, rispondere

a/o, account of . . . (fin), conto nm di . . .

A/P, Additional Premium (ins), premio nm supplementare

apologise vb, **1** (orally), chiedere scusa; **I apologise about . .,** chiedo scusa per . . . **2** (corr) scusarsi; **we apologise for the delay,** ci scusiamo per il ritardo

apology n, scusa nf; **please accept our apologies,** vi preghiamo di accettare le nostre scuse

appeal vb, **1** (law), **appeal against,** fare appello. **2** (be attractive), attirare; **the shape of the packet appeals to children,** la forma del pacchetto attira i bambini

applicant n, candidato(-a) nm/f

application n, **1** (request for a job, loan), domanda nf; **application form** (exhibitions, etc), modulo nm di richiesta; **job application form,** domanda nf d'impiego; **please complete the enclosed application form for a stand,** preghiamo di completare l'accluso modulo di richiesta per lo stand. **2** (use of a product), uso nm; **our new product has many applications,** il nostro nuovo prodotto ha molti usi

apply vb, **1** (something), applicare. **2** (for job), chiedere impiego. **3** (work hard) dedicarsi; **apply oneself to one's work,** dedicarsi al proprio lavoro. **4** (relevant to), riferirsi; **this does apply to you,** ciò si riferisce a lei

appoint vb, **1** nominare; **he has been appointed chairman** è stato nominato presidente. **2** stabilire; **on the appointed place,** sul luogo stabilito

appointment n, **1** (meeting), appuntamento nm; **make an appointment** (offce), fissare un appuntamento. **2** (to a job), nomina nf; **appointment as chairman,** nomina di presidente

appraisal n (pers), valutazione nf

appreciate vb, **1** (understand), rendersi conto; **we appreciate your situation,** ci rendiamo conto della vostra situazione. **2** (be grateful) apprezzare; **I appreciate your kindness,** apprezzo la sua gentilezza

appreciation n (fin), (increase in value), aumento nm di valore

approach vb, (figures), raggiungere; **the rate is approaching the 3% mark,** il tasso raggiunge il 3%

appropriation n (balance sheet), stanziamento nm (di una somma)

approval n, **1** benestare nm; **we have the approval of . .,** abbiamo il benestare di . . . **2** (on approval) (mktg, sales), in prova; **we agree to send you the goods on approval**, siamo d'accordo nell'inviarvi la merce in prova

approved *adj*, approvato(-a); **approved retailer**, dettagliante *nm* approvato; **approved supplier**, fornitore *nm* approvato

A/R, all risks (ins), tutti i rischi

arbitration *n*, **I** (gen) arbitraggio *nm*. **2** (law), arbitrato *nm*

arcade *n* (mktg, sales), galleria *nf*; **shopping arcade**, galleria di negozi

area *n*, **I** (geographical), area *nf*. **2** (sales), settore *nm*; **sales area**, settore vendite. **3** (territory), zona *nm*; **area manager**, direttore *nm* di zona

argument *n*, **I** (gen), argomento *nm*. **2** (law), disputa *nf*; **have an argument**, avere una disputa

armchair *n* (offce), poltrona *nf*

around *adv*, (roughly), circa *adv*; **the price is around £5000**, il prezzo è circa £5000

arr, arrival, arrivo *nm*

arrange for *vb*, predisporre; **we have arranged for the goods to reach you tomorrow**, abbiamo predisposto la consegna delle merci per domani

arrangements *npl*, preparativi *nmpl*

arrears *n* (of payment), arretrati *nmpl*, **in arrears**, in arretrato

arrival *n*, arrivo *nm*; **the arrival of the consignment**, l'arrivo *nm* della spedizione

arrive *vb* (transp), arrivare

articulated lorry *n*, (transp), camion *nm* semi rimorchio

artwork *n* (mktg, sales), documento *nm* (recommended term)

A/S, account sales (mktg, sales),

conto *nm* vendite

a/s, after sight *n* (fin), dalla vista; **30 days after sight**, a 30 giorni dalla vista

assemble *vb*, **I** (eg kits), montare; **easy to assemble**, facile da montare. **2** (for a meeting), riunirsi; **the representatives have assembled in . .**, i delegati si sono riuniti in . . .

assembled *adj*, montato(-a)

assembler *n*, (gen), montatore *nm*

assembly *n*, **I** (completed assembly of parts), montaggio *nm*; **assembly line**, catena *nf* di montaggio. **2** (formal meeting, politics), assemblea *nf*

assess *vb*, valutare

assessment *n* (pers), **I** valutazione *nf*; **assessment centre**, centro di valutazione. **2** (fin), ripartizione *nf*; **tax assessment**, ripartizione tasse

assessor *n* (ins), assessore *nm*

asset *n*, **I** (gen), risorsa *nf*; **his main asset is . .**, la sua risorsa principale . . . **2** (balance sheet), attivo *nm*; **fixed assets**, attivo immobilizzato

assist *vb*, assistere

assistant *n*, **I** (gen), assistente *nm/f*; **manager's assistant**, assistente del direttore. **2** (assistant to someone), vice; **assistant manager**, vice direttore *nm*

ATM, Automatic Teller Machine (fin), distributore *nm* automatico di banconote, bancomat *nm*

attach *vb*, **I** (gen), attaccare. **2** (corr), accludere; **we attach . .**, accludiamo . . .

attractive *adj*, attraente; **available in attractive colours**, disponibile in colori attraenti

auction *n*, asta *nf*

audiotypist *n*, dattilografa *nf* specializzata

audit *n*, revisione *nf*

audit *vb*, **1** (gen), verificare, **carry out a computer systems** verificare i sistemi informatici. **2** (fin), rivedere (i conti)

auditor *n* (fin), revisore *nm* (di conti)

authorise *vb*, (to do something), autorizzare

authorised capital *n* (fin), capitale *nm* sociale

Automatic Teller Machine *n* (fin), distributore *nm* automatico di banconote, bancomat *nm*

A/V, ad valorem (imp/exp), secondo il valore

av, average *n*, media *nf*

average *n*, **1** (maths), media *nf*; **sales reached an average of 1000 per month**, le vendite hanno raggiunto una media di 1000 al mese; **on average**, in media. **2** (transp), avaria *nf*

average *vb* (calculate the average), fare la media

aviation *n*, aviazione *nf*

avoid *vb*, evitare

aware of *adj*, consapevole di *adj* **1 be aware of**, essere consapevole di. **2 make aware of** (mktg, sales), sensibilizzare; **make customers aware of**, sensibilizzare i clienti su

AWB, air waybill *n* (imp/exp), lettera *nf* di trasporto aereo

B

BA, Bachelor of Arts, laureato(a) *nm/f* in lettere

back *vb*, **1** (support), sostenere. **2** (fin), (guarantee), garantire. **3** (written guarantee), avallare; **the bill has been backed by . .**, la fattura è stata avallata da . . .

back up *vb* (comp), salvaguardare

backer *n* (fin), finanziatore *nm*

backing *n* (gen), sostegno *nm*

back load *n* (transp), carico *nm* di ritorno;

back-to-back credit *n* (fin), credito *nm* appoggiato

badge *n*, distintivo *nm*

BAF, bunker adjustment factor (imp/exp), sovraccarico *nm* di deposito combustibile

bag *n*, **1** (gen), borsa *nf*. **2** (small sealed bag), sacchetto *nm*

bail *n* (law), cauzione *nf*; **release on bail**, libertà provvisoria su cauzione

bailiff *n* (law), ufficiale *nm* fiscale

balance *n*, **1** (fin), bilancio *nm*; **balance sheet**, bilancio d'esercizio. **2** (orders), saldo *nm*; **the balance of the order will be sent shortly**, il saldo dell'ordine sarà spedito in breve tempo; **balance due**, saldo da pagare

balance *vb*, equilibrare

bale *n* (imp/exp), balla *nf*

ban *n* **(on)**, (on publication, export, etc), bando *nm*; **they have put a ban on the press release**, il comunicato è stato messo al bando

ban vb, proibire

bank n, banca; **Bank for International Settlements**, Banca nf dei Saldi Internazionali; **bank charges** (in a particular transaction), spese nfpl bancarie; **bank deposit**, deposito nm bancario; **bank draft**, tratta nf bancaria; **bank note**, banconota nf; **bank rate**, tasso nm bancario

bank vb, depositare in una banca

bank on vb, contare su

bankrupt adj, **go bankrupt**, fare fallimento

bar n (for drinks), bar nm

bar chart n, grafico nm a sbarre

bar code n (gen, comp), codice nm a sbarre

bargain n (gen), **1** buon affare nm; **get a bargain**, fare un buon affare. **2** occasione nf; **it is a good bargain**, è una buona occasione

bargain vb (mktg, sales), negoziare

barge n (transp), chiatta nf

barrel n, **1** (of oil), fusto nm. **2** (gen), barile nm

barrister n (law), avvocato nm

barter n (imp/exp), baratto nm; **barter trade** (imp/exp), accordo nm di compensazione

barter vb (gen), barattare

base rate n (fin), tasso nm di base

based adj, **based in**, situato(-a) in; **the company is based in . .**, la società è situata in . .; **based on**, basato(-a) su; **the assessment is based on . .**, la valutazione è basata su . . .

basic adj, essenziale; **basic equipment**, attrezzatura nf essenziale; **basic point**, punto essenziale

batch n (gen), lotto nm; **batch processing** (comp), trattamento nm in lotto

battery n (electr), **1** (small), pila nf. **2** (large, multicell), batteria nf

B + B, Bed and Breakfast, pensione nf con prima colazione

bbl, barrel, **1** (oil), fusto nm. **2** (gen), barile nm

B/D, bank draft (fin), tratta nf bancaria

bd, b/d, brought down, balance brought down (fin), saldo nm a nuovo

B/E 1 bill of entry (imp/exp), bolletta nf di entrata. **2 bill of exchange** (fin), cambiale nf

bear n (stock market), ribassista nm

bear vb (stand, put up with), sopportare

bearer n (of a document), portatore nm; **bearer securities**, titoli nmpl al portatore

Bed and Breakfast n, pensione nf con prima colazione

before adv, prima adv; **before 5 June**, prima del 5 giugno, **before ordering . .**, prima di ordinare . . .

behalf n, **on behalf of . . . 1** (gen), da parte di . . . **2** (fin), per conto di . . .

below prep, sotto; **below the bed**, sotto il letto; **below 5%**, al di sotto adv del 5%

benefit n (gen), vantaggio nm; **one of the benefits of our service is . .**, uno dei vantaggi del nostro servizio è . . .

benefit from vb, profittare del

berth n, **1** (in harbour), ancoraggio nm. **2** (in trains), cuccetta nf

berth vb (transp), ancorare

between prep (transp), fra

bf, b/f, brought forward (fin, acct), riporto nm

bid n (fin), offerta nf

bid for . . . vb (fin), offrire un prezzo per . . .

big *adj*, **1** (size), grande.
2 (reputation), importante

bill *n*, **1** (to be paid), conto *nm*, fattura
nf. **2** (negotiable), tratta *nf*.
3 (politics), progetto *nm* di legge.
4 (commercial documents), **bill of
entry** (imp/exp), bolletta *nf* di
entrata; **bill of exchange** (fin),
cambiale *nf*; **bill of lading**
(imp/exp), polizza *nf* di carico;
clean bill of lading, polizza di
carico senza clausola; **bill of sale**,
atto *nm* di vendita

billboard *n* (mktg, sales), pannello *nm*
pubblicitario

binding *adj* (law), **1** obbligatorio(-a);
binding agreement, contratto *nm*
obbligatorio. **2** (gen), impegnativo
(-a); **binding offer**, offerta *nf*
impegnativa

biro *n*, biro *nf*

**BIS, Bank for International
Settlements**, Banca *nf* dei Saldi
Internazionali

Bk, bank (fin), banca *nf*

B/L, bill of lading (imp/exp), polizza
nf di carico

bl (imp/exp), **1** (gen), **barrel**, barile
nm. **2** (oil), **barrel**, fusto *nm*.
3 (fibre, cloth), **bale**, balla *nf*

blackboard *n*, lavagna *nf*

blister pack *n* (mktg, sales),
pacchetto a 'bolla' (in cartoncino e
plastica trasparente)

blue-chip *adj* (fin), (share) valore *nm*
di primo ordine; **blue-chip
company**, società *nf* di primo
ordine

blue collar *n* (pers), colletto *nm* blu

blurb *n* (mktg, sales), notizia *nf*
pubblicitaria

board of directors *n*, consiglio *nm*
d'amministrazione; **board
director**, direttore *nm* del
consiglio d'amministrazione;
**member of the board of
directors**, membro *nm* del

consiglio d'amministrazione

boat *n* (transp), barca *nf*

bolt *vb* (eng), imbullonare

bolted *adj* (eng), imbullonato(-a)

bond *n*, **1** (stock market),
obbligazione *nf*. **2** (guarantee),
cauzione *nf*

bonded warehouse *n* (imp/exp),
magazzino *nm* doganale

bonus *n* **1** (ins), premio *nm*. **2** (extra
payment), indennità *nf*

book *vb* (accommodation), prenotare;
book a stand, riservare uno stand;
book an order, registrare un
ordine

booking *n*, prenotazione *nf*

booking form *n*, **1** (hotels, etc)
modulo *nm* di prenotazione.
2 (exhibitions, etc), modulo di
iscrizione; **please complete the
enclosed booking form**, si prega
di compilare l'accluso modulo di
iscrizione

book value *n* (acc, ins), valore *nm*
contabile

boom *n* (mktg, sales, fin), aumento
nm improvviso; **we have seen a
boom in sales**, abbiamo notato un
improvviso aumento nelle vendite

booming *adj* (mktg, sales, fin), in
pieno sviluppo *nm*

boot up *vb* (comp), caricare il
programma

born *adj* (pers), nato(-a); **born 12
June 1972**, nato il 12 giugno 1972

borrow *vb*, prendere a prestito

borrowings *npl* (fin), prestiti *nmpl*

box *n*, **1** (gen), scatola *nf*. **2** (on a
form), quadratino *nm*; **tick the
appropriate box**, contrassegnare
il quadratino giusto

brain storm *n*, attacco *nm* di pazzia,
colpo *nm* di genio; **brainstorming
session**, discussione *nf* a ruota
libera/per associazione di idee

brake *vb*, frenare

branch *n*, **1** (part of retail chain), succursale *nf*. **2** (part of group of companies), filiale *nf*

brand *n* (mktg, sales), marca *nf*; **brand image**, concetto *nm* di marca; **brand loyalty**, fedeltà alla marca; **brand name**, nome di marca

breach *n*, **1** **a breach of contract**, una rottura di contratto. **2** (law), violazione *nf*; **breach of the law**, violazione della legge

break *vb* (gen), rompere; **break the law** (law), infrangere la legge

break even *vb* (fin), chiudere a pareggio

break in *vb* (law), scassinare

breakdown *n*, **1** (of car), guasto *nm*. **2** (analysis of figures), analisi *nf*

break down *vb*, **1** (car), avere un guasto. **2** (figures), classificare i conti. **3** (analysis of accounts), analizzare i conti

breakeven point *n* (fin), pareggiare le entrate e le uscite

break in *n* (law), apertura *nf* con scasso

bridge *vb*, **1** (differences, gap between positions), stabilire un collegamento. **2** (eng) collegare

brief *vb* **(on/about)**, mettere al corrente

briefing *n*, **1** (general information), riunione *nf* d'informazione. **2** (before a meeting), riunione di preparazione

bring *vb* (gen), portare

bring out *vb* **(a new model)**, esporre (un nuovo modello)

broadcast *vb* (telec), trasmettere per radio; trasmettere per televisione

brochure *n*, opuscolo *nm*

broken *adj*, rotto(-a)

broker *n*, **1** (gen), mediatore *nm*. **2** (fin), (stockbroker), agente *nm* di cambio. **3** (ins), broker *nm*

bros, brothers *npl*, fratelli *nmpl*

brown goods *npl* (mktg, sales), settore *nm* del bruno

B/S *n* **1** (fin), **balance sheet**, bilancio *nm*. **2** (fin, imp/exp), **bill of sale**, atto *nm* di vendita

BS 5750, la norma britannica per l'assicurazione qualità

bt fwd, brought forward (fin), riporto *nm*

budget *n* (fin), bilancio *nm* preventivo

budget for *vb* (fin), stanziare una somma; **we have budgeted for an increase in overheads**, abbiamo stanziato una somma per l'aumento delle spese

build *vb*, costruire

building *n*, **1** (accommodation), edificio *nm*. **2** (activity), costruzione *nf*; **building industry**, industria *nf* edile; **building site**, **1** (gen), zona *nf* da costruzione. **2** (being built on), cantiere *nm*

bulk *adj* (transp), **1** (gen), in grande quantità. **2** (sales), all'ingrosso; **bulk buying** (mktg, sales), acquisti *nmpl* all'ingrosso

bulk carrier *n* (transp) (naut), spedizioniere *nm* di grandi quantità

bulk storage *n*, **1** (transp) immagazzinamento *nm* di massa. **2** (comp), memoria in massa

bull *n* (stock market), rialzista *nm*

buoyant *adj* (mktg, sales), alto(-a); **the market is buoyant**, il mercato è alto

burglary *n* (law), furto *nm* con scasso

burgle *vb* **1** (break in), svaligiare. **2** (break in and steal), (law), commettere un furto con scasso

bus *n* (transp), autobus *nm*; **bus station**, stazione *nf* degli autobus

business *n*, **1** (gen), affari *nmpl*; **how is business?**, come vanno gli affari?; **do business**, fare affari; **businessman**, uomo d'affari; **businesswoman**, donna d'affari **business trip**, viaggio d'affari. **2** (mktg, sales), attività *nf* commerciale; **I am in business**, ho un'attività commerciale. **3** (offce), ufficio; **business address**, indirizzo dell'ufficio

bust, go bust *vb* (fin), **1** (file for bankruptcy), dichiarare fallimento. **2** (business failure), fare fallimento

busy *adj* (telec) occupato(-a); **the line is busy**, la linea è occupata; **I am not available, I am very busy**, non sono libero, sono molto occupato

buy *vb*, comprare

buy out *vb* (gen), rilevare; **we bought out W's share in XYZ in 1993**, abbiamo rilevato la quota W nella XYZ nel 1993

buyer *n*, **1** (gen), compratore *nm*. **2** (property), acquirente *nm/f*. **3** (in charge of purchasing), addetto(-a) *nm/f* agli acquisti

by-product *n*, sottoprodotto *nm*

C & F, cost and freight *n* (imp/exp), costo *nm* e nolo *nm*

CA, chartered accountant *n*, ragioniere *nm* diplomato commercialista

cable *n* (comp), **1** (gen), cavo *nm*. **2** (electr), raccordo *nm*

CAC, currency adjustment charge *n* (fin, imp/exp), sovraccarico *nm* monetario

CAD, Computer Assisted Design *n* (comp), concetto *nm* assistito da computer

CAD/CAM, Computer Assisted Design and Manufacture *n* (comp), concetto e manifattura assistiti da computer

CAF, currency adjustment factor (fin, imp/exp), sovraccarico *nm* monetario

calculate *vb* (fin), calcolare

calculator *n* (offce), calcolatore *nm*

calendar *n* (offce), calendario *nm*; **calendar year**, anno *nm* civile

call *n*, **1** (telephone), telefonata *nf*. **2** (visit), visita *nf*

call *vb*, **1** (gen), chiamare; **call a committee meeting**, convocare una riunione di comitato. **2** (phone), telefonare. **3** (give a name to something) chiamarsi; **the new product is called 'Luxus'**, il nuovo prodotto si chiama 'Luxus'

call at *vb* (travel), fermarsi

call back *vb*, (telephone), richiamare (al telefono)

call for vb, I (a load, a person), passare a prendere; **our driver will call for the load**, il nostro autista passerà a prendere il carico; **I will call for you at your hotel**, passerò a prenderla all'albergo. **2** (political change), **call for changes**, richiedere dei cambiamenti

call in vb **(a loan)**, chiedere (il rimborso di un prestito)

call in vb **the receiver** (fin), nominare un curatore fallimentare

call on vb, I (visit), fare visita a. **2** (request support), fare appello; **we shall call on the chamber of commerce to support the exhibition**, faremo appello alla camera di commercio per assistenza all'esibizione

camera n, I (photographs), macchina nf fotografica. **2** (video), video camera nf. **3** (cinema), cinepresa nf

campaign n, campagna nf

campaign vb, fare una campagna

can n, I (tin), barattolo nm. **2** (larger metal container), bidone nm

can vb, mettere in conserva

canal n (transp), canale nm

cancel vb, annullare

cancellation n (reservation), annullamento nm

canvass vb, I (mktg, sales), sollecitare. **2** (political), fare un giro elettorale

capacity n, I (volume held), capacità nf; **production capacity**, capacità di produzione. **2** (potential), abilità nf; **he has the capacity to . .**, ha l'abilità di . . . **3** (role), in qualità; **in the capacity of**, in qualità di . .; **he is acting in the capacity of . .**, agisce in qualità di . . .

capital n, I (fin), capitale nm; **capital assets**, capitale fisso; **capital gains tax**, imposta sul sopravalore; **capital goods**, beni di capitale;

capital intensive, industria del capitale; **capital investment**, spese d'investimento; **capital outlay**, spese d'impianto; **called-up capital**, revoca di capitale. **2** (letter), maiuscola nf. **3** (main town), capitale nf; **Rome is the Italian capital**, Roma è la capitale d'Italia

captain n (transp), capitano nm

car n, macchina nf, automobile nf; **car hire**, noleggio nm auto; **car parking**, parcheggio nm auto

card n, I (gen), carta nf, cartoncino nm. **2** (business card), biglietto nm da visita

cardboard box n (imp/exp), scatola nf di cartone

card index n, schedario nm

care n, cura nf; **with care**, con cura; **take care of**, prendersi cura di . .; **our agent will take care of the . .**, il nostro agente si prenderà cura di . . .

career n (pers), carriera nf; **career objective** (pers), I (gen), obbiettivo nm di carriera. **2** (admin, ads), pretese nfpl

cargo n (transp), carico nm; **cargo handler**, incaricato nm manutenzione merci

carousel n (slide projector), proiettore nm diapositive

carphone n, (telefono) cellulare nm

carriage n (transp), porto nm; **carriage forward** (imp/exp), porto nm assegnato; **carriage free** (transp), franco di porto; **carriage paid** (fin), porto affrancato; **carriage paid to . .**, (imp/exp), porto affrancato fino a . . .

carried forward adj (acc), riporto nm

carrier n (transp), vettore nm, trasportatore nm

carry vb, I (on a vehicle), trasportare. **2** (with your hands), portare. **3** (have in store), avere uno stock;

carry a stock of . ., avere uno stock di . . .

carry forward vb **(to)** (fin), riportare

carry out vb (gen), (accomplish), eseguire; **carry out a project**, eseguire un progetto; **carry out instructions**, eseguire le istruzioni

carton n (imp/exp), cartone nm

case n, **1** (gen), caso nm; **the case of the stolen lorry**, il caso del camion rubato. **2** (suitcase), valigia nf. **3** (cardboard box), cartone nm; **a case of wine**, un cartone di vino. **4** (wooden box), cassa nf, **a case of wine**, una cassa di vino

cash n (notes and coins), contanti nmpl; **pay cash**, pagare in contanti; **I have £220 in cash**, ho 220 sterline in contanti; **cash before delivery**, in contanti prima della consegna; **cash in advance**, contanti in anticipo; **cash on delivery**, contanti alla consegna; **cash on shipment**, contanti all'imbarco; **cash with order**, contanti all'ordine; **cash sale/purchase**, vendita/acquisto in contanti; **cash desk** (gen), cassa nf; **pay at the cash desk**, pagare alla cassa; **cash discount**, sconto nm cassa; **cash dispenser** (bank), bancomat nm; **cash receipts** (acc), entrate nfpl in contanti

cash in vb, (fin), incassare

cash-and-carry n, (mktg, sales), 'cash and carry' nm

cash flow n (fin), movimento nm di cassa nf; **cash flow problems** (fin), difficoltà nei movimenti di cassa; **cash flow projection** (fin), previsioni di movimenti di cassa

cashier n (fin), cassiere nm

cast vb (eng), fondere

casting n, **1** (eng), getto nm. **2** (cinema), distribuzione nf di parti

catalogue n, (mktg, sales), catalogo nm

catch vb **(a train/plane)**, prendere (un treno/un aeroplano)

catch up vb (gen), riguadagnare (il tempo perduto)

cater for vb (food), provvedere

caterer n (gen), fornitore nm di cibo e bevande

cause n, causa nf

cause vb, causare

CBD, cash before delivery (mktg, sales), contanti nmpl prima della consegna

CBI, Confederation of British Industry = Federazione nf Industrie Britanniche

cc, charges collect (imp/exp), spese nfpl dovute

cc, cubic centimetre, centimetro nm cubo

CCTV, closed circuit television, televisione nf a circuito chiuso

CD-ROM n, CD-ROM nm

cease vb, **1** (gen), cessare. **2** (cease production), interrompere (la produzione). **3** (cease trading), ritirarsi dagli affari

ceiling n, (maximum), **1** (gen), soffitto nm. **2** (maximum limit) limite nm massimo; **go through the ceiling**, arrivare al limite massimo

central adj, centrale

centralise vb, centralizzare

CEO, Chief Executive Officer, Presidente nm Direttore nm Generale

certificate n, certificato nm; **certificate of origin** (imp/exp), certificato d'origine

certification n, certificazione nf

certified adj, **1** (gen), attestato(-a). **2** (law), autenticato(-a); **certified copy**, copia autenticata

certify vb, **1** (gen), attestare. **2** (law), autenticare

CF, cost and freight (imp/exp), costo e nolo

cf, carried forward (fin), riporto *nm*

CR, current rate *n* (fin), tasso *nm* in vigore

cge pd, carriage paid (mktg, sales), porto *nm* pagato

chain *n*, (gen), catena *nf*; **chain store**, magazzino *nm* con succursali *nfpl*

chair *vb*, (a meeting), presiedere (un'assemblea)

chairman *n*, (pers), presidente *nm/f*

chalk *n*, (mktg, sales), gesso *nm*

challenge *n*, sfida *nf*

challenging *adj*, stimolante; **a challenging job**, un posto stimolante

chamber *n*, **1** (gen), camera *nf*; **chamber of commerce**, camera di commercio. **2** (large room), sala *nf*

change *n*, resto *nm*; **have you got change for lire 10.000?**, ha i resto di Lit 10.000?

change *vb*, cambiare

channel *n*, **1** (gen), canale. **2** (radio), stazione *nf*. **3** (TV), canale

channel *vb* (gen), dirigere; **to channel the . . . towards . .**, dirigere il . . . verso

character *n*, **1** (gen), carattere *nm*. **2** (references, morals), reputazione *nf*; **of good character**, di buona reputazione. **3** (personality), personalità *nf*; **a pleasant character**, una personalità gradevole

charge *n*, **1** (cost), prezzo *nm*. **2** (accusation), capo *nm* d'accusa.

charge *vb* **1** (fin), addebitare; **please charge it to my account**, lo addebiti per favore sul mio conto; **2 charge somebody (with a crime)**, accusare qualcuno (di un delitto)

charge for *vb*, far pagare; **we will have to charge you for . .**, dovremo farvi pagare . .;

charges *npl*, **1** (fin), spese *nfpl*; **charges payable** (fin), spese da pagare; **charges collect** (imp/exp), spese dovute. **2** (at bank), commissioni *nfpl* bancarie

chart *n*, (offce), grafico *nm*

chart *vb* **(results)**, fare il grafico

charter *n* (transp), nolo *nm*; **time charter**, nolo a tempo; **charter party** (transp), contratto *nm* di noleggio

charter *vb* (transp), noleggiare

chartered accountant *n* (fin), commercialista *nm/f*

chartered flight *n*, volo *nm* 'charter'

chartering *n* (transp), nolo *nm*

cheap *adj*, **1** (cost), a buon mercato/a basso prezzo. **2** (quality), di cattiva qualità

check *vb*, **1** (monitor regularly), controllare. **2** (make sure), verificare. **3** (stop), far fermare; **check inflation**, controllare l'inflazione

check in *vb*, registrare i bagagli

check out *vb*, pagare il conto e lasciare l'albergo

check in desk *n*, ufficio *nm* registrazione, 'check in' *nm*

checklist *n*, lista *nf* di controllo

chemicals *npl*, prodotti *nmpl* chimici

chemist *n*, **1** (gen), chimico *nm*. **2** (dispensing chemist), farmacista *nm/f*

cheque *n* (fin), assegno *nm* bancario; **crossed cheque**, assegno sbarrato; **cash a cheque**, cambiare un assegno; **cheque book**, libretto *nm* d'assegni

children *npl* (forms, CV), **1** (gen), figli *nmpl*. **2** (small children), bambini *nmpl*. **3** (older children), ragazzi *nmpl*

choose *vb*, scegliere

chq, cheque (fin), (GB), assegno *nm* bancario

CIA, cash in advance (mktg, sales), contanti *nmpl* in anticipo

CIF, cost, insurance, freight (imp/exp), costo *nm*, assicurazione *nf*, nolo *nm*

CIF & E, cost, insurance, freight and exchange variations/bankers' charges (imp/exp), costo, assicurazione, nolo e fluttuazione di cambio/commissioni bancarie

CIP, carriage, freight and insurance paid to . . . (imp/exp), porto *nm* pagato, inclusa assicurazione *nf* fino a . . .

circle *vb*, **I** (forms), fare un cerchio. **2** (surround), circondare

circuit *n*, circuito *nm*

circulate *vb*, (a document), mettere in circolazione

circulation *n*, **I** (gen), circolazione *nf*. **2** (of newspaper), (distribution), diffusione *nf*. **3** (print run), tiratura *nf*; **large circulation**, grande tiratura

circumstances *npl*, circostanze *nfpl*

claim *n*, **I** (gen), richiesta *nf*. **2** (ins), reclamo *nm*; **claims department** (ins), sezione reclami. **3** (law), diritto *nm*; **have a claim on . .**, avere un diritto su . . .

claim *vb*, **I** (claim to be true), asserire. **2** (a right), reclamare. **3** (damages), fare una richiesta d'indennizzo. **4** (responsibility), rivendicare. **5** (better rights or conditions), chiedere; **the union is claiming a wage increase**, i sindacati chiedono un aumento di salario

clause *n*, clausola *nf*

clean *adj* (gen), pulito; **clean bill of lading**, polizza *nf* di carico senza clausola

clear *adj*, **I** (gen), chiaro(-a), **it is clear that . .**, è chiaro che . . . **2** (transparent), transparente. **3** (obvious), evidente, **a clear increase/decrease**, un aumento/una diminuzione evidente

clear *vb* **customs** (imp/exp), sdoganare

clear *vb* **stocks** (mktg, sales), liquidare lo stock

clearance *n*, (of customs), sdoganamento *nm*; **clearance sale** (mktg, sales), vendita *nf* di liquidazione

clerical assistant *n* (offce), impiegato(-a) d'ufficio

client *n*, cliente *nm*

client database *n*, (mktg, sales), schede *nfpl* clienti *nmpl*

climb *vb*, arrampicarsi

clip *vb* **the coupon** (mktg, sales), ritagliare il tagliando; **just clip the coupon and return it to the address at the top of the advertisement**, ritagliare semplicemente il tagliando e rinviarlo all'indirizzo indicato in cima all'annuncio

clock *n* (offce), orologio *nm*

clone *n* (comp), 'clone' *nm*

close *vb*, chiudere

close down *vb*, **I** (a computer), spegnere. **2** (company), chiudere (una ditta)

closing data *n*, data *nf* di chiusura

C/N, credit note (mktg, sales), nota *nf* di credito

C/O, care of . . . (transp), presso . . .

Co, company, società *nf*, ditta *nf*, compagnia *nf*

coach *n* (transp), carrozza *nf*, pulmann *nm*, corriera *nf*; **coach station**, stazione *nf* pulmann

COD, cash on delivery (mktg, sales), contanti *nmpl* alla consegna

code n, 1 (software, security, gen), codice nm. 2 (of practice), etichetta nf professionale

code vb, 1 (law), codificare. 2 (messages), cifrare

coin n, moneta nf

cold calling n, (mktg, sales), 1 (visiting possible customers), visitare clienti senza appuntamento. 2 (telephoning possible customers), telefonare clienti eventuali

cold storage n (transp), deposito nm frigorifero

collapse vb, (sales), crollare; **the price of 32 bit microchips has collapsed**, il prezzo dei '32 bit microchip' è crollato

collateral n (fin), garanzia nf addizionale

collect vb, 1 (hobby), fare una collezione. 2 (a load), prelevare un carico

collection n (of loads) prelievo nm, raccolta nf

column n (of figures, etc), colonna nf

combine vb, unire, combinare

combined adj, combinato(-a), misto(-a); **combined efforts**, sforzi nm combinati; **combined transport bill of lading** (imp/exp), polizza nf di carico con trasporto misto; **combined transport operator** (imp/exp), agente nm di trasporto misto

come out vb, uscire; **the new model will come out next month**, il nuovo modello uscirà il mese prossimo

command n (comp), ordine nm

comment (on) vb, commentare

commercial n, 1 (TV advertisement), pubblicità commerciale nf

commercial adj, commerciale

commission n, (sales, fin), commissione nf, provvigione nf

commodities npl (fin), merci nfpl

communicate vb, comunicare

communication n, comunicazione nf; **corporate communication** (pers), comunicazione della società

compact disc n, disco compatto nm, 'cd'

company n, (Plc, Ltd, etc), società nf; **company accommodation** (pers), uffici della società; **company car**, macchina/auto della società; **company secretary**, segretario(-a) di società

comparative adj, comparativo(-a)

compare vb (with), paragonare (a); **compared with . .**, paragonato (-a) a . . .

comparison n (gen, fin), paragone nm; **in comparison with . .**, in paragone a . . .

compensate vb, 1 (gen), ricompensare. 2 (ins), indennizzare; **we would like to compensate you for . .**, vorremmo indennizzarvi per . . .

compensation n, 1 (gen), compenso nm. 2 (law), indennizzo nm

competition n (mktg, sales), concorrenza nf

competitive adj, 1 (gen), competitivo(-a) 2 (mktg, sales), di concorrenza; **competitive price**, prezzo di concorrenza

competitor n, concorrente nm

complain vb, 1 (gen, about pain), lamentarsi. 2 (mktg, sales), fare le rimostranze

complaint n, 1 (gen, mktg, sales), reclamo nm; **make a complaint**, fare un reclamo. 2 (law), querela nf; **lodge a complaint**, sporgere querela, presentare una querela

complete adj, completo(-a); **a complete set of documents**, una serie completa di documenti

complete *vb*, I (a document, job), completare. **2** (a manufacturing process), finire. **3** (form), riempire

complimentary ticket *n*, biglietto *nm* omaggio

comply with *vb*, (law), conformarsi a . . .

component *n*, componente *nm*

composed *adj* of, be composed of, composto(-a) di, essere composto di

comprehensive *adj*, I (understanding), comprensivo(-a). **2** (complete) completo(-a); **a comprehensive report**, un rapporto completo

comprehensive insurance *n*, assicurazione *nf* casko

compromise *n*, compromesso *nm*

computer *n*, (comp), computer; **computer manager** (pers), direttore d'informatica; **computer operator**, operatore *nm* di computer

computing *n*, informatica *nf*

concessionaire *n*, concessionario *nm*

condition *n* (general state, agreements, etc), condizione *nf*; **market conditions are . .**, le condizioni del mercato sono . .; **the machinery is in good condition**, il macchinario è in buone condizioni; **conditions of sale**, condizioni di vendita; **on condition that . .**, a condizione che . . . .

conduct *vb* (a survey), condurre

conference *n*, conferenza *nf*; **conference hall**, sala *nf* conferenze

confidence *n*, (be sure of), avere fiducia; **have confidence in . .**, abbia fiducia in . . . .

confidential *adj*, confidenziale; **a confidential document**, un documento confidenziale

confirm *vb*, confermare

confiscate *vb* (law), confiscare

congratulate *vb*, congratularsi con

congratulations *npl*, congratulazioni *nfpl*

connect *vb* (comp), collegare

connection *n*, I (gen), collegamento *nm*; **make a connection**, fare un collegamento. **2** (travel), coincidenza; **catch a connection**, prendere una coincidenza

consider *vb*, considerare

considerably *adv*, considerevolmente *adv*; **considerably higher/lower than . . .** (gen, fin), considerevolmente più alto/più basso del . .; **considerably more/less than . . .** (gen, fin), considerevolmente di più/di meno del . . .

consignee *n*, (imp/exp), destinatario *nm*

consignment *n* (transp) I (gen), spedizione *nf*. **2** (one of a series of shipments), consegna *nf*

consignor *n* (transp), mittente *nm*

construction industry *n*, fabbrica *nf* di costruzioni

consular invoice *n* (imp/exp), fattura *nf* consolare

consultancy *n*, consulenza *nf*; **on a consultancy basis**, su una base di consulenza

consultant *n*, (gen), consulente *nm/f*; **a firm of consultants**, una ditta di consulenti

consumer *n* (fin), consumatore *nm*; **consumer goods** (gen), beni di consumo; **consumer protection**, protezione del consumatore

consumption *n* (fin), consumo *nm*

cont, to be continued, cont., continua

contact *vb* (gen), contattare; **please contact me on this number . .**, mi contatti per favore a questo numero; **contact our office**, contatti il nostro ufficio

container n (transp), contenitore nm; **container lorry**, camion nm con contenitore; **container ship**, nave nf con contenitori; **refrigerated container**, contenitore refrigerato; **sealed container**, contenitore sigillato

containerised adj (transp), contenitorizzato(-a)

continuous adj, continuo(-a); **continuous production** (gen), produzione continua; **continuous stationery**, carta nf continua

contract n, contratto nm; **fixed-term contract**, contratto a durata determinata; **contract of employment** (pers), contratto d'impiego

contract out vb, subappaltare; **the company intends to contract out assembly work**, la società ha intenzione di subappaltare il lavoro di assemblaggio

contracted adj, contrattato(-a)

contractor n (gen), contraente nm

contravene vb (law), contravvenire

control vb, controllare

convenient adj, conveniente; **be convenient**, essere conveniente; **when would it be convenient?**, quando sarebbe conveniente?

cooling-off period n (gen), fase nf di raffreddamento

copy n, **1** (gen), copia nf. **2** (photocopy, carbon copy), fotocopia, copia carbone. **3** (of journal or newspaper), numero nm

copy vb, (a file/document), copiare

copyright adj (law), protetto(-a) dai diritti d'autore

copyright n (law), riproduzione nf vietata

copyright vb (law), proteggere con i diritti d'autore

copywriter n (mktg, sales), redattore nm pubblicitario

cordless telephone n, (telec), telefono nm senza fili

corporate adj, **1** (gen), corporativo (-a). **2** (mktg, sales), **corporate identity**, identità della società; **corporate strategy**, strategia della società

corporation tax n (companies), imposta nf sulle società

correspond to vb, **1** (equivalent to), corrispondere a. **2** (meet legal requirement), essere conforme a

COS, **cash on shipment** (imp/exp), contanti nmpl alla spedizione

cost n, **1** (gen), costo nm; **cost and freight** (imp/exp), costo e nolo; **cost, insurance, freight** (imp/exp), costo, assicurazione e nolo; **cost-effective**, rendibile; **cost of living**, costo della vita; **cost of living index**, indice del costo della vita; **cost price** (fin), prezzo del costo; **cost savings** (gen), economie; **achieve cost savings**, fare delle economie. **2** (recurring expenses), spese nfpl

cost vb, **1** (calculate expenditure), valutare il costo; **the project has been costed at 200.000 lire**, il costo del progetto è stato valutato a Lit 200.000. **2** (price), costare; **the machinery cost 40.000.000 lire**, il macchinario costa lire 40.000.000

costly adj, costoso(-a), caro(-a)

counsel n (law), avvocato nm, avvocatessa nf; **counsel for the defence**, avvocato della difesa

count vb, contare

count on vb, contare su . . .

counter n, **1** (shop), banco nm. **2** (bank, post office), sportello nm. **3** (where one pays), cassa nf

countersign vb, contrassegnare

countertrade n (imp/exp), accordo

nm di compensazione

country *n*, 1 (nation) paese *nm*, nazione *nf*; **country of origin** (imp/exp), paese d'origine. 2 (out of town), campagna *nf*; **live in the country**, vivere in campagna

coupon *n* (mktg, sales), tagliando *nm*

course *n*, 1 (in restaurant), piatto *nm*, portata *nf*. 2 (in education), corso *nm*

court *n* (law), corte *nf*

cover *n* (fin, ins), copertura *nf*; **cover note** (ins), nota *nf* di copertura; **issue a cover note**, rilasciare una nota di copertura

cover *vb* (gen), coprire; **be covered for £2000 risks** (ins), essere coperto(-a) per £ 2000 di rischi

CP, carriage paid (mktg, sales), porto *nm* pagato

CP, charter-party *n* (imp/exp), contratto *nm* di noleggio

CPT, cost per thousand (mktg, sales), costo *nm* per migliaia

CPU, central processing unit (comp), unità *nf* centrale di trattamento

Cr, credit *n* (fin), credito *nm*

CR, creditor (fin), creditore *nm*

craft *n*, 1 (profession, trade), mestiere *nm*. 2 (handcrafts), artigianato *nm*

crane *n*, (transp), gru *nf*

crash *n* (vehicle), scontro *nm* violento; **the lorry carrying your order has had a crash**, il camion che trasportava il vostro ordine ha avuto uno scontro violento

crash *vb*, (vehicles), scontrare violentemente

crate *n* (imp/exp), cassa *nf*

create *vb*, 1 (gen), creare. 2 (a company), fondare; **the company was created in 1991**, la società è stata fondata nel 1991

creation *n*, 1 (gen, artistic, fashion), creazione *nf*. 2 (of a company), fondazione *nf*

credit *n* (fin), credito *nm*; **credit advice** (imp/exp), avviso *nm* di credito; **credit balance** (fin), saldo *nm* creditore; **credit card** (fin), carta *nf* di credito; **credit note** (fin), nota *nf* di credito; **credit rating** (fin), solvibilità *nf*; **credit terms** (mktg, sales), termini *nmpl* di credito; **on credit**, a credito; **be in credit**, essere in credito; **credit transfer** (fin, gen), trasferimento *nm* di credito

credit *vb* (fin), accreditare

creditor *n* (fin), creditore *nm*; **creditors** (on balance sheet), crediti *nmpl*

crew *n*, 1 (gen), personale *nm*. 2 (of ship, train, etc), equipaggio *nm*

crime *n* (law), 1 (minor), reato *nm*. 2 (serious), crimine *nm*

crisis *n*, crisi *nf*; **go through a crisis**, attraversare una crisi; **be in a crisis**, essere in una crisi

critical path analysis *n*, analisi *nf* della strada critica; **carry out a CPA**, effettuare un'analisi della strada critica

criticise *vb*, criticare

cross *vb*, 1 (in documents), fare una croce. 2 (a country, a frontier), attraversare. 3 (a cheque), sbarrare

cross out *vb*, cancellare; **please cross out the parts which do not apply**, si prega di cancellare le sezioni non pertinenti

crossroad *n*, incrocio *nm*

CT, combined transport (imp/exp), trasporto *nm* misto

CTC, combined transport document (imp/exp), documento *nm* di trasporto misto

CTO, combined transport operator, (imp/exp), agente *nm* di trasporto misto

cu ft, cubic foot (gen), piede *nm* cubo

cupboard *n* (offce), armadio *nm*

curr, currt, current (fin), corrente

currency *n*, valuta *nf*; **currency dealer** (fin), cambiavalute *nm*; **foreign currency**, valuta straniera

current *adj*, **1** (current period), corrente; **current account** (fin), conto *nm* corrente. **2** (fin), circolante; **current assets** (fin), attivo circolante; **current liabilities**, debiti a breve termine; **current ratio** (fin), tasso *nm* di liquidità generale; **current value** (ins), valore *nm* corrente

currently *adv*, attualmente

curve *n* (gen, fin), curva *nf*

customer *n*, cliente *nm*; **customer loyalty** (mktg, sales), fedeltà *nf* del cliente; **customer services** (offce), servizi *nmpl* alla clientela

customised *adj*, **1** (appearance of a product), personalizzato(-a). **2** (made to special requirements), fatto(-a) su ordinazione, fatto(-a) su misura

customs *npl* (imp/exp), dogana *nf*; **customs clearance** (imp/exp), sdoganamento *nm*; **customs officer** (gen, imp/exp), doganiere *nm*

cut *n*, **1** (reduction), sconto *nm*, riduzione *nf*. **2** (stop electricity, etc), interruzione *nf* energia elettrica

cut *vb*, **1** (prices, costs, production), ridurre. **2** (gen, comp), tagliare; **cut and paste commands**, comandi di taglio e incollatura

cut out *vb*, eliminare

cutback *n*, riduzione *nf*; **a cutback in production**, una riduzione nella produzione *nf*

cut-off date *n* (fin), data *nf* interruzione

CV, curriculum vitae (pers), curriculum vitae *nm*

CWE, cleared without examination (imp/exp), sdoganato(-a) senza ispezione preliminare

CWO, cwo, cash with order (mktg/sales), contanti *nmpl* all'ordine

cwt, hundredweight, misura di peso = 50.7 kg

cycle *n*, ciclo *nm*

cyclical *adj*, ciclico(-a)

D

DA, deposit account n (fin), conto nm di deposito

D/A, documents against acceptance n (imp/exp), documenti nmpl contro accettazione

DAF, delivered at frontier (imp/exp), consegna nf alla frontiera

daily adj, quotidiano(-a); **the daily newspaper**, il quotidiano nm

dairy products npl, prodotti nmpl derivati dal latte

damage n, 1 (gen), danno nm. 2 (ins), avaria nf

damaged adj (gen), danneggiato(-a)

damages npl (law), indennizzo nm, risarcimento nm danni

damp adj (gen), umido(-a)

damp n (gen), umidità nf; **the goods have been spoilt by damp**, le merci hanno sofferto l'umidità

damp-proof adj, a prova di umidità; **damp-proof packing**, imballaggio a prova d'umidità

danger n, 1 (gen), pericolo nm. 2 (risk of), rischio nm; **there is a danger of contamination**, c'è il rischio di contaminazione

dangerous adj, pericoloso(-a)

data n (comp), dati nmpl; **data capture**, cattura nf dati; **data processing**, trattamento nm dati; **data protection** (law), protezione nf dati; **data transmission**, trasmissione nf dati; **database**, base nf dati; **database manager**, direttore nm della base dati;

database software, software della base dati

date n, 1 data nf; **date of birth**, data di nascita. 2 **be up to date**, essere aggiornato(-a)

date vb (document), datare

day n, 1 (day in week), giorno nm; **at . . . days after sight** (fin), a . . . giorni dalla vista; **the first day of the month**, il primo giorno del mese; **day book** (accounts), giornale nm; **day return ticket**, biglietto nm andata e ritorno valido per un giorno; **day to day management of . .**, la gestione quotidiana. 2 (length of time) giornata nf; **a day of meetings**, una giornata di riunioni

DC, direct current, corrente nf diretta

DCP, freight/carriage paid to . . . (imp/exp), nolo/trasporto pagato fino a . . .

dd, d/d, del'd, delivered (imp/exp, transp), consegnato(-a)

DDP, delivered duty paid (imp/exp), consegnato adj franco dogana

dead adj, morto(-a)

deadline n, data nf limite; **deadline for delivery . .**, la data limite per la consegna . . .; **meet a deadline**, rispettare la data limite

deal n, affare nm, **it's a deal**, affare fatto

deal in . . . vb, commerciare in

deal with . . . vb, 1 (eg a report), occuparsi; **the report deals with . .**, il rapporto si occupa di . . . 2 (with a customer), trattare. 3 (negotiate with), commerciare con

dealer n, (mktg, sales), 1 (gen), rivenditore nm. 2 (exclusive), concessionario nm. 3 (retail), dettagliante nm. 4 (wholesale) grossista nm

dear adj, caro

debate n, dibattito nm

debate vb, discutere, dibattere

debit n, debito nm

debit vb, debitare; **debit an account** (fin), debitare un conto

debt n, debito nm; **be in debt**, essere indebitato(-a)

debtor n, debitore nm

debug vb, I (sort out problems), fare la messa a punto. 2 (comp), testare un programma software

decide vb, decidere

decision n, decisione nf

deck n, ponte nm; **cargo deck** (transp), ponte da carico; **deck cargo** (transp), carico nm di coperta

declaration n, dichiarazione nf

declare vb, I (gen), dichiarare. 2 (a result), rendere noto

decline n, I (gen), declino nm. 2 (sales), diminuzione nf

decline vb, I (say no), declinare. 2 (get worse), diminuire; **business is declining**, gli affari diminuiscono

decrease n, diminuzione nf

decrease vb, diminuire

dedicated adj, scrupoloso(-a)

deduct vb, detrarre; **please deduct the cost of . . . from . .**, si prega di detrarre il costo di. . . . da. . . .

deductible adj, detraibile

deduction n (fin), detrazione nf

deed n (law), atto nm; **draw up a deed**, redigere un atto

defect n, difetto nm

defective adj, difettoso(-a)

defence n (gen, law), difesa nf

defend vb **(against)** (law), difendere (contro)

defer vb (put off), rimandare; **defer a decision**, rimandare una decisione

deferred adj, (gen), rimandato(-a); **deferred payment**, pagamento nm a rate

definite adj, preciso(-a); **be definite about . .**, essere preciso su . . .

definitely adv, definitivamente

delay n, ritardo nm

delay vb, ritardare

delayed adj, in ritardo nm

deliver vb (transp), consegnare

delivered adj (imp/exp), consegnato(-a); **delivered at frontier** (imp/exp), consegnato(-a) alla frontiera; **delivered duty paid** (imp/exp), consegnato(-a) franco dogana

delivery n (transp), consegna nf; **delivery arrangements**, termini nmpl di consegna; **delivery date**, data nf di consegna; **delivery deadline**, data limite di consegna; **delivery note** (imp/exp), nota nf di consegna

demand n, domanda nf, richiesta nf

demand vb, domandare, richiedere

demanding adj, esigente

demonstrate vb, I (a product), esibire. 2 (against), fare una dimostrazione. 3 (prove that), dimostrare

demonstration n, I (of product), esibizione nf, dimostrazione nf. 2 (political), dimostrazione

demurrage n, (transp), controstallia nf

denationalise vb, privare della nazionalità

denial n, rifiuto nm; **self-denial**, abnegazione nf

deny vb, I (as refusal), negare; **I cannot deny it**, non posso negarlo. 2 (as denial), rifiutare, **deny entry**, rifiutare l'entrata.

3 (deny responsibility), declinare la responsabilità

depart vb (transp), partire

department n, 1 (part of a company), reparto. 2 (part of an institute), sezione nf; **the foreign language department**, la sezione lingue straniere

departmental adj, a sezione nf, a reparti nmpl; **departmental manager**, direttore nm di sezione, direttore di reparto

department store n (shop), grande magazzino nm

departure n, partenza nf

depend (on) vb, dipendere (da)

deposit n, 1 (part payment in advance), acconto nm, deposito nm; **pay a deposit**, pagare un acconto; **leave a sum as deposit**, lasciare una somma come deposito. 2 (law, security, guarantee), cauzione nf; **deposit account** (fin), conto nm deposito

deposit vb (fin), depositare

depreciation n, 1 (of goods, cars, etc), svalutazione nf; **the depreciation percentage is low**, la percentuale di svalutazione è bassa. 2 (of plants, machinery, buildings, etc), ammortamento nm; **depreciation fund**, quota nf d'ammortamento

deputy adj, vice nm; **deputy manager**, vice direttore

description n, descrizione nf; **description of goods** (imp/exp), descrizione delle merci

design n, 1 (gen), disegno nm. 2 (ind), costruzione nf; **motor of good design**, motore di buona costruzione. 3 (comm) modello nm; **our latest designs**, i nostri ultimi modelli

design vb, 1 (gen), disegnare. 2 (create, have in mind), progettare

designer n, 1 (gen, original idea),

stilista nm. 2 (art, visual appearance), disegnatore nm, disegnatore grafico. 3 (stage), scenografo(-a) nm/f

desk n, 1 (offce), scrivania nf. 2 (comm), cassa nf; **pay at the desk**, pagare alla cassa

desk top publishing n (comp), desk top publishing nm

despatch vb (imp/exp), spedire

detached house n (gen), casa nf singola, villetta nf

detail n, dettaglio nm; **details** (name and address), 1 (gen), nome nm e indirizzo nm. 2 (comm), dati nmpl; (of a company), dati della società; **customer details** (mktg, sales), i dati del cliente. 3 (of an event), dettagli nmpl

detailed adj, dettagliato(-a)

develop vb, sviluppare

development n, sviluppo nm; **development area**, zona nf di sviluppo

deviation n, deviazione nf

device n, 1 (equipment), dispositivo nm. 2 (gen), mezzo nm

dial vb, **dial a number**, comporre un numero telefonico; **dial the police**, telefonare alla polizia

diary n, 1 (gen), diario nm. 2 (offce), agenda nf

dictate vb (offce), dettare

dictation n, dettatura nf; **dictation machine**, registratore nm

diesel n, diesel nm; **diesel engine**, motore diesel; **diesel oil**, nafta nf, diesel nm

difference n, differenza nf; **the difference between . . . and . . . is . .**, la differenza tra . . . e . . . è

digital adj (comp), digitale, numerico(-a)

digitised adj (comp), numerizzato(-a)

dimensions npl (imp/exp), dimensioni nfpl; **the dimensions of the load are 5 by 6 . .**, le dimensioni del carico sono 5 per 6

direct adj, diretto(-a); **direct current**, corrente nf diretta, corrente continua; **direct debit**, prelievo nm automatico; **direct line** (telephone), linea nf diretta; **direct marketing**, marketing nm diretto; **direct sales**, vendita nf diretta

directions npl, istruzioni nfpl

directions for use npl, modo nm d'impiego

director n (pers), direttore nm/f; **director of communication**, direttore alle comunicazioni; **director's secretary** (offce), segretaria nf di direzione; **marketing director**, direttore del marketing

directorate n (of company), direzione nf

disadvantage n, svantaggio nm

disagree with vb, non essere d'accordo; **we disagree with your analysis**, non siamo d'accordo con la vostra analisi

disc n (comp), disco nm; **disc drive**, 'disc drive' nm

discharge vb (transp), scaricare

discontinue vb, cessare; **discontinue production**, cessare la produzione

discount n (fin), sconto nm; **give a discount**, accordare uno sconto

discounted adj (fin), scontato(-a) adj

discovery n, scoperta nf

discrepancy n (gen), differenza nf

discuss vb (gen), discutere

discussion n (gen), discussione nf

dishonour vb **a bill**, non pagare una cambiale

dishwasher n lavastoviglie nf

dismiss vb, 1 (a person), congedare. 2 (an idea or argument), scartare, mettere da parte

dispatch vb, spedire

display n (of goods), mostra nf

display vb, 1 (a product), esporre. 2 (comp screen), mostrare (sullo schermo)

distribute vb (gen), distribuire

distribution n (mktg, sales), distribuzione nf; **distribution network** (mktg, sales), rete nf di distribuzione; **distribution problems** (gen), problemi nmpl di distribuzione

distributor n (mktg, sales, transp), distributore nm

diversify vb (gen), diversificare

divide vb, dividere

dividend n (fin), dividendo nm

division n, divisione nf

DIY, do-it yourself (mktg, sales), fai da te

do vb **business with . .**, fare affari con . . .

dock vb (transp), attraccare

dock warrant n (imp/exp), certificato nm di deposito

dockyard n, cantiere nm

document n (offce), documento nm; **documents against acceptance** (imp/exp), documenti contro accettazione; **documents against payment** (imp/exp), documenti contro pagamento

domestic adj, 1 (within a country), nazionale. 2 (household), domestico(-a); **domestic appliances** n, elettrodomestici nmpl

dominant adj (market position), dominante

dominate vb **the market**, dominare il mercato

door-to-door *adj*, porta a porta; **door-to-door sales**, vendite *nfpl* porta a porta; **door-to-door salesman**, venditore *nm* porta a porta

double *vb*, raddoppiare

down, be down *vb* (fin, results), essere in ribasso

down time *n*, tempo *nm* passivo

downturn *n* (fin, mktg, sales), abbassamento *nm*

downturn *vb* (fin), abbassare

downward trend *n* (gen, fin), tendenza *nf* al ribasso

dozen *n*, dozzina *nf*; **a dozen bottles**, una dozzina di bottiglie; **by the dozen**, a dozzine

D/P, **documents against payment**, (imp/exp), documenti *nmpl* contro pagamento

DP manager *n* (comp), direttore *nm* d'informatica

Dr to, **draw to . . .** (fin), all'ordine di . . .

Dr, **debtor** (fin), debitore *nm*, debito *nm*

draft *n*, **1** (of letters, reports), bozza *nf*; **draft contract**, bozza di contratto. **2** (fin), tratta *nf*; **bank draft**, tratta bancaria; **sight draft**, tratta a vista. **3** (of plans), progetto *nm*

draft *vb*, **1** (make a first attempt), fare una bozza. **2** (gen, write), redigere. **3** (a plan), disegnare, progettare

draw *n* (competitions), punteggio *nm* pari; **prize draw**, tiro *nm* a sorte

draw up *vb* (agreements), redigere; **draw up an agreement**, redigere un patto; **draw up a contract**, redigere un contratto

drawback *n*, **1** (disadvantage), inconveniente *nm*. **2** (imp/exp), 'drawback' *nm*

drawee *n*, trattario *nm*

drawer *n*, **1** (offce) cassetto *nm*. **2** (fin), traente *nm*

drill *vb* (gen), trapanare

drink *n*, bevanda *nf*; **soft drink**, bevanda analcolica; **strong drink**, bevanda alcolica

drive *n*, **1** (campaign), campagna *nf* di propaganda. **2** (in a vehicle), passeggiata *nf*, giro *nm*. **3** (distance to travel), distanza *nf*; **the office is a short drive from the town**, l'ufficio è a breve distanza dalla città. **4** (personality), iniziativa *nf*; **have plenty of drive**, avere molta iniziativa. **5** (propulsion), trasmissione *nf*; **belt drive**, trasmissione della cinghia

drive *vb* (car), guidare

driver *n* (gen), guidatore *nm*, autista *nm*

driving licence *n*, patente *nf* (di guida)

drop *vb*, cadere

drum *n* (imp/exp), bidone *nm*

dry *adj*, secco(-a)

DTI, **Department of Trade and Industry** = Ministero *nm* dell'Industria e Commercio

DTP, **desk top publishing** (comp), 'desk top publishing' *nm*; **DTP software**, software *nm* per desk top publishing

due *adj*, **1** (fin), da pagarsi; **bill due in two weeks**, conto da pagarsi tra due settimane. **2** (gen), dovuto(-a); **payment is due on 30th of the month**, il pagamento è dovuto al 30 del mese; **due date** (fin), scandenza *nf*

dump *vb* (sell at a loss), vendere in perdita

duplicate *n* (a second copy), duplicato *nm*; **in duplicate**, in duplicato

duplicate *vb* (offce), duplicare

durable *adj*, resistente, durevole

durables *npl*, beni *nmpl* durevoli

duration *n*, durata *nf*

duty *n* (customs duty), dogana *nf*;
duty paid (imp/exp), franco dogana

D/W, dock warrant (imp/exp),
certificato *nm* di deposito

**E + O E, errors and omissions
excepted**, salvo errori ed
omissioni

early *adv* **1** (early in the day), presto,
di buon'ora. **2** (quick), pronto(-a);
**we can guarantee early
delivery**, possiamo garantire una
consegna pronta; **an early reply**,
una risposta pronta. **3** (before
time), in anticipo; **early
repayment**, pagamento *nm* in
anticipo; **early retirement**,
prepensionamento *nm*

earn *vb*, guadagnare

earnings *npl*, utili *nmpl*; **earnings
per share**, utile *nm* per azione

ease *vb*, **1** (make easier), facilitare.
2 (drop in rates, prices) diminuire;
rates have eased, i tassi *nmpl*
sono diminuiti

easy *adj* (not difficult), facile

economic *adj*, economico(-a)

economical *adj*, **1** (saves money),
economico(-a) **2** (uses little),
economo(-a)

economics *n* (subject, study of),
economia *nf*

economise *vb*, economizzare

economy *n* (of a country), economia
nf; **the German/Italian/Spanish
economy**, l'economia tedesca/
italiana/spagnola

EDI, Electronic Data Interchange,
scambio *nm* dati elettronici

edible *adj*, commestibile

editor *n* (of a newspaper), redattore
nm, redattrice *nf*

education n, 1 (gen, teaching), insegnamento nm. 2 (section in CV), studi nmpl

EE, errors excepted, salvo errori

effect n (of . . ./on . . .), effetto nm; **have an effect on . .**, avere un effetto su . . .

effective adj, efficace

efficiency n, efficienza nf

efficient adj, efficiente

electrical equipment n, attrezzatura nf elettrica

electronic adj, elettronico(-a); **electronic mail** (comp), posta nf elettronica; **electronic system**, sistema nm elettronico

electronics npl, elettronica nf

eligible adj, 1 (membership), eleggibile; **be eligible for . .**, essere eleggibile per . . . 2 (rights), avere diritto a . . .

embargo n, embargo nm; **lift an embargo**, togliere un embargo; **place an embargo on . .**, mettere un embargo su . . .

embark vb (goods/passengers), imbarcare

emphasize vb (something), mettere in evidenza

employ vb, impiegare

employee n, impiegato(-a) nm/f, dipendente nm/f; **employees** (staff), personale nm, impiegati nmpl; **number of employees**, numero nm degli impiegati/dei dipendenti

employer n, datore nm di lavoro; **employer's liability insurance**, assicurazione nf (a carico del datore di lavoro) contro gli infortuni sul lavoro

employment n, impiego nm

employment history n (CV), esperienza nf professionale

empty adj, vuoto(-a)

Enc, Encl, enc, enclosure(s) (corr), allegato nm, allegati nmpl

enclose vb (corr), allegare, accludere; **I enclose a copy of our brochure**, allego una copia nf del nostro opuscolo

encounter vb, incontrare; **encounter problems**, incontrare degli ostacoli

end vb (come to the end), finire

endorse vb, 1 (a cheque), girare. 2 (approve an idea), approvare

engine n, motore nm; **internal combustion engine**, motore a combustione interna

enquiry n, 1 (gen), domanda nf (d'informazione). 2 (law), inchiesta nf; **court of enquiry**, commissione nf d'inchiesta

enter vb, (bookkeeping, etc), registrare

enterprise n, 1 (initiative), iniziativa nf. 2 (a company), impresa nf

entrance n, entrata nf

envelope n (stationery), busta nf

equal vb, eguagliare

equal (to) adj, uguale a; **be equal to**, essere uguale a

equity n (ordinary share), azione nf ordinaria

error n, errore nm; **errors and omissions excepted**, salvo errori ed omissioni

established (in) . . . adj 1 (country, region), stabilito(-a); **the company is established in . .**, la società è stabilita in . . . 2 (date), fondato(-a); **this company was established in 1945**, questa società è stata fondata nel 1945

estate agent n, mediatore nm, agente nm immobiliare

estimate n, 1 (quotation), preventivo nm. 2 (rough calculation), valutazione nf

estimate vb, valutare

estimated adj, 1 (fin), preventivato (-a); **estimated cost**, costo preventivo. 2 (gen), previsto(-a) adj; **estimated time of arrival**, ora d'arrivo previsto; **estimated time of departure**, ora di partenza prevista

Ethernet n (comp), 'Ethernet' nm

EU, **European Union**, UE, Unione Europea nf

event n, caso nm, evento nm; **events marketing**, marketing nm di eventi nmpl

eventual adj, 1 (final), finale. 2 (possible), eventuale

eventually adv, infine

examine vb, esaminare

exceed vb, eccedere

exceptional items npl (acct), spese nfpl straordinarie

excess n, eccesso nm

exchange vb **(for)** (gen), 1 (gen), scambiare. 2 (money), cambiare. 3 (from . . . to . . .) passare da . . . a . .; **exchange from one bank to another**, passare da una banca ad un'altra

exchange rate n, tasso nm del cambio

exclusive adj, esclusivo(-a); **exclusive deal**, affare nm esclusivo; **exclusive rights**, diritti nmpl esclusivi

excuse n, scusa nf

executive adj, esecutivo(-a); **executive committee**, comitato nm esecutivo; **executive powers**, poteri nmpl esecutivi; **executive director**, membro nm del consiglio d'amministrazione

executive n, 1 (pers), dirigente nm, direttore nm; **chief executive**, direttore generale. 2 (employee), responsabile; **sales executive**, responsabile nm alle vendite

exhibit vb (mktg, sales), esibire

exhibition n (mktg, sales), esposizione nf; **exhibition centre**, centro nm esposizione

exhibitor n (mktg, sales), espositore nm

expanding adj, in espansione; **expanding company**, società nf in espansione; **expanding market**, mercato nm in espansione

expansion n, espansione nf

expect vb, 1 (hope for), sperare; **we expect to sign a contract with . .**, speriamo di firmare un contratto con . . . 2 (something to happen), aspettarsi; **we expect rates to fall**, ci aspettiamo che i tassi diminuiscano. 3 (wait for), aspettare; **we will expect you at the hotel at 7 pm**, vi aspettiamo all'albergo alle sette di sera

expenditure n, spesa nf

expenses npl, spese nfpl; **travelling expenses**, spese di viaggio

experience n, esperienza nf; **gain experience in marketing**, acquistare esperienza nel marketing

experienced adj, esperto(-a); **we are looking for an experienced manager**, cerchiamo un direttore esperto

experiment n, esperimento nm

expert n, esperto nm

export n, esportazione nf; **export manager**, direttore nm all'esportazione

export vb, esportare

exporter n, esportatore nm

express n (train) (transp), espresso nm

express adj (direct), espresso(-a) **express delivery** (transp), consegna nf per espresso

express adv, per espresso

ExQ, **Exq**, **ex quay** (imp/exp), ex molo

EXS, **ex ship** (imp/exp), ex nave

external disc drive *n*, disc drive *nm* all'esterno

extra charge *n* (fin), supplemento *nm*

extrude *vb* (gen), estrudere

extruded *adj*, in estrusione *nf*

extrusion *n* (gen), estrusione *nf*

EXW, **ex works** (imp/exp), ex stabilimento

eyecatching *adj* (mktg, sales), attraente

FAA, **faa**, **free of all average** (ins), franco d'avaria

fabric *n* (eg cloth), tessuto *nm*

fabricate *vb*, **1** (imagine), inventare. **2** (falsify a document), falsificare. **3** (build), fabbricare, costruire

fabrication *n*, **1** (fig), invenzione *nf*. **2** (falsify), falsificazione *nf*. **3** (building), fabbricazione *nf*, costruzione *nf*

face *vb*, **1** (in front of), essere di fronte; **I am facing the building**, sono di fronte all'edificio. **2** (go through) attraversare; **the company faces a difficult period**, la società attraversa un periodo difficile

face value *n* (fin, stock market), valore *nm* nominale

facilitate *vb*, facilitare

facilities *npl*, **1** (of hotel), amenità *nfpl*; **among the facilities offered by our . . . are . .**, tra le amenità offerte dal nostro . . . . ci sono . . . **2** (fin), facilitazioni *nfpl*; **a comprehensive range of facilities**, una gamma completa di facilitazioni

factor *n* (gen, maths), fattore *nm*; **decisive factor**, fattore determinante; **a major factor in the decision was . .**, uno dei fattori principali nella decisione è stato quello di . . . .

factory *n*, stabilimento *nm*; **factory gate price**, prezzo *nm* all'uscita stabilimento; **factory production**, produzione *nf* dello stabilimento

fail vb, **1** (fin), (go bust), andare in fallimento. **2** (not succeed), fallire, **all our plans failed**, tutti i nostri piani fallirono. **3** (fail to do something promised), non riuscire a; **they failed to deliver by the agreed date**, non sono riusciti a fare le consegne alla data convenuta

failure n, **1** (mech), avaria nf. **2** (business failure), fallimento nm

fair adj, giusto(-a)

fair n, fiera nf

FAK, freight all kinds (imp/exp), nolo nm per tutti i generi di merci

fall n, **1** (gen), caduta nf. **2** (fin), ribasso nm; **a rapid fall in prices**, un ribasso rapido nei prezzi

fall vb, **1** (gen), cadere. **2** (fin), diminuire; **prices have fallen this year**, i prezzi sono diminuiti quest'anno; **we expect the rate to fall to . .**, ci aspettiamo che il tasso diminuisca fino a . .; **sales have fallen by 15%**, le vendite sono diminuite del 15%

fall due (in, on) vb (fin), venire a scadenza; **payment falls due in May**, il pagamento viene a scadenza in maggio

fall off vb, diminuire; **demand is beginning to fall off**, le richieste cominciano a diminuire

fall through vb, fallire; **the negotiations fell through because of . .**, le trattative sono fallite a causa di . . .

fall-off n (reduction, slackening), diminuzione nf; **a fall-off in orders**, una diminuzione negli ordini

FAQ, faq, 1 free alongside quay (imp/exp), franco banchina. **2 fair average quality** (mktg, sales), qualità corrente

fare n, tariffa nf; **the fare to London is £14**, la tariffa per Londra è di 14 sterline; **half fare**, mezza tariffa; **second class fare**, la tariffa di un biglietto in seconda classe; **single fare**, tariffa singola; **return fare**, tariffa di un biglietto andata e ritorno

farmer n, agricoltore nm, fattore nm

farming n, agricoltura nf, coltivazione nf

FAS, free alongside ship (imp/exp), franco lungo la nave

fast adj, veloce; **the fast food industry**, l'industria nf del 'fast food'; **fast delivery guaranteed**, garantita consegna veloce

fast adv, velocemente; **he works fast**, lavora velocemente

fault n, **1** (machines, products), difetto nm; **we believe the problem is due to a fault in the system**, pensiamo che il problema sia dovuto a un difetto nel sistema. **2** (mistake), errore nm; **we must apologise, the fault was ours**, ci scusiamo, l'errore è stato nostro

faulty adj, difettoso(-a)

fax n (message), fax nm; **fax machine**, macchina nf fax; **fax number**, il numero di fax

fax vb, inviare un fax

FBL, FIATA, combined transport bill of lading (imp/exp), polizza nf di carico di trasporto misto

FCL, full container load (transp), contenitore nm completo

feasibility n, possibilità nf; **a feasibility study**, uno studio di possibilità

feasible adj, possibile, fattibile

feature n (of a product), caratteristica nf; **a key feature**, una caratteristica chiave; **a unique feature**, una caratteristica unica

feature vb (mktg, sales), **1** (programme or article), presentare; **the article will feature our company**, l'articolo presenterà la nostra società. **2** (of a product), mettere in evidenza; **the product features the latest technology**, il prodotto mette in evidenza la tecnologia più avanzata

fee n, **1** (cost of a professional service), onorario nm; **a doctor's fee**, l'onorario di un medico. **2** (regular contribution, club), rata nf; **the annual membership fee includes . .**, la rata annuale di associazione include . . .

feel vb (opinion), pensare; **in view of what you say, we feel that . .**, considerando quanto dite, pensiamo che . . .

female adj (human gender), femminile

ferry n, traghetto nm

fga, free of general average (ins), franco avaria comune

field n, campo nm; **field survey**, indagine di campo; **in the field** (mktg, sales), nel campo; **a specialist in the field of . . .** uno specialista nel campo di . . .

fight vb, lottare

figure n (1,2,3 . . .), cifra nf, numero nm

file n, **1** (single card), cartellino nm, scheda nf. **2** (collection of information on a subject), scheda nf. **3** (container for storage files), schedario nm. **4** (binder to hold documents), raccoglitore nm, schedario nm. **5** (comp), archivio nm, schedario nm; **file management**, gestione nf archivio

file vb (offce), archiviare

filing cabinet n (offce), schedario nm

filing clerk n (offce), archivista nm

fill in vb, **(a form)**, riempire, compilare

fill up vb **1** (gen), riempire. **2** (with petrol), fare il pieno

film n, **1** (photos), rullino nf. **2** (cinema), film nm. **3** (thin layer or covering), pellicola nf, strato nm

sottile. **4** (cling film), pellicola nf

final adj, finale, ultimo(-a)

finally adv, finalmente

finalise vb, finalizzare, completare

finance n, finanza nf

finance vb, finanziare

financial adj, finanziario(-a); **the financial arrangements**, le disposizioni nfpl finanziarie; **financial director** (fin), direttore finanziario; **financial manager** (fin), direttore finanziario; **financial year** (fin), esercizio nm

financier n, **1** (somebody who is in finance), finanziere nm. **2** (somebody who can finance someone), finanziatore nm

financing n, finanziamento nm

find vb, trovare

fine adj, **1** (small particles), fine. **2** (appearance), bello(-a)

fine n (law), multa nf; **pay a fine**, pagare una multa

fine vb, multare

finish n (on a product), finitura nf

finish vb, finire

finished adj (completed), finito(-a); **finished goods/products** (fin), prodotti nmpl finiti

FIO, free in and out, (imp/exp), nolo più spese di carico e scarico

fire n, **1** (gen), fuoco nm. **2** (accidental), incendio nm

firm adj, **1** (compact), compatto; **firm ground**, un terreno compatto. **2** (fixed), fisso(-a); **firm prices**, prezzi nmpl fissi. **3** (decisive), deciso(-a); **firm character**, carattere nm deciso. **4** (definite), definito(-a); **a firm order**, un ordine definito

firm n (business), ditta nf, società nf

first adj, primo(-a); **the first time**, la prima volta

fit *vb*, **1** (be the right size), andar bene. **2** (fix on), montare. **3** (adjust and assemble), regolare

fix *vb*, **1** (make arrangements), fissare, stabilire; **fix an appointment**, fissare un appuntamento; **fix a date**, fissare una data; **fix a plan**, stabilire un piano. **2** (eg assembly), montare. **3** (repair), riparare

fixed *adj*, **fixed assets** (fin), immobili *nmpl*; **fixed rate** (fin), tasso *nm* fisso; **fixed-term contract** (pers), contratto a durata determinata

flat *adj*, **1** (gen), piatto(-a), piano; **flat foot**, piede *nm* piatto; **flat ground**, terreno, piano. **2** (with no life)(-a) scialbo *nm*; **a flat person**, una persona scialba. **3** (depressed), depresso(-a); **the market is flat**, il mercato è depresso; **I feel a bit flat**, mi sento un po' depresso. **4** (tyres), sgonfio(-a); **I have got a flat tyre**, ho una ruota sgonfia

flat *n* (accommodation), appartamento *nm*

flat rate *n*, tasso *nm* uniforme

flatten *vb*, appiattire

flaw *n*, difetto *nm*, imperfezione *nf*

flexible *adj*, flessibile; **flexible working hours**, orario flessibile; **thanks to our flexible production system** . ., grazie al nostro sistema di produzione flessibile . . . . .

flier/flyer *n* (leaflet), volantino *nm*

flip chart *n*, lavagna *nf* a fogli volanti

float *vb* **a company** (fin), lanciare una società

floating *adj*, fluttuante; **floating rates**, tassi *nmpl* fluttuanti

floor *n*, **1** (first, second floor), piano *nm*; **first floor**, primo piano; **ground floor**, pianterreno. **2** (of a room or a street), pavimento *nm*. **3** (floor/ceiling), soffitto *nm*

flow chart *n* (fin), diagramma *nm* di flusso

flow of capital *n*, flusso *nm* di capitale

fluctuate *vb*, fluttuare

fluctuations *npl*, fluttuazioni *nfpl*; **the change in price is due to fluctuations in the interest rate**, il cambio dei prezzi è dovuto alle fluttuazioni nel tasso d'interesse

fly *vb* (transp), volare

FM, frequency modulation, modulazione *nf* di frequenza

FMCG, fast moving consumer goods (mktg, sales), beni *nmpl* di consumo corrente

FOB, free on board (imp/exp), franco a bordo

focus on *vb* (gen, non-tech), concentrarsi su

fold *vb* (documents), piegare

folder *n*, **1** (product information, mktg, sales), volantino *nm*. **2** (contains documents), cartella *nf*

follow *vb*, seguire

follow up *vb* (contact who has not responded) (mktg, sales), ricontattare; **follow up a lead** again (mktg, sales), riattivare un contatto; **follow up after a meeting** (mktg, sales), dare seguito a una riunione

food *n*, cibo *nm*, alimento *nm*; **food industry**, industria *nf* alimentare; **food products**, prodotti *nmpl* alimentari

FOR, FOT, free on rail, free on truck (imp/exp, transp), franco vagone

forecast *n* (fin), previsione *nf*

forecast *vb* (fin), prevedere

foreign *adj*, **1** (from another place), straniero(-a), estero(-a); **this is a foreign engine**, questo è un motore straniero; **foreign currency**, valuta *nf* estera; **foreign trade**, commercio *nm* estero. **2** (does not belong to something), estraneo(-a); **a foreign body**, un corpo estraneo

foreman n, capo-reparto nm

forklift (truck) n, carrello nm elevatore

form n (imp/exp), modulo nm; **fill in a form**, riempire un modulo

forward vb (imp/exp), 1 (corr) inoltrare; **please forward the letter to the above address**, si prega inoltrare la lettera all'indirizzo sopra indicato. 2 (send to new address), far pervenire. 3 (dispatch, send), spedire, mandare

forwarding agent n (transp), spedizioniere nm

founded adj **in (1900)**, fondato(-a) nell (1900)

fountain pen n, (penna) stilografica nf

four-colour process n (ad) (mktg, sales), quadricromia nf; **a four-colour advertisement**, un'inserzione nf in quadricromia

FPA, free of particular average (imp/exp), franco avaria particolare

FPAD, freight payable at destination (imp/exp), nolo nm pagabile a destinazione

franchise n (mktg, sales), franchigia nf

franchise vb (mktg, sales), dare una franchigia

frank vb (corr), affrancare

franking machine n (offce), macchina nf affrancatrice

FRC, free carrier (imp/exp), franco trasportatore

free adj (mktg, sales), gratuito(-a); **free admission**, entrata nf gratuita; **free carrier** (imp/exp), franco trasportatore nm; **free delivery** (imp/exp), consegna nf franca; **free on board** (imp/exp), franco a bordo; **free gift** (mktg, sales), regalo nm; **free sheet** (mktg, sales), pubblicazione nf gratuita

freebie n (mktg, sales), regalo nm pubblicitario

freephone number n (mktg, sales), numero nm verde

freeze vb, 1 (weather), gelare. 2 (deep freeze), congelare. 3 (prices, rates), bloccare, congelare

freight n (transp), nolo nm; **freight paid to . . .** (imp/exp), nolo nm pagato fino a . .; **fast freight**, nolo veloce; **freight car** (transp), carro nm merci; **freight train** (transp), treno nm merci; **freight plane** (transp), aereo da trasporto; **dead freight** (transp), nolo vuoto per pieno; **freight paid** (fin), nolo pagato; **freight payable at destination** (imp/exp), nolo pagabile a destinazione

frequency n, frequenza nf

frequent adj, frequente

fridge n, frigorifero nm

fringe benefits npl, gratifiche nfpl extra

fuel n, combustibile nm, carburante nm; **fuel oil** (imp/exp), nafta nf, olio nm pesante

full adj, completo(-a)

full-time adj (pers), a tempo pieno; **a full-time job/position**, un lavoro/un posto a tempo pieno

future adj, futuro(-a); **future developments may include . .**, è possibile che i futuri sviluppi includano . . .

future n, futuro nm; **in the future**, nel futuro

futures market n (fin), mercato nm di merci vendute con consegna a termine

G

GA, ga, general average (ins), avaria *nf* comune

gadget *n*, **1** (unflattering), aggeggio *nm*, (colloquial), coso *nm*. **2** (small piece of equipment), dispositivo *nm*, arnese *nm*

gain *n*, **1** (gen, fin), guadagno *nm*. **2** (increase), aumento *nm*; **a gain in weight**, un aumento di peso

gain *vb*, **1** (gen, fin), guadagnare. **2** (increase), aumentare. **3** (obtain), ottenere; **gain experience** (CV), acquistare esperienza

gamble *n*, **1** (gen), gioco *nm* d'azzardo. **2** (risk), rischio *nm*. **3** (speculation), speculazione *nf*

gamble *vb*, **1** (gen), giocare d'azzardo. **2** (gamble on), giocare; **he gambles on the Stock Exchange**, gioca in Borsa. **3** (gamble away), perdere al gioco

gap *n*, **1** (opening), apertura *nf*. **2** (interval), intervallo *nm*, pausa *nf*. **3** (difference of opinions), divergenza *nf*; (cultural gap), lacuna *nf*

garden *n*, giardino *nm*; **garden centre**, centro *nm* giardinaggio, 'garden centre' *nm*; **garden bed**, aiuola *nf*; **kitchen garden**, orto *nm*; **garden furniture**, mobili *nmpl* per giardino

gas *n*, gas *nm*

gather *vb*, **1** (gen), riunire. **2** (pick), cogliere; **gather information**, raccogliere informazioni; **gather speed**, aumentare di velocità; **gather strength**, riprendere forza; **gather ground**, guadagnare terreno

GCR, general cargo rates (transp), tariffe *nfpl* generali di carico

GDP, Gross Domestic Product, PIL, Prodotto *nm* Interno Lordo

general *adj*, generale; **general cargo rates** (transp), tariffe *nfpl* generali di carico; **general manager**, direttore *nm* generale

get *vb*, ottenere; **get ahead**, far progressi; **get in touch with**, contattare, entrare in contatto con

get off *vb* (a train), scendere

gift *n*, regalo *nm*

gift wrap *vb*, fare un pacchetto regalo

Giro cheque *n*, assegno *nm* postale

give *vb*, **1** (gen), dare; **give credit** (fin), far credito; **give a talk to . .**, parlare a . .; **give notice** (pers), (to an employer), dare le dimissioni; (to an employee), licenziare con preavviso. **2** (formal gifts), offrire

giveaway *n* (mktg, sales), regalo *nm*

gloomy *adj* (financial outlook), pessimistico(-a)

glossy *n* (magazine), (rivista) di lusso *nm*

glue *n*, colla *nf*

glue *vb*, incollare

glut *n* (of), sovrabbondanza *nf* (di)

GNP, Gross National Product, PNL, Prodotto *nm* Nazionale Lordo

go *vb*, andare; **go public** (fin, stock market), essere introdotto in borsa; **go to law**, ricorrere alla legge; **go to the dogs**, andare in rovina

go ahead, *vb*, fare progressi; **go ahead!**, avanti!

go down by . . . *vb* (rates, prices), calare; **sales have gone down by 2%**, le vendite sono calate del 2%

go down to *vb*, scendere; **inflation will go down to 5%**, l'inflazione scenderà fino al 5%

go up *vb*, **1** (gen), montare. **2** (fin),

salire; **prices have gone up by 10%**, i prezzi sono saliti del 10%

go-ahead, *adj*, intraprendente; **a go-ahead businesswoman**, una donna d'affari intraprendente

go-between *n*, intermediario *nm*

goods *n* (fin), merci *nfpl*; **goods wagon** (transp), vagone *nm* merci; **manufactured goods**, merci lavorate; **imported goods**, merci importate; **luxury goods**, merci di lusso

goodwill *n*, **1** (gen), fiducia *nf*, buona volontà *nf*. **2** (comm), avviamento *nm* (di una ditta)

GP, **general practitioner**, medico *nm* generico

grade *n*, **1** (gen), grado *nm*. **2** (quality), qualità

grade *vb* (quality of goods), selezionare

graph *n* (chart), grafico *nm*, diagramma *nm*; **graph paper**, carta *nf* millimetrata

graph *vb*, tracciare il grafico

graphics *npl*, rappresentazioni *nfpl* grafiche

green *adj* (colour), verde; **green card** (ins), carta verde

greet *vb*, **1** (gen), salutare. **2** (visitor), accogliere

grievance *n*, lagnanza *nf*, reclamo *nm*

gross *adj* (fin), lordo(-a) *adj*; **gross earnings**, reddito *nm* lordo; **gross national product**, prodotto nazionale lordo; **gross profit**, profitto lordo; **gross revenue**, entrata lorda; **gross weight**, peso lordo

gross *n*, **1** (12 × 12), grossa *nf*. **2** in massa, all'ingrosso; **by the gross**, all'ingrosso

grow *vb*, crescere

growth *n*, **1** (gen), crescita *nf*, sviluppo *nm*. **2** (fin), aumento *nm*;

the growth of trade, l'aumento del commercio

guarantee *n*, garanzia *nf*; **the product comes with a two-year guarantee**, il prodotto ha due anni di garanzia

guarantee *vb*, garantire; **we can guarantee that . .**, possiamo garantire che . . .

guaranteed *adj*, garantito(-a); **guaranteed delivery**, consegna *nf* garantita

guess *n*, ipotesi *nf*, supposizione *nf*

guess *vb*, supporre

guest *n*, **1** (hotel), cliente *nm*. **2** (invited for meal or stay), invitato *nm*, ospite *nm*

H

haggle vb, mercanteggiare sul prezzo

half adj, 1 (gen), mezzo(-a); **half-measures**, mezze misure; **half-pay**, mezzo stipendio

half n, metà nf; **half of the work**, metà del lavoro; **half-price**, metà prezzo

half-brother n, fratellastro nm

half-dozen n, mezza dozzina nf

half-sister, n, sorellastra nf

half-year n, semestre nm; **the half-year results**, i risultati nmpl del semestre

half-yearly adv, semestralmente

hall n, sala nf, salone nm; **concert hall**, sala da concerto; **conference hall**, sala conferenze; **exhibition hall**, salone esposizioni; **main hall**, sala principale

halve vb (reduce by half), dividere a metà

hampered, be hampered by vb, essere ostacolato(-a) da . . .

hand over vb (documents), consegnare

handbook n, manuale nm

handle vb, 1 (see to), occuparsi . . . di . . . 2 (move goods), (transp), maneggiare vb

handling n, 1 (gen), manutenzione nf; **handling truck**, carrello nm di manutenzione; **handling costs**, costi nmpl, di manutenzione. 2 (goods handling), trattamento nm. 3 (fin), gestione nf; **handling charges**, spese nfpl di gestione

handout n (printed information), documento nm (da distribuire)

hard adj, 1 (gen), duro(-a); **hard times**, tempi duri. 2 (difficult), difficile; **hard problem**, problema nm difficile

hard copy n (comp), copia nf su carta

hard disc n (comp), 'hard disc' nm

hardware n, 1 (shop), ferramenta nm; **hardware shop**, negozio, nm di ferramenta. 2 (comp), hardware nm

haulage n, transporto nm

haulier n (transp), trasportatore nm

head n (leader), capo nm, responsabile nm; **head of department**, capo dipartimento; **head of marketing**, responsabile del marketing; **head office** (fin), sede nf (di una ditta)

headed paper n (offce), carta nf intestata

headhunter n, 1 (gen), cacciatore nm di teste. 2 (mktg, sales) chi è alla ricerca di personale altamente specializzato

headline n, titolo nm

headquarters npl, 1 (registered office), sede nf sociale. 2 (head office), direzione nf

heat n, calore nm

heated adj, accaldato(-a), animato (-a); **heated body**, corpo nm accaldato; **heated discussion**, discussione nf animata

heating n, riscaldamento nm; **central heating**, riscaldamento centrale

heavy adj (weight), pesante

heavy duty adj, 1 (type of use), per uso intensivo. 2 (strong construction), solido(-a)

height n, altezza nf

help n, aiuto nf; **thank you for your help**, vi ringraziamo per il vostro aiuto

help vb, aiutare; **our agent in . . . will be able to help you**, il nostro agente in . . . sarà in grado di aiutarvi

HGV, heavy goods vehicle = veicolo nm per trasporti pesanti

hi-fi n (mktg, sales), (strumento nm) ad alta fedeltà

high adj (price), alto(-a); **the price is very high**, il prezzo è molto alto; **a high level of . .**, un alto livello di . . .

highlighter n (offce), evidenziatore nm

hire adj (fin), in affitto nm; **hire car**, macchina nf in affitto

hire vb, **1** (employ), assumere. **2** (equipment), prendere in affitto

hired adj **1** (equipment), in affitto nm. **2** (employed), assunto(-a)

hire purchase n, acquisto nm a rate

hit n (success), successo nm

hit, be hit by . . . vb (affected), essere colpito da . . . ; **we have been hit by the high price of fuel**, siamo stati colpiti dal fattore dell'alto prezzo del carburante

hoarding n (mktg, sales), tabellone nm pubblicitario

hobbies npl (CV), passatempi nmpl

hold n (of a ship), stiva nf

hold vb (stocks), contenere; **our warehouse holds considerable stocks of . .**, il nostro deposito contiene scorte considerevoli di . . .

holding company n, società nf finanziaria

hold up n, **1** (in traffic), ingorgo nm. **2** (of car), panna nf. **3** (in production), ritardo nm

hole n, foro nm; buco nm; **hole puncher** (offce), bucatrice nf

holiday n, vacanza nf, ferie nfpl; **it is a lovely holiday**, è una bella vacanza; **Mr Bright is on holiday until**

the end of the month, il signor Bright sarà in ferie fino alla fine del mese; **the holiday period**, il periodo festivo

home n, casa nf, abitazione nf

home adj, domestico(-a), nazionale

home address n (offce), indirizzo nm privato, domicilio nm

home market n, mercato nm nazionale

honest adj, onesto(-a)

hospital n, ospedale nm

hospitality n, ospitalità nf; **hospitality tent** (mktg, sales), tenda nf di ricevimento

hour n, ora nf

hourly adj (every hour), orario; **hourly flights**, voli orari; **hourly rate**, tariffa oraria

hourly adv, ad ogni ora, una volta all'ora

household equipment/goods npl, articoli nmpl casalinghi

household word n, parola nf d'uso comune

hovercraft n (transp), hovercraft nm

HP, hp, horse power, potenza nf in cavalli

HP, hire-purchase (fin), acquisto nm a rate

huge adj, enorme

human resources npl, risorse nfpl umane

hypermarket n (mktg, sales), ipermercato nm

I

ignore *vb*, ignorare

illegal *adj*, illegale

illegible *adj*, illeggibile; **the second page of the fax is illegible**, la seconda pagina del fax è illeggibile

image *n*, immagine *nf*

import *vb*, importare

importance *n*, importanza *nf*

important *adj*, importante

imported *adj*, importato(-a); **imported goods**, merci *nfpl* importate

impound *vb* (imp/exp), sequestrare

incentive *n* (mktg, sales), incentivo *nm*

include *vb*, **1** (correspondence, enclose), allegare, accludere; **please include . .**, si prega di accludere . . . **2** (gen), includere; **the contract includes a clause on . .**, il contratto include una clausola su . . .

inclusion *n*, inclusione *nf*

inclusive *adj* (**of**), compreso(-a); **inclusive of delivery**, consegna *nf* compresa; **inclusive terms**, tutto compreso

income *n*, reddito *nm*; **regular income**, reddito regolare; **income tax**, imposta *nf* sul reddito

incomings *npl*, entrate *nfpl*

increase *n*, aumento *nm*; **increase in value**, aumento di valore

increase *vb* (gen, fin), aumentare; **the production has been increased**, la produzione è stata aumentata; **increase the prices**, aumentare i prezzi; **increase by** (gen, fin), aumentare del . .; **the cost of hire has been increased by 8%**, il costo d'affitto è stato aumentato dell' 8%

independence *n*, indipendenza *nf*

independent *adj*, indipendente

indicate *vb*, indicare

indication *n*, indicazione *nf*

indispensable *adj*, indispensabile

industrial *adj*, industriale; **industrial dispute**, disputa *nf* industriale; **industrial relations**, relazioni *nfpl* industriali; **industrial estate**, zona *nf* industriale

industrialist *n*, industriale *nm*

industry *n*, industria *nf*; **domestic industry**, industria nazionale; **the service industries**, le industrie del settore servizi

inflation *n*, inflazione *nf*

influence *n*, influenza *nf*; **have an influence on . .**, avere un'influenza su . . .

influenced, be influenced by *vb*, essere influenzato(-a) da

inform *vb*, informare

informal *adj*, non ufficiale, senza formalità; **an informal visit**, una visita non ufficiale; **an informal discussion**, una discussione senza formalità

information *n*, **1** (gen), informazione *nf*; **some information about . .**, delle informazioni su . . . **2** (comp), dato *nm*; **information systems**, sistemi *nmpl* d'informatica

infra-red control *n*, comando *nm* a raggi infrarossi

infringe *vb* **a patent** (law), contraffare un brevetto

in-house *adj*, interno(-a); **an in-house magazine**, una rivista interna

initial adj, iniziale

Inland Revenue n (fin), fisco nm

innovate vb, fare innovazioni

innovation n, innovazione nf

innovative adj, innovativo(-a)

input vb (comp), entrare dei dati

inquiry n 1 (investigation), (law), inchiesta nf; **carry out an inquiry**, fare un'inchiesta. 2 (request for information), richiesta nf d'informazioni; **thank you for your inquiry about . .**, vi ringraziamo per la vostra richiesta di informazioni su . . . 3 (gen), informazione nf; **make enquiries about . .**, assumere informazioni su . .,

insert n (mktg, sales), inserzione nf

insert vb (mktg, sales), inserire; **insert an ad in . .**, inserire un annuncio sul . . .

insertion rate n (mktg, sales), tariffa nf annunci pubblicitari

insist (on) vb, insistere (su)

inspect vb, ispezionare

inspection n, ispezione nf

install vb, installare

installation n, installazione nf

instalment n (fin), 1 (part of amount due for a purchase), acconto nm. 2 (part payment of a loan to a borrower), rata nf; **the first instalment is due to be paid on 1 June**, la prima rata dovrà essere pagata il primo giugno; **payment by instalments**, pagamento nm a rate

institute vb **proceedings against** (law), intentare un processo contro

instruct vb (give an order), dare istruzioni

instructions npl, istruzioni nfpl; **give instructions**, dare istruzioni; **the instructions for use**, le istruzioni d'uso

insulated adj, 1 (electr), isolato(-a). 2 (heat), con isolazione nf termica

insulation n, 1 (electr), isolazione nf. 2 (heat), isolazione termica

insurance n, assicurazione nf; **insurance policy**, polizza d'assicurazione; **insurance sector**, settore nm assicurativo

insure vb (**against**), assicurare (contro)

insured, be insured vb (**against**), essere assicurato(-a) (contro)

insured n ('The Insured'), assicurato nm ('L'Assicurato')

insurer n, assicuratore nm

intangible adj (acct), intangibile; **intangible assets**, attività nf intangibile

interest n, 1 (financial interest), investimento nm. 2 (shares in), partecipazione nf; **a 10% interest in . .**, una partecipazione del 10% in . . . 3 (return on capital), interesse nm; **at 10% interest**, al 10% di interesse. 4 (money paid for capital on a % basis), interessi nmpl

interested adj, interessato(-a); **be interested in . .**, essere interessato in . . .

interests npl (CV), interessi nmpl

interface vb (comp), interfacciare

intervene vb, intervenire

intervention n, intervento nm

interview n, 1 (gen), intervista nf. 2 (pers), colloquio nm

interview vb, 1 (gen), intervistare. 2 (pers), avere un colloquio; **interview an applicant** (pers), avere un colloquio con un candidato

in-tray n, posta nf in arrivo

introduce vb, 1 (suggest) introdurre; **introduce a new idea**, introdurre una nuova idea; **introduce a new product** (mktg, sales), introdurre

sul mercato un nuovo prodotto.
2 (get something adopted) fare
adottare; **introduce a new policy**,
fare adottare una nuova politica.
3 (a person to someone),
presentare (una persona a
qualcuno); **I will introduce you to
our new director, Mr Collins**, la
presenterò al Signor Collins, il
nostro nuovo direttore

introductory price n (fin), prezzo
nm introduttivo

inventory n, inventario nm; **make an
inventory**, fare un inventario;
inventory turnover (fin),
rotazione nf scorte

invest in vb (fin), investire

investigate vb (law), investigare

investment n (fin), investimento nm

invitation n, invito nm; **an invitation
to tender** (mktg, sales), un invito a
concorrere per un appalto; **send
an invitation**, inviare un invito

invite vb, invitare

invoice n, fattura nf; **invoice value**
(fin, mktg, sales), valore nm della
fattura; **pro forma invoice**, fattura
pro forma

invoice vb, fatturare

invoicing n (fin), fatturazione nf

involve vb, coinvolgere

involved, be involved in vb (be
active in), essere coinvolto(-a) in

IQ, intelligence quotient,
quoziente nm d'intelligenza

iron n, ferro nm

ironmonger n, negoziante nm di
ferramenta

irrevocable letter of credit n (fin),
lettera nf di credito irrevocabile

issue n, **1** (of magazine), numero nm.
2 (of new shares), emissione nf.
3 (subject, subject of discussion),
questione nf; **we must discuss
the issue of the maintenance**,

dobbiamo discutere la questione
della manutenzione

issue vb, **1** emettere; **issue a bill of
lading**, emettere una polizza di
carico; **issue a press release**,
emettere un comunicato stampa.
2 rilasciare; **issue a receipt**,
rilasciare una ricevuta

item n, **1** (eg goods), articolo nm;
luxury item, articolo di lusso;
missing items, articoli che
mancano. **2** (part of an agenda),
questioni nfpl; **items on the
agenda** (of a meeting), questioni
all'ordine del giorno (di
un'assemblea). **3** (fin), voce nf; **this
item does not appear in the
books**, questa voce non appare nei
libri contabili

itemise vb, dettagliare; **itemised
bill/invoice**, fattura nf dettagliata

J

jam *vb* (mechanical), bloccare; **the machine is jammed**, la macchina è bloccata

jam *n* (traffic), ingorgo *nm* (stradale)

jeopardise *vb*, mettere a repentaglio, mettere in pericolo

JIT, Just in Time, giusto in tempo

job *n*, **1** (pers), impiego *nm*; **job advertisement**, offerta d'impiego; **part-time job**, impiego a tempo determinato; **full-time job**, impiego a tempo pieno. **2** (specific position in company), mansione *nf*; **job description**, descrizione delle mansioni. **3** (piece of work to do), lavoro *nm*; **this is a very difficult job**, questo è un lavoro molto difficile

join *vb*, unire, partecipare; **join two cables**, unire due cavi; **join in an enterprise**, partecipare ad un'impresa

joint *adj*, **joint account**, conto *nm* di partecipazione; **joint action**, azione *nf* collettiva; **joint decision**, decisione *nf* collettiva; **joint interests**, interessi *nmpl* comuni; **joint stock company**, società *nf* per azioni; **joint venture**, compartecipazione *nf*

judge *n* (law), giudice *nm*

judge *vb* (law), giudicare

judgment *n* (law), giudizio *nm*

junior *adj*, **1** (younger), giovane; **junior employee**, impiegato *nm* giovane. **2** (younger and with less experience), meno anziano; **junior partner**, il socio meno anziano;

junior manager, il direttore meno anziano. **3** (with brothers or sisters), minore

jury *n* (law), giuria *nf*

just *adv*, **1** (barely), appena; **just enough**, appena abbastanza; **they just managed to . .**, sono appena riusciti a . . . **2** (a short while ago), proprio, giusto; **just as I came in**, proprio quando sono entrato; **just in time (production)**, giusto in tempo

justice *n*, giustizia *nf*

justify *vb*, giustificare

K

keep *vb*, **1** (gen), tenere; **you can keep it**, può tenerlo; **keep the books**, tenere la contabilità. **2** (retain, preserve), conservare; **keep in a dry place**, conservare in luogo asciutto; **keep the receipt**, conservare la ricevuta. **3** (maintain), mantenere; **keep a promise**, mantenere una promessa; **he has two families to keep**, ha due famiglie da mantenere; **keep cool**, mantenersi calmo. **4** (stay), stare restare; **keep standing**, stare in piedi; **keep awake**, stare sveglio; **keep quiet**, stare/restare tranquillo

keep ahead of . . . tenersi in testa a . . . **keep to a deadline**, rispettare la data limite

keep up appearances, salvare le apparenze

keep up with . . . *vb*, **1** (stay informed), stare al passo, tenersi al corrente. **2** (maintain the same level, price, rate) tenere lo stesso livello di . . .

key *n*, **1** (gen), chiave *nf*. **2** (comp), tasto *nm*

key *adj*, chiave *nf*; **key part**, parte *nf* chiave; **key feature**, caratteristica *nf* chiave; **key factor**, fattore *nm* chiave

key in *vb* (comp), battere a macchina

keyboard *n* (comp), tastiera *nf*; **keyboard operator**, dattilografo (-a) *nm/f*

keyboard *vb*, battere a macchina

kind *adj*, gentile; **kind person**, persona *nf* gentile

kind *n* (type), specie *nf*; **this is a good kind of material**, questa è una buona specie di materiale; **payment in kind**, pagamento *nm* in natura. **2 in kind**, nello stesso modo; **repay in kind**, ripagare nello stesso modo

kind of *adv*, quasi; **he kind of knew it**, quasi lo sapeva

kit *n* (mktg, sales), corredo *nm*; **kit form**, tipo *nm* di corredo

know-how *n*, abilità *nf*

knowledge *n*, conoscenza *nf*; **a good knowledge of the market**, una buona conoscenza del mercato

L

label n, 1 (on goods), etichetta nf;
sticky label, etichetta autoadesiva.
2 (name, make), marca nf; **sold
under the Prestige label**,
venduto(-a) sotto la marca Prestige

label vb (goods), etichettare, marcare;
please label the boxes clearly, si
prega di marcare le scatole in modo
chiaro

labour n, 1 (gen), lavoro nm. 2 (pers),
mano d'opera nf; **labour force**,
mano nf d'opera; **labour market**,
mercato nm della mano d'opera

labour costs npl, 1 (acct, pers), spese
nfpl del personale. 2 (specific
projects), costo nm della mano
d'opera

lack n, mancanza nf; **lack of . . .** (e.g.
materials), mancanza di . . .

lack vb, mancare (di); **the report
lacks detail**, la relazione manca di
dettagli

laminate vb, laminare

land n, 1 (gen), terra nf. 2 (acct),
proprietà nf fondiaria

land vb, 1 (aeroplane), atterrare.
2 (naut), sbarcare. 3 (a cargo),
scaricare

landing charges npl, spese nfpl di
sbarco

language n, lingua nf; **foreign
language**, lingua straniera;
languages spoken (CV),
conoscenza nf di lingue

LAN network n (comp), rete nf
locale

laptop n (comp), computer nm
portatile

large adj, grande

last adj, ultimo(-a)

last vb, durare

late adj, 1 (for a deadline), in ritardo;
late payment (fin), pagamento nm
in ritardo; **arrive late**, arrivare in
ritardo; **be late**, essere in ritardo.
2 (towards the end of), verso la
fine di; **in late May**, verso la fine di
maggio. 3 (former), ex, precedente;
the late director, l'ex direttore.
4 (a person who is dead), defunto(-
a); **the late president**, il defunto
presidente

lately adv, ultimamente,
recentemente

latest adj (model, figures), ultimo(-a);
the very latest model,
l'ultimissimo modello nm; **the
latest results**, gli ultimi risultati
nmpl

launch n, lancio nm; **launch price**,
prezzo nm di lancio; **the product
launch will be in September**, il
lancio del prodotto avverrà in
settembre

launch vb (a product), lanciare

law n, legge nf

lawyer n, 1 (practising), avvocato nm.
2 (law expert), giurista nm

lay days npl (transp), stallie nfpl

lay off vb (pers), licenziare

layoffs npl (pers), licenziamenti nmpl

LC, L/C, letter of credit (fin),
lettera nf di credito

LCL, less than container load
(transp), carico nm incompleto del
container

lead n, **sales lead** (mktg, sales),
prospetto nm (di vendita); **lead
time** (gen), tempi nmpl di
realizzazione

lead vb (be ahead), essere il primo d la
prima

leader n, all'avanguardia, in testa, leader; **the company is a leader in the field of technology**, la società è all'avanguardia nel campo della tecnologia; **leader company**, società nf leader

leading adj, importante; **leading producer of . .**, produttore nm importante di . . .

leaflet n (mktg, sales), volantino nm

leakage 1 (gen, imp/exp), colaggio nm. 2 (from specific container), perdita nf di liquido

learn vb, imparare

lease n, contratto nm d'affitto

lease vb, 1 (to someone), affittare. 2 (lease from someone), prendere in affitto

leaseback n, cessione nf contratto d'affitto

leasing n, 'leasing' nm

leather n, pelle nf; **leather goods**, articoli nmpl di pelle

leave vb, 1 (a place), partire; **the lorry has left**, il camion è partito. 2 (leave behind), dimenticare; **the driver left the customs documents**, l'autista ha dimenticato i documenti doganali. 3 (gen), lasciare; **please leave a copy of the report at the office**, si prega di lasciare una copia del rapporto nell'ufficio

leave, be on leave vb, congedarsi

ledger n (offce), libro nm mastro

left adj (direction), sinistro(-a)

left n, sinistra nf

legal adj, legale; **legal adviser**, consigliere nm legale

leisure n (mktg, sales), ricreazione nf, passatempo nm; **leisure centre**, centro ricreativo; **leisure market** (mktg, sales), mercato nm del passatempo

lend vb, prestare

lender n, prestatore nm

length n, lunghezza nf

less adv, meno; **five is less than ten**, cinque è meno di dieci; **it is less than I thought**, è meno di quanto pensassi; **in less than no time**, in men che non si dica

lessee n, locatario nm

lessor n, locatore nm

let vb (property to someone), affittare

letter n, lettera nf; **letter of application** (pers), domanda nf d'impiego; **letter box**, cassetta nf postale; **letter of credit** (imp/exp), lettera di credito

level n, livello nm, piano nm

level out vb (gen, fin), stabilizzarsi

leverage n (fin), azione nf di leva

LGV, **large goods vehicle** = veicolo nm per trasporti ingombranti

liabilities npl, 1 (gen), obblighi nmpl. 2 (acct), passività nfpl

liability n (legal liability), responsabilità nf

liable, be liable to vb, 1 (likely to), essere soggetto(-a) a. 2 (legal implication), essere responsabile di

library n, biblioteca nf

licence n, 1 (gen), permesso nm, licenza nf. 2 (driving), patente nf

license vb (a process), autorizzare, accordare una licenza

life n, vita nf; **product life**, vita del prodotto nm; **shelf life**, durata nf; **life insurance**, assicurazione nf sulla vita

lift n, ascensore nm

lift vb (transp), sollevare

light vb, accendere, illuminare

lighten vb, 1 (take some weight off), alleggerire. 2 (give some comfort), alleviare

lighting n, illuminazione nf

limit n, limite nm

limit vb, limitare

limited company, private limited company n, società nf a responsabilità limitata

line n, linea nf; **product line**, linea dei prodotti; **production line**, linea di produzione

liquidation n, liquidazione nf; **go into liquidation**, andare in liquidazione

liquidity n, 1 (gen), liquidità nf; **liquidity problems**, problemi nmpl di liquidità. 2 (solvability), solvibilità nf

list n, lista nf; **price list**, listino nm prezzi

list vb, elencare; **the catalogue lists all the sales points**, il catalogo elenca tutti i punti di vendita

literature n, 1 (gen), letteratura nf. 2 (on a product), opuscoli nmpl pubblicitari

litigation n (law), lite nf

live adj, 1 (telec), dal vivo, in diretta. 2 (electr), sotto tensione. 3 (living), vivo(-a)

load n (on a vehicle), carico nm; **a load of . .**, un carico di . .; **please collect the load from . .**, si prega di ritirare il carico da . . .

load vb (transp, comp), caricare

loan n, prestito nm

local adj, locale; **local radio**, radio nf locale

locate vb, 1 (find), trovare. 2 (place), situare; **the machine is located in a corner**, la macchina è situata in un angolo

location n, posizione nf

lodge vb **a complaint against** . . . 1 (gen), presentare un reclamo contro . . . 2 (law), sporgere querela contro . . .

logo n, emblema nm, simbolo nm, 'logo' nm

long adj, lungo(-a); **long distance**, a lunga distanza; **long-term loan** (fin), mutuo nm a lunga scadenza

loose adj, 1 (gen), sciolto(-a); **loose goods**, merci sciolte. 2 (free), libero(-a); **a loose translation**, una traduzione libera. 3 (large), ampio(-a); **a loose shirt**, una camicia ampia

lorry n (transp), camion nm, autocarro nm; **lorry driver** (transp), autista nm di camion; **lorry load** (transp), carico nm del camion

lose vb (gen), perdere

loss n, perdita nf; **make a loss**, avere una perdita; **loss adjuster** (ins), liquidatore nm d'avaria

lost adj, perduto(-a)

lot n, **a lot of . .**, molto(-a); **a lot of experience**, molta esperienza; **a lot of people**, molta gente; **a lot of figures**, molti numeri nmpl

low adj, basso(-a); **low voice**, voce nf bassa; **low interest loan** (fin), mutuo nm a basso interesse; **low prices**, prezzi nmpl bassi

lower vb, abbassare; **lower prices**, abbassare i prezzi

LPG, liquified petroleum gas (transp), gas nm di petrolio liquefatto

LSD, loading, storage and delivery (imp/exp, transp), carico nm, immagazzinamento e consegna

Ltd, private limited company, società nf a responsabilità limitata

luggage n, bagaglio nm

lump sum n, somma nf globale pagata con un versamento unico

luxury adj, di lusso; **luxury goods**, articoli nmpl di lusso

luxury n, lusso nm

LV, luncheon voucher n, tagliando nm per ristorante

M

machine n, macchina nf; **machine tool**, macchina utensile

machinery n, 1 (several machines), macchinario nm. 2 (working parts), meccanismo nm

made adj, **made in . . .** (imp/exp), fabbricato(-a) in . .; **made of** (imp/exp), fatto(-a) di; **made to measure**, fatto(-a) su misura; **made up of . . .**, essere composto da . . .

magazine n (gen), rivista nf, periodico nm

magistrate n (law), magistrato nm

mail n, posta nf, corrispondenza nf; **mail order** (mktg, sales), ordinazione nf per corrispondenza

mail vb, mandare per posta

mailing company n, società nf di servizi postali

mailing list n, elenco nm di indirizzi

main adj, principale; **main activity**, attività nf principale

mains n (electr), conduttura nf principale; **it runs on mains electricity**, funziona sulla conduttura principale

maintain vb, 1 (keep), mantenere. 2 (affirm), affermare

maintenance n, assistenza nf; **site maintenance**, assistenza su luogo

major adj, 1 (gen), maggiore; **the major part of our production is sold abroad**, la maggior parte della nostra produzione è venduta all'estero. 2 (more important), più importante; **the major delivery will be made next month**, la consegna più importante sarà effettuata il mese prossimo; **the major manufacturer**, il fabbricante nm più importante

majority n, maggioranza nf

make n (of goods), marca nf

make vb, 1 (manufacture), fare, fabbricare. 2 (oblige), far fare; **make an application**, fare una domanda d'impiego; **make an appointment**, prendere un appuntamento; **make an offer** (fin), fare un'offerta; **make redundant** (pers), licenziare; **make up for (a loss)** compensare; **make up one's mind**, decidersi

maker n, fabbricante nm

malpractice n (law), pratica nf illecita, azione nf disonesta; **be guilty of malpractice**, essere colpevole di pratiche illecite; **be accused of malpractice**, essere accusato di azioni disoneste

manage vb, 1 (gen), dirigere, amministrare. 2 (fin), gestire. 3 **manage to do something**, riuscire a fare qualcosa

management n, 1 (managers of a company), direzione nf. 2 (the activity of managing), gestione nf; **management accounting**, contabilità nf di gestione; **management information system** (comp), sistema nm d'informatica per la gestione; **management problems**, problemi nmpl di gestione

manager/manageress n (pers), direttore nm/f

managing director n (pers), consigliere nm delegato

manifest n (transp), manifesto nm

manifest adj, manifesto(-a)

man-made adj, 1 (gen), artificiale. 2 (fabrics), sintetico(-a)

manpower n, mano nf d'opera

manual *adj*, manuale; **manual control**, controllo *nm* manuale

manual *n*, manuale *nm*; **user manual**, manuale del consumatore

manufacture *vb* (gen), fabbricare

manufacturer *n*, fabbricante *nm*

manufacturing industries *npl*, industrie *nfpl* manufatturiere

margin *n* (fin), margine *nm*; **margin ratio** (fin), tasso *nm* di margine; **profit margin**, margine di profitto

marginal *adj*, marginale; **marginal profit**, profitto *nm* marginale

marina *n*, darsena *nf*

marine *adj*, marittimo(-a), marino(-a); **marine insurance** (ins), assicurazione *nf* marittima; **marine station**, stazione *nf* marittima

mark *vb*, marcare

mark down *vb* (prices), ridurre

mark up *vb* (prices), rialzare

marker pen *n*, penna *nf* evidenziatrice

market *n* (potential customers, market place, etc) mercato *nm*; **there is a big market for . .**, c'è un enorme mercato per . .; **market analysis**, analisi *nf* di mercato; **market demand**, domanda *nf* di mercato; **market penetration**, penetrazione *nf* di mercato; **market price**, prezzo *nm* di mercato; **market research**, ricerca *nf* di mercato; **market sector** (mktg, sales), settore *nm* di mercato; **market share**, parte *nf* di mercato; **market trend**, tendenza *nf* di mercato; **market value**, valore *nm* di mercato; **be in the market for . .**, essere nel mercato per . . . .

market *vb* (a product), mettere sul mercato, lanciare un prodotto

marketing *n* (mktg, sales), marketing *nm*, ricerca *nf* di mercato; **marketing department** (pers),

servizio *nm* di marketing

mark-up *n* (increase in price), rialzo *nm*

married *adj* (CV), sposato(-a)

mass *n*, (gen), massa *nf*. **2** (religious), messa *nf*; **mass attack** attacco *nm* in massa

mass memory (comp), memoria *nf* di massa

mass production *n*, produzione *nf* in serie

match *vb*, **1** (gen), accoppiare. **2** (colours), accompagnare, andar bene; **the red and the blue match well with the other colours**, il rosso e il blu vanno bene con gli altri colori; **the dress and the shoes match well**, il vestito e le scarpe si accompagnano bene; **matching colours**, colori *nmpl* che vanno bene. **3** (offer an equal price), offrire lo stesso prezzo;

mate *n*, compagno *nm*; **mate's receipt** (imp/exp), ricevuta *nf* di bordo

material *n* (cloth), materiale *nm*; **raw materials**, materiali *nmpl* grezzi

mature *adj* (personal quality), maturo(-a)

mature *vb* (fin), maturare, scadere

maximise *vb*, massimizzare

maximum *adj*, massimo(-a)

maximum *n*, massimo *nm*

md, months after date (fin), a . . . mesi dalla data

mean *n* (maths), (average), medio(-a)

means *npl*, mezzi *nmpl*

measure *n*, misura *nf*

measure *vb*, misurare

measurement *n*, misura *nf*, dimensione *nf*; **pay by measurement** (transp), pagare per cubatura

mechanical *adj*, meccanico(-a)

mechanism *n*, meccanismo *nm*

media, the media *npl*, i media *nmpl*

medical *adj*, medico(-a); **medical board**, corpo *nm* medico; **medical officer**, ufficiale *nm* sanitario; **medical student**, studente *nm* in medicina

medicine *n*, medicina *nf*

meet *vb*, **1** (have a meeting), vedersi. **2** (at the station), andare a prendere. **3** (meet someone), incontrarsi. **4** (meet a target), far onore; **meet one's commitments**, far fronte ai propri impegni; **meet the requirements/the conditions**, soddisfare le richieste/le condizioni

memo *n*, memorandum *nm*, appunto *nm*, nota *nf*; **an internal memo**, una nota interna; **write a memo to . . . /about . .**, scrivere un appunto a . . . / su . .; **send a memo**, inviare un memorandum

memory *n* (comp), memoria *nf*

mend *vb*, riparare

menu *n* (comp), menu *nm*

merchandising *n*, commercio *nm*

merchant *adj*, mercantile; **merchant ship**, nave *nf* mercantile

merge *vb* (fin), fondere; **merge with . .**, fondere con . . .

merger *n* (gen), fusione *nf*

message *n* (offce), messaggio *nm*; **send a message**, inviare un messaggio; **receive a message**, ricevere un messaggio

meter *n*, contatore *nm*

method *n*, metodo *nm*; **methods of payment**, metodo di pagamento; **method of production**, metodo di produzione

metre *n*, metro *nm*

microphone *n* (mktg, sales), microfono *nm*

mile *n*, miglio *nm*

mileage *n*, distanza *nf* in miglia (in Italy: chilometraggio *nm*)

minicomputer *n* (comp), mini-computer *nm*

minimal *adj*, minimo; **maintenance costs are minimal**, i costi *nmpl* di manutenzione sono minimi

minimise *vb*, minimizzare

minimum *adj*, minimo(-a)

minor *adj*, minore

minority *n*, minoranza *nf*; **be in a minority**, essere in minoranza

minus *prep*, meno

minutes *npl* (of meetings), verbale *nm* di riunione

miscellaneous *adj*, miscellaneo(-a), misto(-a)

mislead *vb*, sviare, ingannare

misleading *adj*, ingannevole, menzognero(-a); **misleading advertising**, pubblicità *nf* menzognera

miss *vb*, mancare, perdere, fallire; **we miss the sun**, ci manca il sole; **miss the flight**, perdere il volo; **miss the train**, perdere il treno; **miss the target**, fallire il bersaglio

missing *adj*, che mancano; **missing articles**, articoli che mancano; **only one person is missing**, manca solo una persona; **a missing person**, un disperso *nm*

mistake *n*, errore *nm*; **make a mistake**, fare un errore

mobile phone *n* (gen), telefono *nm* portatile

model *n*, **1** (scale model), campione *nm*. **2** (version of a product), modello *nm*; **the latest model is more powerful**, l'ultimo modello è più potente

mode of transport *n* (imp/exp, transp), modo *nm* di trasporto

modification n, modifica nf; **make a modification to . .**, apportare una modifica a . . .

modify vb, modificare

modular adj, modulare

module n, modulo nm

money n, 1 (capital), capitale nm. 2 (coins, notes), denaro nm

monitor n (comp), 1 (gen), monitor nm. 2 (process control), apparecchio nm di controllo

monitor vb, controllare

month n, mese nm; **at . . . months after date** (fin), a . . . mesi dalla data

monthly adj, mensile adj; **monthly deliveries**, consegne nfpl mensili; **monthly paid** (pers), pagato mensilmente; **monthly payments** (fin), pagamenti nmpl mensili

moor vb (transp), ormeggiare

mooring n, ormeggio nm

more adj/adv, più; **please send more copies**, si prega di inviare più copie; **more attractive**, più attraente; **more economical**, più economico(-a); **more expensive**, più caro(-a)

more than . . . (gen, fin), più di; **more than 20 million**, più di venti milioni

more . . . than . ., più . . . che . .; **more milk than coffee**, più latte che caffè; **this product is more attractive than useful**, questo prodotto è più attraente che utile; **more . . . than . .**, più di quanto; **more interesting than we thought**, più interessante di quanto pensassimo; **more useful than I could possibly demonstrate**, più utile di quanto possa dimostrare

mortgage n, ipoteca nf; **mortgage loan**, mutuo nm ipotecario

mortgage vb, ipotecare

motivate vb, motivare

motivation n, motivazione nf

motor n, 1 (engine), motore nm. 2 (automobile), automobile nm; **motor insurance** (ins), assicurazione nf automobilistica; **motor show**, salone nm dell'automobile

motorist n, automobilista nm

motorway n (transp), autostrada nf; **motorway junction**, nodo nm autostradale

mouse n (comp), mouse nm

move vb (offices, house), trasferirsi

MP, Member of Parliament = Deputato nm

mpg, miles per gallon, consumo di miglia per gallone (1 gallone = litri 4,546)

Ms, no exact equivalent in Italian, use either Signora or possibly Signorina

m/s, months after sight (fin), a . . . . mesi dalla vista

MTO, multimodal transport operator (imp/exp), trasportatore nm multimodale

multiple copies npl (imp/exp), copie nfpl multiple

multiply vb (by), moltiplicare (per)

N

NA, N/A, not applicable (form filling), non pertinente

name *n*, nome *nm*; **company name**, nome della società; **trade name**, ragione *nf* sociale

name *vb*, nominare

narrow *adj*, stretto(-a)

national *adj*, nazionale; **national insurance contributions**, contributi *nmpl* assicurativi; **national reputation**, reputazione *nf* nazionale

nationalise *vb*, nazionalizzare

nationalised *adj*, nazionalizzato(-a)

nationality *n*, nazionalità *nf*

naval *adj*, navale

NCV, no commercial value (imp/exp), senza valore commerciale

near *adj*, 1 (distance) vicino(-a); **near the airport**, vicino all'aeroporto. 2 (time) prossimo(-a) *adj*; **in the near future**, in un prossimo futuro

nearly *adv*, quasi

need *n*, bisogno *nm*; **we think there is a need for . .**, pensiamo che ci sia un bisogno per . . .

need *vb*, aver bisogno; **he needs an analysis**, ha bisogno di un' analisi

needs analysis *n*, analisi *nf* dei bisogni

neglect *vb*, 1 (not look after something) trascurare. 2 (forget to do) tralasciare

negotiable *adj*, negoziabile

negotiate *vb*, negoziare, trattare

negotiation *n*, trattativa *nf*

net *adj*, netto(-a); **net contribution**, contribuzione *nf* netta; **net income**, reddito *nm* netto; **net result**, risultato *nm* netto; **net weight** (imp/exp), peso *nm* netto; **net worth**, valore *nm* netto

net *vb* (receive a net amount), ricavare un guadagno netto

network *n* (comp), rete *nf*

network *vb* (comp), mettere in rete

networked system *n* (comp), sistema *nm* di rete

networking *n* (cooperation between companies), cooperazione *nf*

new *adj*, nuovo(-a)

news *n*, 1 notizie *nfpl*. 2 (news programme–TV), telegiornale *nm*. 3 (news programme–radio), giornale radio *nm*. 3 (in newspaper), notizie d'attualità. 4 (particular event), annuncio *nm*; **the news of the merger . .**, l'annuncio della fusione . . .

newsletter *n* (mktg, sales), foglio *nm* d'informazioni

niche *n*, nicchia *nf*

nil *adj* (figures), zero *nm*

no-claims bonus *n* (ins), indennità *nf*

no commercial value *n* (imp/exp), senza valore *nm*

non-payment *n* (fin), nessun pagamento *nm*

non-returnable *adj*, 1 (disposable), da non restituire. 2 (no deposit on container), non consegnato(-a)

not applicable *adj* (forms), non pertinente

not as ordered *adj* (mktg, sales), non conforme all'ordine

note *n*, 1 (short message), nota *nf*. 2 (banknote), banconota *nf*

note *vb*, 1 (be aware of), notare. 2 (write down), prendere nota.

3 (see) osservare

noted *adj* **for** rinomato(-a) per

note-pad *n* taccuino *nm*, blocco note *nm*

notice *vb*, osservare

notification *n* **(of)**, notifica *nf*; **receive notification (of)**, ricevere la notifica (di)

notify *vb*, notificare

novel *adj*, **1** (new), nuovo(-a). **2** (unusual), insolito(-a)

novelty *n*, novità *nf*

null and void *adj*, senza valore legale

number *n*, **1** (ref no, phone), numero *nm*; **our fax number is . .**, il nostro numero di fax è . .; **the product number is . .**, il numero del prodotto è . . . **2** (figures in accounts, results) cifra *nf*. **3** (quantity), numero *nm*

number *vb*, numerare; **we have numbered the boxes 1 to 15**, abbiamo numerato le scatole da 1 a 15

number plate *n*, targa *nf*

numerical order *n*, ordine *nm* numerico; **in numerical order**, in ordine numerico

o/a, on account of (fin), per conto di . . .

object *n*, **1** (gen), oggetto *nm*. **2** (purpose), scopo *nm*; **the object of the meeting is . .**, lo scopo della riunione è . . .

object *vb* **(to)** obiettare

objection *n*, obiezione *nf*; **make an objection**, fare un'obiezione

objective *n*, obiettivo *nm*; **the sales team reached their objectives**, il reparto vendite ha raggiunto il suo obiettivo

objective *adj*, oggettivo(-a); **objective case**, caso oggettivo

obligatory *adj*, obbligatorio(-a)

oblige *vb*, obbligare

obsolete *adj*, in disuso, fuori moda

obstacle *n*, ostacolo *nm*; **an obstacle to . .**, un ostacolo a . . .

obtain *vb*, ottenere

obtained *adj*, ottenuto(-a), **qualification obtained in . .**, (CV), diploma *nm* ottenuto nel . . .

occupation *n* (pers, forms), professione *nf*

occupy *vb* (premises), occupare

OD, O/D, overdrawn *adj* (fin), scoperto(-a)

odd numbers *npl*, numeri *nmpl* dispari

offence *n* (law), infrazione *nf*; **commit an offence**, commettere un'infrazione

offer *n*, offerta *nf*; **make an offer**,

fare un'offerta; **receive an offer**, ricevere un'offerta; **refuse an offer**, rifiutare un'offerta

offer *vb*, offrire; **offer a discount of 4.000 lire**, offrire uno sconto di Lit 4.000; **offer to take back the goods**, offrire di riprendere indietro la merce

office *n*, ufficio *nm*; **office block**, immobile *nm* con uffici; **office equipment**, attrezzatura *nf* d'ufficio; **office furniture**, mobili *nmpl* d'ufficio; **office manager**, direttore *nm* di sezione

official *adj*, ufficiale

offset *vb*, (fin), controbilanciare; **offset the cost of advertising**, per controbilanciare il costo della pubblicità

OHP overhead projector *n* (mktg, sales), lavagna *nf* luminosa

oil *n* 1 (crude oil), petrolio *nm*; **oil tanker** (ship), petroliera *nf*. 2 (lubricant) olio *nm*

O-levels, Ordinary levels, *npl*, esami del quinto anno di scuola media/superiore

omission *n*, omissione *nf*

on, be on *vb* (electr), essere acceso; **the light is on**, la luce è accesa; **the computer is on**, il computer è acceso

on demand, payable on demand (fin), pagabile a vista

one-man business *n*, azienda *nf* individuale

one-way street *n*, strada *nf* a senso unico

on line *adj* (comp, network), in linea

o/o, order of (fin), all'ordine di

open *adj*, aperto(-a); **open account**, conto *nm* aperto; **open market**, mercato *nm* libero; **have an open mind**, non avere preconcetti; **open scandal**, scandalo *nm* pubblico

open *vb*, aprire; **open a**

programme (comp), aprire un programma; **open the mail** (offce), aprire la posta; **open a branch in . .**, aprire una filiale in . . .

opening *n* (of sales point, of an event), apertura *nf*; **an opening in the market**, un'apertura nel mercato

operate *vb* (a machine), operare, far funzionare; **the system is operated by hydraulic pressure**, il sistema è fatto funzionare a mezzo di pressione idraulica

operating *n*, 1 (fin, acct), esercizio *nm*; **operating budget**, bilancio *nm* d'esercizio; **operating capital**, capitale *nm* d'esercizio; **operating costs**, costi *nmpl* d'esercizio. 2 (gen/machinery) funzionamento *nm*; **operating instructions**, istruzioni *nfpl* di funzionamento; **operating system** (comp), sistema *nm* di funzionamento

operations *npl* (of a company), attività *mfpl*

operator *n* 1 (telephone), telefonista *nm*. 2 (of machines), operatore *nm*. 3 (tour operator), agente *nm*

operator's manual *n*, manuale *nm* d'istruzioni

opportunity *n*, occasione *nf*

optimise *vb*, essere ottimista

optimum *adj*, optimum *nm*

option *n*, 1 (gen), scelta *nf*. 2 (fin), opzione *nf*

optional *adj*, facoltativo(-a)

OR, owner's risk (ins), a rischio del proprietario

order *n* (imp/exp), 1 ordine *nm*; **export order**, commessa *nf*; **telephone/fax order**, ordine per telefono/per fax. 2 **in order** (in the right place), in ordine; **in alphabetical order**, in ordine alfabetico; **out of order**, guasto(-a)

order *vb* (sales), ordinare

ordinary adj, ordinario(-a)

ore n, minerale nm

organic adj, organico(-a); **organic products**, prodotti nmpl organici

organisation n, organizzazione nf; **organisation chart**, organigramma nm

organise vb, organizzare

origin n, origine nf

original adj, originale; **original equipment**, attrezzatura nf originale; **original writer**, scrittore nm originale

other adj, altro(-a)

out adv, fuori; **out of breath**, senza fiato; **out of mind**, dimenticato(-a); **out of order**, guasto(-a); **out of print**, fuori stampa; **out of stock**, esaurito(-a)

outbid vb, sorpassare; **they outbid XYZ Plc**, hanno sorpassato XYZ Plc

outburst n, esplosione nf

outcast n, esiliato nm

outcome n, risultato nm

outfit n, corredo nm

outgoings npl (fin), uscite nfpl

outlaw n, fuorilegge nm

outlay n (initial capital spent), spesa nf

outlet n (sales outlet), sbocco nm

outline vb (a plan), abbozzare, delineare

outlook n (the future), prospettiva nf; **the outlook is good**, la prospettiva è buona

outperform vb, dare dei risultati migliori (che)

output n, 1 (factory), rendimento nm. 2 (electr), potenza nf sviluppata

outsell vb, 1 (higher prices), vendere a prezzo superiore. 2 (higher quantities), vendere in quantità superiore

outsider n, estraneo nm

outside use n, per uso esterno

outstanding adj 1 (quality), notevole. 2 **outstanding items** (not delivered), articoli nmpl in sospeso; **outstanding payment** (unpaid), pagamento nm in arretrato

out tray n (offce), posta nf in partenza

over prep (above), al di sopra; **over 10%**, al di sopra del 10%; **over target**, al di sopra dell'obbiettivo

overbook vb, prendere un impegno al di sopra delle capacità

overcapacity n, capacità nf in eccesso

overcharge vb, sovraccaricare

overdraft n, scoperto nm

overdrawn adj (fin), scoperto(-a); **be overdrawn**, essere scoperto(-a) (in banca)

overdue adj, 1 (gen), in ritardo; **the order is overdue**, l'ordine è in ritardo. 2 (fin), in sofferenza; **the invoice payment is overdue**, il pagamento della fattura è in sofferenza

overheads npl, spese nfpl generali

overload vb, sovraccaricare

overlook vb, trascurare; **this account has been overlooked**, questo conto è stato trascurato

overpayment n, (fin), pagamento nm eccessivo

overprice n (mktg, sales), sovrapprezzo nm

overprice vb (mktg, sales), dare in sovrapprezzo

overtime n, straordinari nmpl; **work overtime**, fare degli straordinari

owe vb, dovere

own vb, 1 (gen), possedere. 2 (own to), confessare

own brand n (mktg, sales), marca nf

del distributore

owner *n*, proprietario *nm*; **owner's equity to debt** (acct), tasso *nm* di solvibilità; **owner's risk** (ins), a rischio del proprietario

P

pa, **per annum**, per anno

pack *n* (mktg, sales), pacco *nm*; **a 5 kg pack**, un pacco da 5 kg

pack *vb*, **1** (imp/exp), imballare. **2** (items of clothing, etc) fare i bagagli

package *n*, **1** (transp, post) pacco *nm*, pacchetto *nm*. **2** (mktg, sales), imballaggio *nm*. **3** (comp, eg bundling), involto *nm*. **4 package tour**, viaggio *nm* organizzato

packet *n* (mktg, sales), **1** (gen), pacchetto *nm*. **2** (bag containing a small, measured amount of contents), sacchetto *nm*

packing note/list *n* (imp/exp), lettera *nf* di accompagnamento

pad *n* (for writing), taccuino *nm*, blocco *nm* note

padded *adj* (imp/exp), imbottito(-a) *adj*

padding *n* (imp/exp), imbottitura *nf*

page *n* (of a book), pagina *nf*

pager *n*, ricevitore *nm* tascabile

paging *n* (telec), ricerca *nf* di persone

paid *adj* (on bills), pagato(-a); **paid in advance** (fin), pagato(-a) in anticipo; **paid on delivery**, pagato(-a) alla consegna

paid-up capital *n* (fin), capitale *nm* versato

pallet *n* (transp), pallet *nm*

P + D, **pickup and delivery** (imp/exp, transp), prelievo *nm* e consegna *nf*

paper n, 1 (newspaper), giornale nm. 2 (to write on), carta nf

paper clip n (offce), graffetta nf

paperwork n, 1 (admin), lavoro nm amministrativo. 2 (documents, forms), documenti nmpl

par n (stock market), pari nf; **above par** (stock market), sopra la pari; **at par**, alla pari; **below par** (stock market), sotto la pari

parcel n (offce, transp), pacco nm, pacchetto nm

parent company n, società nf madre

park n, 1 (gen), parco nm; **leisure park**, parco nm divertimenti. 2 (car park), parcheggio nm

park vb (vehicles), parcheggiare

part n, 1 (spare part), pezzo nm di ricambio. 2 (component), parte nf, componente nm

part adj (incomplete), parziale; **part delivery** (transp), consegna nf parziale; **part load** (transp), carico nm parziale; **part payment**, pagamento nm parziale; **part time** (pers), a tempo determinato

participate vb (**in**), partecipare (a)

particular n, particolare nm; **particular average** (ins), avaria nf particolare

partner n, socio nm

partnership n, società nf

pass vb, 1 (overtake), sorpassare. 2 (tests), passare; **pass an exam**, passare un esame

passenger n, passeggero nm

password n (comp), parola nf d'ordine

past adj, passato(-a), scorso(-a)

past n, passato nm

paste vb (comp), incollare

patent n, brevetto nm

patent vb, brevettare

patented adj, brevettato(-a)

pattern n, 1 (design, ornamentation), disegno nm, motivo nm. 2 (model), modello nm

pay n, paga nf, salario nm

pay vb (fin), 1 pagare; **pay back**, rimborsare; **pay cash**, pagare in contanti; **pay for itself** (fin), ammortizzare; **the machine will pay for itself in two years**, tra due anni la macchina sarà ammortizzata; **pay in money**, versare (denaro), fare un versamento; **pay into an account**, (fin), versare in un conto; **pay on delivery** (transp, mktg, sales), pagare alla consegna. **2 pay a visit (to . . .)**, far visita a . . .

payable adj (fin), pagabile; . . . **payable at the end of June**, . . . pagabile alla fine di giugno

payee n, beneficiario nm

payload n (transp), carico nm pagante

payment n (fin), pagamento nm; **part payment**, pagamento parziale; **payment against documents** (fin), pagamento contro documenti; **payment in instalments** (fin), pagamento a rate; **payment on delivery** (mktg, sales), pagamento alla consegna

payphone n, telefono nm pubblico

payroll n (fin), libro nm paga

PC, **personal computer**, PC nm

peak n (results), massimo nm; **exports reached peak in March**, le esportazioni hanno raggiunto il massimo in marzo

peak vb (gen, fin), raggiungere il massimo; **we believe that demand has peaked**, riteniamo che la domanda ha raggiunto il massimo

peg vb prices (mktg, sales), stabilizzare i prezzi

penalise vb, penalizzare

penalty n, 1 (gen), ammenda nf, multa nf. 2 (sports), rigore nm

pencil n, matita nf; **pencil sharpener** (offce), temperamatite nm

pending prep, 1 (during), durante; **pending this debate**, durante questo dibattito. 2 (up to), fino a; **pending your departure**, fino alla sua partenza

pending adj, in sospeso

pension n, pensione nf; **pay a pension**, pagare una pensione; **receive a pension**, ricevere una pensione

per prep, per; **per year**, per anno; **per quarter**, per trimestre

percentage n, percentuale nf; **a high percentage of . .**, un'alta percentuale di . .; **a small percentage of . .**, una piccola percentuale di . . .

performance n (of a company), risultato nm; **performance-related pay** (pers), salario in relazione al risultato

period n, periodo nm; **period of probation** (pers), periodo di prova

periodicals npl (eg magazines), periodici nmpl

peripherals npl (comp), periferici nmpl

perishable adj, deperibile

perks npl (pers), vantaggi nmpl; **receive perks**, ricevere dei vantaggi

permanent adj, permanente

permission n, permesso nm; **obtain permission**, ottenere il permesso

permit n, 1 (gen), permesso nm. 2 (authorisation), autorizzazione nf. 3 (driving permit), patente nf

permit vb, permettere

personal adj, personale; **personal assistant** (pers), assistente nm

personale; **personal computer**, PC; **personal details** (forms, curriculum vitae), informazioni nfpl personali; **personal organiser** (paper based), agenda nf a fogli mobili; **personal property** (customs), proprietà nf personale; **personal secretary** (pers), segretaria nf personale

personalise vb (mktg, sales), personalizzare

personnel n (staff), personale nm; **personnel manager** (pers), direttore nm del personale

PERT n (fin), il metodo PERT

petrol n, benzina nf

petroleum products npl, prodotti nmpl petroliferi

pharmaceutical industry n, industria nf farmaceutica

pharmaceutical products npl, prodotti nmpl farmaceutici

phase n, fase nf; **the first phase of the project**, la prima fase del progetto

phase in vb, introdurre a tappe

PhD, n, Dottorato nm; **a PhD in . .**, un dottorato in . . .

phone n, telefono nm; **phone card**, carta nf telefonica; **phone number**, numero nm telefonico

phone vb, telefonare

photocopier n, fotocopiatrice nf

photocopy n, fotocopia nf

photocopy vb, fotocopiare

pick vb, 1 (choose), scegliere. 2 (a crop), cogliere

pick up vb, 1 (a load), (transp) caricare, prelevare; **please pick up the goods from . .**, si prega di caricare la merce da . .; **pick-up and delivery** (transp), carico nm e consegna nf. 2 (improve, sales, profits, economy), riprendersi; **sales picked up in the second**

quarter, le vendite si sono riprese nel secondo trimestre

picket n, picchetto nm; **strike picket** (pers), picchetto di scioperanti

picket vb (pers), organizzare picchetti; **picket a factory**, organizzare picchetti a una fabbrica

pie chart n (fin), grafico nm a settori

piggyback vb (transp), trasportare un rimorchio per ferrovia

pile n, mucchio nm

pile up vb (transp), ammucchiare

pilfering n (imp/exp), furterello nm

place vb **an order** (mktg, sales), passare un ordine

placement n (work placement), collocamento nm

plan n, **1** (gen), piano nm, progetto nm; **a strategic plan**, un piano strategico; **a marketing plan**, un progetto di marketing, **2** (drawing), disegno nm

plan vb (gen, fin), progettare

planner n (offce), progettista nm

planning n (gen), progettazione nf

plant n, **1** (factory), fabbrica nf; **the company has a new plant in Dortmund**, la società ha una nuova fabbrica in Dortmund. **2** (production unit), stabilimento nm; **the packing plant**, lo stabilimento per l'imballaggio. **3** (number of large machines, earthmoving machines), impianto nm

plastic n (gen), plastica nf

plastic adj, plastico(-a); **plastic-covered . .**, coperto(-a) in plastica

plate vb (gen), placcare

platform n, **1** (railway), banchina nf. **2** (comp), piattaforma nf

Plc, plc, public limited company, società nf anonima

plot n, **1** (conspiracy), complotto nm.

2 (intrigue), intrigo nm. **3** (of a film, opera, etc), trama nf. **4** (piece of land), appezzamento nm; **building plot**, terreno nm da costruzione

plug in vb (comp), inserire la corrente

plummet vb (gen, fin), cadere

plunge vb (figures, rates), precipitare

PM, Prime Minister, Presidente nm del Consiglio

poach vb, **1** (gen, mktg, sales), cacciare furtivamente. **2** (recruitment), indurre qualcuno a cambiare posto di lavoro

POD, pay on delivery (transp, mktg, sales), pagamento nm alla consegna

POE, 1 port of embarkation (imp/exp), porto nm d'imbarco. **2 port of entry**, porto d'entrata

point n, punto nm; **make a point**, fare un punto; **a major point**, un punto principale; **this is an interesting point**, questo è un punto interessante; **point of sale**, punto di vendita; **decimal point**, virgola nf; **23 point zero three (23.03)**, ventitrè virgola zero tre

pointer n, **1** (sign), indicatore nm. **2** (presentations), bacchetta nf

police n (law), polizia nf

policy n, **1** (gen), linea nf di condotta, sistema nm; **our policy is well known**, la nostra linea di condotta è ben conosciuta; **the company's policy is to satisfy the customers**, il sistema della società è di soddisfare i clienti. **2** (ins), polizza nf

poll n, **1** (after the elections), votazione nf. **2** (before the elections), inchiesta nf

poll vb, **1** (after the elections), raccogliere voti. **2** (opinion), fare un'inchiesta

pollute vb, **1** (the atmosphere), inquinare. **2** (food or something else), contaminare

pollution n, 1 (of the atmosphere), inquinamento nm. 2 (of food or something else), contaminazione nf

pool n, 1 (swimming), piscina nf. 2 (shared resource), fondo nm comune

pool vb, mettere in un fondo comune; **pool equipment**, mettere l'attrezzatura in un fondo comune

poor adj, 1 (no money), povero(-a). 2 (not very good), inferiore, scadente; **poor quality** (imp/exp), qualità nf scadente; **poor results**, risultati nmpl scadenti, risultati inferiori

popular adj (goods), 1 (fashionable), in voga nf. 2 (in demand), ricercato(-a); **this type of garment is very popular**, questo tipo di indumento è molto in voga; **popular fashion**, moda in voga; **our goods are very popular**, le nostre merci sono molto ricercate

population n, popolazione nf

port n, porto nm; **port of call** (transp), scalo nm; **port of entry** (imp/exp), porto d'entrata; **port charges** (transp), tasse nfpl portuali

portable adj, portatile

portfolio n, 1 (gen), portafoglio nm. 2 (for documents, drawings) cartella nf

POS advertising n (mktg, sales), pubblicità nf sul luogo di vendita

position n, posizione nf; **the site is in an ideal position**, il luogo è in una posizione ideale

position n, **be in a position to . .**, essere in grado di . .; **we are not in a position to reduce the prices**, non siamo in grado di ridurre i prezzi

post n, 1 (letters delivered), posta nf; **post code**, codice nm postale; **post office**, ufficio nm postale. 2 (job, position) posto nm

post vb, 1 (a letter), imbucare.

2 (figures in accounts), registrare (sui libri contabili)

postage n (rate), tariffa nf postale

postal service n, servizio nm postale

poster n (mktg, sales), affisso nm

postman n (offce, gen), postino nm

postmark n, timbro nm postale

postpone vb, posporre

potential n, potenziale nm; **the product has great potential**, il prodotto ha un potenziale enorme

potential adj, potenziale; **there is a potential market of 3 million units**, c'è un mercato potenziale di 3 milioni di unità

power n (electr), energia nf, corrente nm; **power cut**, interruzione nf della corrente; **power point** (electr), presa nf di corrente

powerful adj, potente

PR, **port risks** (ins), rischi nmpl di porto

practise vb, 1 (gen), fare pratica; esercitarsi. 2 (a profession), esercitare

precedent n, precedente nm

precision n, precisione nf; **high precision**, alta precisione; **precision casting**, colata nf di precisione

prefer vb, preferire; **we would prefer to . .**, preferiremmo . .; **our customers prefer branded goods to unbranded goods**, i nostri clienti preferiscono merci di marca alle merci non di marca

preference n, preferenza nf; **there is a preference for . .**, c'è una preferenza per . . .

premises npl, 1 (building), edificio nm; **off the premises**, fuori dall'edificio. 2 (place), posto nm; **on the premises**, sul posto

premium n (ins), premio nm

prepacked *adj*, pre-imballato(-a)

prepaid *adj* (fin), pagato(-a) in anticipo

prescription *n* (med), ricetta *nf*

present *n*, regalo *nm*

present *vb*, presentare; **present a bill for acceptance** (fin), presentare una fattura all'accettazione

presentation *n*, presentazione *nf*; **make a presentation** (give a talk about a product, company), fare una presentazione

president *n* (of company), presidente *nm*

press *n* ('the press'), stampa *nf*; **an article in the press**, un articolo nella stampa; **press coverage of the exhibition**, un esteso servizio d'informazioni sulla mostra

pressure *n*, pressione *nf*; **high/low pressure**, alta/bassa pressione; **be under pressure**, essere sotto pressione

price *vb*, valutare

price *n* (eg of goods), prezzo *nm*; **price cut** (special offer), ribasso *nm*; **price/earnings ratio** (fin), rapporto prezzi/redditi; **price freeze** (fin), blocco *nm* dei prezzi; **price increase**, aumento *nm* dei prezzi; **price list**, listino *nm* prezzi; **the price is very high/low**, il prezzo è molto alto/basso

pricing policy *n*, politica *nf* dei prezzi

prime *adj*, **1** (gen) primo(-a). **2** (1st class), di prim'ordine; **prime site** (property), un luogo *nm* di prim'ordine

prime time *n* (TV, mktg, sales), ore *nfpl* di grande ascolto

print (off/out) *vb* (comp), stampare

printer *n*, **1** (comp), stampante *nf*. **2** (occupation), stampatore *nm*

printing *n* (gen), stampa *nf*

printout *n* (comp), stampato *nm*

priority *adj*, di precedenza; **priority order**, ordine *nm* di precedenza

priority *n*, precedenza *nf*; **we would be grateful if you would give priority to . .**, vi saremmo grati se voleste dare precedenza a . . .

private *adj*, privato(-a); **private limited company**, società *nf* a responsabilità limitata

privatise *vb*, privatizzare

prize *n*, premio *nm*; **prize draw**, estrazione *nf* del premio

procedure *n*, procedimento *nm*; **please follow the correct procedure for . .**, si prega di seguire il procedimento giusto per . .; **the procedure for ordering is set out at the back of the catalogue**, il procedimento per le ordinazioni è spiegato nel retro del catalogo

proceedings *npl* (law), azione *nf* legale

proceeds *npl* (acct), ricavo *nm*

process *n* (industrial, eg manufacturing), procedimento *nm*

process *vb*, **1** lavorare, trattare; **process wool**, lavorare la lana; **process minerals**, trattare i minerali. **2 process an order**, eseguire un ordine

processing *n*, lavorazione *nf*, trattamento *nm*; **waste processing**, lavorazione degli scarti; **data processing**, trattamento dei dati

procurement *n* (purchasing), acquisizione *nf*

produce *n*, prodotto *nm*; **farm produce**, prodotti agricoli; **home produce**, prodotto locale

produce *vb*, produrre

producer *n*, produttore *nm*

product *n*, prodotto *nm*; **product benefits** (mktg, sales), vantaggi *nmpl* del prodotto; **product liability** (law), responsabilità *nf* del fabbricante; **product line**, linea *nf* di prodotti

production *n* (pers), produzione *nf*; **production cost**, costo *nm* di produzione; **production line** (gen), catena *nf* di produzione; **production manager**, direttore *nm* alla produzione

productivity bonus *n* (pers), premio *nm* di produzione

professional *n*, professionista *nm*

professional *adj*, professionale; **he is a professional translator**, è un traduttore professionale; **professional experience** (CV), esperienza *nf* professionale

profile *n* (gen, pers), profilo *nm*; **high/low profile**, alto/basso profilo

profit *n*, profitto *nm*, utile *nm*; **gross/net profit**, profitto lordo/netto; **a high level of profits**, un alto livello di profitti; **profit/earnings per share** (fin), profitto/utile per azione; **a profit of 10%**, un utile del 10%; **profit margin**, margine *nm* di profitto

profitable *adj*, vantaggioso(-a)

profit-sharing *n* (pers), partecipazione *nf* agli utili

pro forma invoice *n*, fattura *nf* pro forma

programme *n*, programma *nm*

programmer *n* (comp), programmatore *nm*

progress *n*, progresso *nm*; **make progress**, fare progressi

prohibit *vb*, proibire

prohibitive *adj*, proibitivo(-a); **the cost of airfreighting goods is prohibitive**, il costo del trasporto aereo delle merci è proibitivo

project *n*, progetto *nm*; **an interesting project**, un progetto

interessante; **project manager** (pers), direttore *nm* alla progettazione

project *vb* (result, fin), proiettare

promise (to) *vb*, promettere

promote *vb*, (pers/mktg, sales), promuovere; **she has been promoted to the post of manager**, è stata promossa al posto di direttrice

promoter *n* (starts businesses), promotore *nm*

promotion *n* (mktg, sales), promozione *nf*

property *n*, proprietà *nf*; **private property**, proprietà privata

proposal *n* (meetings), proposta *nf*; **make a proposal**, fare una proposta; **we have studied your proposal and . .**, abbiamo studiato la vostra proposta e . . .

propose *vb*, proporre; **I would like to propose a solution**, vorrei proporre una soluzione

proposition *n*, proposta *nf*

prospect *vb* (mktg, sales), esplorare

prospection *n*, previsione *nf*

prove *vb*, provare

provision *n* (fin), provvedimento *nm*; **make provision for bad debts**, prendere provvedimenti per i debiti insolvibili

provisional *adj*, provvisorio(-a)

proviso *n* (law), clausola *nf* condizionale; **with the proviso that . .**, con la clausola condizionale che . . .

public *adj*, pubblico(-a); **public prosecutor** (law), pubblico ministero, pubblico accusatore; **public relations** (mktg, sales), relazioni *nfpl* pubbliche; **public transport**, trasporto *nm* pubblico; **public works**, lavori *nmpl* pubblici

publishing house *n*, casa *nf* editrice

pump *n*, pompa *nf*

pump *vb* (transp), pompare

purchase *vb*, acquistare

purchase price *n* (fin), prezzo *nm* d'acquisto

purchaser *n*, acquirente *nm*, compratore *nm*

purpose *n*, scopo *nm*; **the purpose of the visit will be to . .**, lo scopo della visita sarà di . . .

put *vb* (gen), mettere

put off *vb* (eg a meeting), rinviare; **the meeting has been put off until 5 September at 2 pm**, la riunione è stata rinviata fino al 5 settembre, alle due del pomeriggio

put up *vb*, **1 put up a stand** (mktg, sales), montare uno stand. **2 put up prices**, alzare i prezzi

qualifications *npl* (CV), **1** (academic qualifications), titoli *nm* di studio. **2** (other qualifications), qualifica *nf*

qualified acceptance *n*, accettazione *nf* con riserva

qualify *vb*, **1** (get a diploma), diplomarsi. **2** (specialise in something), specializzarsi. **3 qualify for (a grant)**, possedere i requisiti per (una borsa)

quality *n*, qualità *nf*; **best quality**, la migliore qualità; **a high quality product**, un prodotto di alta qualità; **of poor quality**, di qualità scandente; **quality control** (gen), controllo qualità

quantity *n*, quantità *nf*; **a small/large quantity**, una piccola/grande quantità

quarter *n*, **1** (maths) quarto *nm*. **2** (fin), trimestre *nm*. **3** (part of a town), quartiere *nm*; **the business quarter**, il quartiere degli affari

quarterly *adj*, trimestrale

quay *n* (transp), banchina *nf*

query *n*, quesito *nm*; **have a query about . .**, avere un quesito su . . .

query *vb* (an order, a figure), porre dei quesiti

questionnaire *n* (mktg, sales), questionario *nm*; **fill in a questionnaire**, riempire il questionario

quick *adj*, veloce; **a quick reply**, una risposta veloce

quickly *adv*, velocemente

quota *n* (imp/exp), contingente *nf*;

impose a quota, imporre una contingente

quotation *n*, **quote** *n* (quoted price for a contract), quotazione *nf*; **send a quote**, inviare una quotazione

quote *vb*, **quote a price**, quotare un prezzo; **I** (prices, figures, etc), quotare; **quoted on the stock exchange**, quotato in borsa. **2** (names), citare; **quote a famous writer**, citare uno scrittore famoso

R

R and D, Research and Development, ricerca *nf* e sviluppo *nm*

radio *n*, radio *nf*; **on the radio**, alla radio; **radio pager**, ricevitore *nm* tascabile

radio *vb*, **I** (send a message), diramare per radio. **2** (to contact), contattare per radio

rail *n*, ferrovia *nf*; **by rail** (transp), per ferrovia; **rail freight**, nolo *nm* ferroviario; **rail transport**, trasporto *nm* ferroviario

railway *n* (transp), ferrovia *nf*; **railway station**, stazione *nf* ferroviaria

raise *vb*, **I** (gen), alzare; **raise prices**, alzare i prezzi. **2** (money), procurarsi; **raise a loan**, procurarsi un prestito

RAM *n* (comp), RAM

range *n*, **I** (of goods), gamma *nf*. **2** (of a vehicle or machine), raggio *nm*

rapid *adj*, rapido(-a); **rapid delivery** (transp), consegna *nf* rapida

rate *n*, tasso *nm*; **daily rate**, tasso giornaliero; **rate of interest** (fin), tasso d'interesse

rate, at the rate of . ., **I** (percentage), al tasso. **2** (regular amount/time), a un ritmo di . . .. **3** (speed), velocità *nf*

ratings *npl* (TV, radio), indice *nm* d'ascolto

ratio *n* (maths), rapporto *nm*

ration *n*, razione *nf*

ration vb, razionare

rationalisation n (pers),
razionalizzazione nf

rationalise vb, razionalizzare

raw adj, **1** (not cooked), crudo(-a);
raw meat, carne cruda.
2 (natural), greggio(-a); **raw
materials**, materie nfpl prime

reach vb (level), raggiungere; **reach
an agreement**, raggiungere un
accordo; **reach break even** (fin),
raggiungere un pareggio di conti

read vb, leggere

reader n, lettore nm

readership n (number of readers),
numero nm di lettori

ready adj, pronto(-a); **the order is
now ready**, l'ordine adesso è
pronto; **ready for use**, pronto per
l'uso

reassess vb, rivalutare

reassessment n, rivalutazione nf;
make a reassessment of . ., fare
una rivalutazione di . . .

rebate n (mktg, sales), **1** (money
back), rimborso nm. **2** (discount),
riduzione nf; **give a rebate**,
concedere una riduzione

receipt n, **1** (document), ricevuta nf;
make out a receipt, emettere
una ricevuta. **2** (delivery of the
goods), ricevimento nm; **payment
on receipt of goods**, pagamento
nm al ricevimento merci

receipted invoice n, fattura nf
quietanzata

receive vb, ricevere

receiver n (law, fin), curatore nm
fallimentare

reception n, **1** (reception desk),
ricezione nf; **reception area**,
(small area), zona di ricezione; (big
area), sala di ricezione. **2** (for
drinks, snacks), ricevimento nm;
hold a reception, dare un
ricevimento

receptionist n, impiegato(-a) nm/f

recession n, recessione nf

recharge vb (batteries), ricaricare

reciprocal adj (gen), reciproco(-a);
reciprocal agreement, accordo
nm reciproco

recognise vb, riconoscere

recognition n, riconoscimento nm

recommend vb, raccomandare

recommended price n (fin), prezzo
nm raccomandato

record adj (best), primato nm, record
nm; **declare record results**,
dichiarare risultati di primato;
record exports, esportazioni nfpl
di primato; **record sales**, vendite
nfpl record; **a record number of
sales**, un numero record di vendite

record n (offce), **1** (written record),
registrazione nf. **2** (track), traccia nf;
**we have no record of your
letter**, non abbiamo nessuna
traccia della vostra lettera.
3 records (offce), archivi nmpl

record vb, **1** (electronically),
registrare; **record a message**,
registrare un messaggio. **2** (write
down, make a note of . . .),
prendere nota di . . .

recorded message n, messaggio nm
registrato

recruit vb, **1** (soldiers), reclutare.
2 (pers), assumere del personale

recruitment n, **1** (soldiers),
reclutamento nm. **2** (pers),
assunzione nf di personale;
recruitment agency, agenzia per
la ricerca e assunzione di personale

recycle vb (gen), riciclare

recycling n (gen), riciclo nm;
recycling plant, impianto nm di
riciclo

red adj, rosso(-a); **be in the red** (fin),
avere il conto scoperto
(colloquially: essere in rosso)

reduce vb, ridurre; **we have reduced our prices by 10%,** abbiamo ridotto i nostri prezzi del 10%; **we have reduced costs by using . .,** abbiamo ridotto i costi con l'uso di . .; **the rate has been reduced by 4%,** il tasso è stato ridotto del 4%

reduction n, riduzione nf; **price reduction,** riduzione di prezzo; **a reduction in the price of . .,** una riduzione nel prezzo di . . .

redundancy n (pers), licenziamento nm

redundant adj (pers), licenziato(-a); **make redundant,** licenziare

refer to vb, riferirsi . . . a

references npl, referenze nfpl

refine vb, raffinare

refrigerate vb, refrigerare; **refrigerated container** (imp/exp), contenitore nm refrigerato; **refrigerated lorry** (transp), camion nm frigorifero

refuel vb (ship, a plane), rifornire di carburante

refund vb, rimborsare

refuse vb, rifiutare

region n, regione nf

regional adj, regionale; **regional manager,** direttore nm regionale

register n, registro nm

register vb, 1 (gen), registrare; **register a company,** registrare una società. 2 (education), iscriversi, **register for a language course,** iscriversi ad un corso di lingue

registered capital n (fin), capitale nm sociale

registered office n (fin), sede nf sociale

registration form n (at exhibitions), modulo nm d'iscrizione

registration number n, 1 (gen),

numero nm di registrazione. 2 (cars), numero d'immatricolazione

regret vb, rimpiangere

regulation n, regolamento nm

reimburse vb, rimborsare

reinforce vb, rinforzare; **reinforced with . .,** (imp/exp), rinforzato(-a) con . . .

reject n (goods), scarto nm

reject vb, rifiutare

related charges npl (fin), spese nfpl connesse

relationship n, relazione nf, rapporto nm

release vb **(the goods)** (imp/exp), rilasciare (le merci)

relevant adj (eg details, facts), pertinente

reliability n (of product), affidamento nm

reliable adj, fidato(-a)

relocate vb (move premises), trasferirsi; **the company is relocating to . .,** la società si trasferisce a . . .

rely on . . . vb, fare affidamento su . . .

remind vb, rammentare; **I must remind him that . .,** devo rammentargli di . . .

reminder n, promemoria nm

reminder letter n, lettera nf di sollecito

remit vb (send money), rimettere, effettuare il pagamento

remittance n (fin), rimessa nf

remote control n, telecomando nm

renew vb, rinnovare

rent n, affitto nm

rent vb, affittare; **rent a stand** (mktg, sales), affittare uno stand; **rent offices in . .,** affittare uffici in . . .

rental n, pagamento nm affitto

reorganisation n, riorganizzazione nf

reorganise vb, riorganizzare

repair n, 1 (place of repair), riparo nm. 2 (make good), riparazione nf

repair vb (make good), riparare

replace vb (gen, ins), sostituire

reply n, risposta nf; **receive a reply**, ricevere una risposta; **reply coupon** (mktg, sales), cedola nf di risposta

reply vb **(to)**, rispondere(-a); **reply to a job advertisement**, rispondere ad un annuncio d'impiego

report n (on, about), rapporto nm (su); **write a report**, scrivere un rapporto

report on vb (gen), fare un rapporto su . . .

report to vb (inform someone of an event), riferire, informare di . . .

reputable adj, rispettabile

reputation n, reputazione nf; **have a good reputation**, avere una buona reputazione

reschedule vb, 1 (fin, repayments), riprogrammare. 2 (eg to modify a plan), modificare

research n, ricerca nf; **market research**, ricerca di mercato; **research and development**, ricerca e sviluppo nm

research vb, fare ricerche

reservation n, (in hotels, on trains, etc) prenotazione nf; **have a reservation**, avere una prenotazione; **make a reservation**, fare una prenotazione; **cancel a reservation**, annullare una prenotazione

reserve vb, prenotare; **reserve a seat**, prenotare un posto; **reserve a room for one night**, prenotare una camera per una notte

resign vb (a post), dimettersi, dare le dimissioni

resignation n, dimissioni nfpl

responsible adj, **be responsible for . . .** (pers), essere responsabile per . . .

restock vb, riapprovvigionare

restructure vb, ristrutturare

restructuring n (pers), ristrutturazione nf

results npl (fin), risultati nmpl

retail n (sales), (vendita) al dettaglio; **retail price** (fin), prezzo nm al dettaglio; **retail trade**, commercio nm al dettaglio

retail vb, vendere al dettaglio; **the product retails at a recommended price of . .**, il prodotto è venduto al dettaglio a un prezzo raccomandato di . . .

retailer n, dettagliante nm

retire vb (pers), andare in pensione; **retire from business**, ritirarsi dagli affari

retirement n, pensionamento nm; **early retirement**, pre-pensionamento nm

retraining n, riaddestramento nm

return vb, 1 (gen), ritornare; **he will return to Pavia shortly**, ritornerà a Pavia tra breve. 2 (goods), ritornare, restituire

return n (fin), ritorno nm; **return on investment** (fin), ritorno sull'investimento; **return ticket**, biglietto nm di andata e ritorno

revenue n (fin), entrata nf

reverse vb, 1 (gen), invertire; **the trend has reversed**, la tendenza si è invertita. 2 (car), innestare la retromarcia

reverse-charges call n, chiamata nf a carico del destinatario

revise vb, rivedere; **revise terms of payment**, rivedere i termini di pagamento

revision n, revisione nf

revival n (fin, trends), ripresa nf; **a revival in sales**, una ripresa nelle vendite

revolving credit n (fin), credito nm permanente

revolving letter of credit n (imp/exp), lettera nf di credito rinnovabile

rider n (law), clausola nf addizionale

right n, diritto nm; **have the right to say . .**, avere il diritto di dire . . .

right adj, **1** (direction), destro(-a). **2** (correct), giusto(-a)

rights issue n (fin), emissione nf di diritti di sottoscrizione

ring vb, **1** (phone), telefonare. **2** (to make a ring round), circondare

ring binder n (offce), classificatore nm ad anelli

rise n, (fin, sales) aumento nm; **a steep rise**, un aumento esorbitante; **a rise in prices**, un aumento nei prezzi

rise vb (fin, sales), aumentare

risk n (ins), rischio nm; **all risks**, tutti i rischi; **take out an all risks policy**, prendere una polizza casko

risk vb, rischiare

rival n, concorrente nm; **the main rival is . .**, il concorrente principale è . . .

road n (transp), strada nf; **road haulage** (transp), trasporto nm stradale

rob vb (law), **1** (rob someone), derubare, rubare. **2** (bank or a shop), svaligiare

robot n, robot nm; **robot assembly**, montaggio nm a mezzo di robot

roll vb (gen), rotolare

rolled steel n, acciaio nm laminato

ROM n (comp), ROM

roro, roll-on, roll-off (imp/exp, transp), carico-scarico

rough adj (finish on goods), ruvido(-a)

roughly adv (approximation), approssimativamente

round adj (shape), rotondo(-a), circolare

roundabout n (traffic), rotonda nf

route n, itinerario nm

row n, fila nf; **a row of . .**, una fila di . .; **in a row**, in fila

rubber n, **1** (board rubber), cassino nm. **2** (offce), gomma nf

rule n, regola nf

run vb, **1** (a department, a company), dirigere. **2 run out of fuel** (vehicle), essere senza benzina

running expenses npl (fin), spese nfpl d'esercizio

rush hour n, ora nf di punta

rust n, ruggine nf; **there were patches of rust on the surface of the product**, c'erano delle macchie di ruggine sulla superficie del prodotto

rust vb, arrugginire

S

sack n (container, imp/exp), sacco nm

sack vb (pers), licenziare, congedare

SAE, stamped addressed envelope, busta nf affrancata con indirizzo

safe adj, sicuro(-a); **safe investment**, investimento nm sicuro

safe n (offce, banks), cassaforte nf

safeguard vb, salvaguardare

safety n, sicurezza nf; **safety standards**, norme nfpl di sicurezza

sag vb, 1 (results, trends), cedere. 2 (shelves, materials), curvarsi

sail vb, 1 (leave port), salpare. 2 (hobby, sailing), fare la vela

salaried adj, stipendiato(-a)

salary n, stipendio nm

salary vb, stipendiare

sale n, 1 (gen), vendita nf; **on sale**, in vendita; **sale by tender**, vendita per appalto; **sales chart**, diagramma nf vendite; **sales department**, sezione nf vendite; **sales engineer**, tecnico nm alle vendite; **sales figure**, cifra nf delle vendite; **sales forecast**, previsioni nfpl vendite; **sales point**, punto nm vendite. 2 (eg Autumn sale), svendita nf, saldo nm

sample n (mktg, sales), campione nm; **free sample**, campione gratuito; **not up to sample**, non conforme al campione

sample vb (mktg, sales). 1 (opinion), **sample opinion**, fare un sondaggio. 2 (try a food product), provare

sampling n (mktg, sales), campionatura nf

satellite TV n (mktg, sales), TV nf a mezzo satellite

satisfied adj, soddisfatto(-a); **according to our research customers are very satisfied with the new service**, secondo le nostre ricerche la clientela è molto soddisfatta del nuovo servizio

satisfy vb, soddisfare; **satisfy conditions**, soddisfare le condizioni

saturated adj, saturato(-a)

saturation n, saturazione nf

save vb, 1 (comp, data), tenere in memoria. 2 (reduce expenditure, use less of something), economizzare; **save electricity**, economizzare sull'elettricità. 3 (money) (obtain something for less than expected price, put money into a savings account, etc), risparmiare; **save 3.000.000 lire on the cost of materials**, risparmiare 3 milioni di lire sul costo dei materiali

scale n (set charges, rates), scala nf; **scale of charges**, tariffa nf scalare; **on a sliding scale**, sulla scala mobile

scanner n (gen, comp), analizzatore nm

scarce adj, raro(-a)

schedule n (gen), programma nm

schedule vb (gen), (plan a series of events) programmare; **the next meeting is scheduled for . .**, la prossima riunione è programmata per . . .

scheduled flight n, volo nm regolare

scheme n, schema nm

scissors npl, forbici nfpl

scrap n, 1 (little piece), pezzetto nm. 2 (rubbish), scarto nm, rottame nm; **scrap iron**, rottame di ferro

scrap vb (a plan, a product), scartare

screen n (gen, comp), schermo nm

screw vb (gen), avvitare

sea n, mare nm; **by sea**, per via marittima

seal n (imp/exp, law), sigillo nm

seal vb, 1 (imp/exp), sigillare; **seal the case**, sigillare la cassa. 2 (law), apporre il sigillo; **seal the document**, apporre il sigillo al documento

sealed adj (imp/exp), sigillato(-a)

season n, stagione nf; **the quiet season**, la stagione morta; **the busy season**, la stagione piena

seasonal adj, stagionale; **seasonal employment**, impiego nm stagionale

second adj, secondo(-a); **the second point is . .**, il secondo punto è . . .

second vb, 1 (give support), appoggiare. 2 (favour and share ideas/opinions), assecondare; **second a motion** (meetings), appoggiare una mozione; **second an idea**, assecondare un'idea; **second a proposal**, appoggiare una proposta

secondly adv, in secondo luogo

secret adj, segreto(-a)

secret n, segreto nm

secretary n, segretario(-a) nm/f

sectorial adj (economics), settoriale

secure vb **an order**, ottenere un ordine

security n, 1 (gen), sicurezza nf. 2 (stock market), titolo nm. 3 (fin, for a loan), garanzia nf, cauzione nf

see vb, vedere; **see to something**, occuparsi di qualcosa

segment n (mktg, sales), segmento nm; **market segment**, segmento di mercato

segmentation n (mktg, sales), segmentazione nf

seize vb, afferrare; **seize an opportunity**, afferrare una opportunità

select vb, selezionare

selection n, selezione nf; **make a selection**, fare una selezione; **selection procedure** (pers, recruitment), procedimento nm di selezione

self-financing n, auto-finanziamento nm

self-service n, auto-servizio nm, 'self service' nm

sell vb, vendere; **sell off** (surplus stock), liquidare

seller n, venditore nm

Sellotape n (offce), scotch nm

semi-detached house n, casa nf bi-familiare

send vb (gen), inviare; **send back** (post), rinviare; **send off** (a letter, a parcel), inviare

sender n, mittente nm

senior executive n, capo nm funzionario

senior partner n, socio nm dirigente

sensitive adj, sensibile; **be sensitive to . .**, essere sensibile a . . .

sensitivity n, sensibilità nf

sentence n (law), sentenza nf

separate vb (copies), separare

serial number n, numero nm di serie

series n, serie nf

service n, servizio nm; **after-sales service**, servizio dopo vendita; **fast service**, servizio veloce; **maintenance service**, servizio di manutenzione; **secretarial service**, servizi di segreteria; **translation service**, servizi di traduzione; **service contract** (mktg, sales), contratto nm d'assistenza

service vb (a machine), **1** (check), controllare. **2** (keep in good order), mantenere in buone condizioni

servicing n, manutenzione nf; **regular servicing is essential**, una manutenzione regolare è essenziale

set n, serie nf; **a complete set of documents**, una serie completa di documenti

setback n, **1** (not a success), insuccesso nm. **2** (fin), (reverse), rovescio nm; **have a financial setback**, avere un rovescio finanziario

settle vb **a bill** (fin), saldare una fattura

settle vb **a dispute**, sistemare una disputa

settlement n (fin), saldo nm

several adj, parecchi(e) mfpl; **several documents**, parecchi documenti; **several machines**, parecchie machine

shade n, **1** (gen), ombra nf; **a shade of doubt**, un'ombra di dubbio. **2** (colour), sfumatura nf; **I prefer this shade of blue**, preferisco la sfumatura di questo blu

share n **1** (gen, share of), parte nf; **have a share of the market** (mktg, sales), avere una parte del mercato. **2** (shareholding), azione nf; **share certificate** (fin), titolo nm azionario

share vb (fin) spartire; **share the cost of repair**, spartire il costo della riparazione

shareholder n, azionista nm

sharp rise n, aumento nm netto

shed vb **a load** (transp), scaricare un carico

shelf n, ripiano nm

shell n (frame), ossatura nf; **the shell of the building**, l'ossatura dell'edificio

shelve vb **a project**, differire un progetto

shelving n, **1** (gen), scaffalatura nf. **2** (postponement), differimento nm

shift n, **1** (gen), cambiamento nm. **2** (at work), turno nm; **the night shift**, il turno di notte; **shift manager**, direttore nm di squadra

shift vb, **1** (change) cambiare; **he shifted place**, ha cambiato posto. **2** (transfer), transferire; **the load has been shifted**, il carico è stato trasferito

ship n (transp), nave nf; **ship's papers**, documenti nmpl di bordo

ship vb, **1** (send off goods), spedire. **2** (load goods), caricare

shipbuilding n, costruzione nf navale

shipment n, spedizione nf

shipped bill of lading n (imp/exp), polizza nf di carico a bordo

shipper n (transp), **1** (loader), caricatore nm. **2** (sender), spedizioniere nm marittimo

shipping agent n (transp), agente nm marittimo

shipping documents npl (imp/exp, transp), documenti nmpl d'imbarco

shipping instructions npl (transp), istruzioni nfpl d'imbarco

shipping note n (imp/exp), nota nf d'imbarco; ricevuta nf di spedizione

shock-absorbent material adj, materiale per ammortizzatori

shock-absorber n, ammortizzatore nm

shock-proof adj, a prova di shock

shop n, negozio nm

shopping centre n (mktg, sales), centro nm commerciale

shop-soiled adj, deteriorato

short adj, **1** (not long), corto(-a); **short dress**, abito corto. **2** (brief), breve; **short-term contract**

(pers), contratto a breve durata. **3** (insufficient), insufficiente; **short delivery**, consegna insufficiente; **short shipment** (imp/exp), spedizione *nf* insufficiente. **4** (not enough), a corto; **be short of . .**, essere a corto di . . .

shortage *n*, mancanza *nf*; **a shortage of . .**, una mancanza di . . .

shorthand *n*, stenografia *nf*; **shorthand notes**, note *nfpl* in stenografia; **shorthand typist** (offce), stenodattilografa *nf*; **shorthand and typewriting** (pers), stenografia *nf* e dattilografia *nf*

show *n*, esibizione *nf*, mostra *nf*, 'show' *nm*; **fashion show**, sfilata *nf* di moda

show *vb* (demonstrate, let see), mostrare; **the figures show that the recession has affected sales**, le cifre mostrano che la recessione ha avuto un effetto sulle vendite; **our agent will be happy to show you the new model**, il nostro agente sarà lieto di mostrarvi il nuovo modello

shrink *vb* (fin) contrarre; **a shrinking market**, un mercato contratto

shut *adj*, chiuso(-a)

shut *vb*, chiudere

shut down *vb* **1** (a company), sospendere l'attività. **2** (car), fermare il motore

shuttle *n*, **1** (gen), navetta *nf*, spola *nf*. **2** (eng), **shuttle mechanism**, meccanismo *nm* alternativo

sick *adj*, malato(-a)

side effect *n*, effetto *nm* secondario

sight *n*, vista *nf*; **payable at sight** (fin), pagabile a vista; **sight draft** (fin), tratta *nf* a vista

sign *n*, **1** (gen), segno *nm*. **2** (in shops, buildings, etc) insegna *nf*; **neon sign**, insegna al neon

sign *vb* (a document), firmare

signature *n*, firma *nf*; **authorised signature**, firma autorizzata

signed copy *n* (documents), copia *nf* firmata; **please return the signed copies**, si prega di ritornare le copie firmate

significant *adj*, significativo(-a); **significant increase**, aumento *nm* significativo; **significant fact**, fatto *nm* significativo

single fare *n*, biglietto *nm* d'andata

single room *n*, camera *nf* singola

sit-down strike *n* (pers), sciopero *nm* bianco

site *n*, luogo *nm*

site *vb*, situare

situation *n*, **1** (gen), situazione *nf*; **the economic situation**, la situazione economica. **2** (work), impiego *nm*; **get a good situation**, ottenere un buon impiego

size *n*, **1** (measurements), dimensioni *nfpl*; **what is the size of the load?**, quali sono le dimensioni del carico? **2** (clothes) taglia *nf*. **3** (shoes), numero *nm*

skilled labour *n*, mano *nf* d'opera specializzata

skills *npl*, competenze *nfpl*

slack *adj*, calmo(-a); **the market is very slack at present**, attualmente il mercato è molto calmo

slacken *vb* (rates, trends), diminuire

slash *vb* **prices**, ridurre i prezzi in modo drastico

sleeper *n* (train), vagone *nm* letto

sleeping partner *n* (fin), socio *nm* accomandante

slide *n* (mktg, sales), (presentations), diapositiva *nf*; **slide projector** (mktg, sales), proiettore *nm* per diapositive

slide *vb*, scivolare

sliding adj (rates), mobile; nf **sliding scale**, scala mobile

slight adj (small), leggero(-a); **a slight fall in profits**, una leggera diminuzione di profitti

slightly adv (gen, fin), leggermente; **slightly higher/lower results than last year**, risultati leggermente più alti/più bassi dell'anno scorso

sling n (transp), braca nf

slip vb, scivolare; **slip down**, cadere

slippage n, slittamento nm

slip road n (gen), strada nf d'accesso

slogan n (mktg, sales), 'slogan' nm, motto nm pubblicitario

slot n, 1 (mktg, sales, TV), spazio nm; **advertising slot**, spazio pubblicitario

slot machine n 1 (for amusement), 'slot machine' nf. 2 (for hot drinks), distributore nm automatico

slow adj, lento(-a)

slow down vb, rallentare

slowdown n, rallentamento nm

sluggish adj (sales), lento(-a)

slump n (fin), ristagno nm

slump vb (mktg, sales, rates, sales), crollare; **profits have slumped**, i profitti sono crollati

small adj (physical size), piccolo(-a); **a small quantity of . .**, una piccola quantità di . .; **small ads** (mktg, sales), piccoli annunci nmpl

smart money n, risarcimento nm

smart set n, il bel mondo nm

SME, Small or Medium-Sized Enterprise, Piccola o Media Impresa nf

smuggle vb, contrabbandare

S/N, SN, shipping note (imp/exp), nota nf d'imbarco, ricevuta nf di spedizione

snowball vb, lanciare palle di neve

soar vb (sales, rates), aumentare incessantemente

soaring (fin), che aumenta incessantemente; **soaring costs**, costi che aumentano incessantemente

social adj, sociale

soft drinks npl, bibite nfpl analcoliche; **carbonated (fizzy) soft drinks**, bibite analcoliche frizzanti

soft furnishings npl (mktg, sales), tessuti nmpl per arredamento

software n (mktg, sales), 'software' nm

soiled adj (goods), 1 (dirty), sporco (-a). 2 (stained), macchiato(-a)

sole agent n (mktg, sales), agente nm esclusivo

sole distributor n (mktg, sales), distributore nm esclusivo

solicitor n (law), avvocato nm

solve vb **a problem**, risolvere un problema

sort vb (comp), selezionare

sound n, suono nm

soundproof adj, antiacustico(-a)

source n, origine nf; **deduction at source** (fin), trattenute nfpl all'origine

space n, 1 (gen), spazio nm. 2 (space occupied by something), posto nm, spazio nm

space out vb, spaziare

spare parts npl (gen), parti nfpl di ricambio

speak vb, parlare; **speak out**, parlare ad alta voce/parlare francamente; **speak (about)**, parlare (di) **(speak) to**, parlare (a)

special adj, speciale; **special offer** (mktg, sales), offerta nf speciale; **special terms** (for the customer), condizioni nfpl speciali

specialise *vb* **(in)**, specializzare, specializzarsi

speciality *n*, specialità

specifications *npl*, **1** (gen), specificazione *nf*; **technical specifications**, specificazioni tecniche. **2** (law), **specification of charge**, capo *nm* d'accusa

specify *vb*, specificare

spectacular *adj*, spettacolare, grandioso(-a)

speculate *vb*, speculare

speed *n*, velocità *nf*

speed *vb*, andare in fretta

speed up *vb*, accellerare

spell out *vb* **(a word)**, compitare, scandire

spend *vb*, **1** (money), spendere. **2** (time), passare, trascorrere

spill *vb* (gen), rovesciare; **our lorry has spilled its load**, il nostro camion ha rovesciato il carico

spin-off *n*, derivato *nm*

split *vb* **(into)**, dividere (in)

spoil *vb* (affect quality), rovinare; **the goods have been spoiled by the damp**, le merci sono state rovinate dall'umido

spokesman *n*, portavoce *nm/f*

sponsor *n* (mktg, sales), patrocinatore *nm*

sponsor *vb* (mktg, sales) patrocinare

sponsoring *n* (mktg, sales), patrocinato *nm*

sport *n* (gen), sport *nm*

sports centre *n* (mktg, sales), centro *nm* sportivo

sports equipment *n*, equipaggiamento *nm* sportivo

spot *n* (mktg, sales), posto *nm*; **on the spot**, sul posto

spray *vb*, spruzzare

spread *vb*, **1** (over), spalmare. **2** (of news), diffondere

spreadsheet *n*, 'spreadsheet' *nm*

square *adj*, quadrato(-a); **the room is square**, la stanza è quadrata; **the rate is 1500 lire per square metre**, la tariffa è 1500 lire per metro quadro

squeeze *vb*, spremere

stabilise *vb*, stabilizzare

stable *adj*, stabile

stack *n* (transp), mucchio *nm*

stack *vb* (transp), ammucchiare

stacked *adj* (transp), ammucchiato(-a)

staff *n* (pers), personale *nm*

stage *n* (of a project), stadio *nm*; **stage report**, rapporto *nm* a tappe

stagnate *vb*, ristagnare, essere inattivo(-a)

stake *n*, partecipazione *nf*; **have a stake in the company**, avere una partecipazione nella società; **at stake**, in giuoco

stamp *n*, francobollo *nm*

stamp *vb*, affrancare

stamped addressed envelope *n*, busta *nf* affrancata e indirizzata

stand *n* (mktg, sales), stand *nm*; **stand manager** (mktg, sales), responsabile *nm* dello stand

stand *vb* (withstand, resist), sopportare; **the case can stand temperatures of up to 100°C**, la cassa può sopportare temperature fino a 100 gradi C

staple *n* (offce), graffetta *nf*

staple *vb* (offce), aggraffare

stapler *n* (offce), graffettatrice *nf*

start *n*, inizio *nm*

start *vb*, iniziare; **start a campaign**, iniziare una campagna; **start a company**, creare una società

start-up costs npl (fin), spese nfpl d'impianto

state adj, statale; **state aid**, aiuto nm statale; **state-controlled**, controllato(-a) dallo stato

state vb, dichiarare; **the report states that . .**, il rapporto dichiara che . . .

State n, Stato nm **The State**, lo Stato

statement n (declaration), dichiarazione nf; **bank statement**, estratto conto nm della banca; **statement in court** (law), dichiarazione in corte; **statement of account** (fin), estratto conto

station n, stazione nf; **station concourse**, atrio nm della stazione

stationary adj, stazionario(-a)

stationery n, cartoleria nf

statistics npl, 1 (gen), statistiche nfpl. 2 (science), statistica nf

status n, 1 (gen), condizione nf sociale. 2 **financial status**, situazione nf finanziaria

statutory adj, statutario(-a)

stay n (period of residence), soggiorno nm

stay vb (spend some time in a place), fermarsi, soggiornare

STD code n, codice nm telefonico

steady adj, 1 (regular), regolare. 2 (stable), stabile

steal vb (gen), (theft), rubare

steam n, vapore nm

steamship n (imp/exp, transp), nave nf a vapore

steel n, acciaio nm; **stainless steel**, acciaio inossidabile; **steel industry**, industria nf dell'acciaio

steep adj, 1 (fin), esorbitante, forte; **a steep rise in prices**, un aumento esorbitante dei prezzi. 2 (slope), ripido(-a), scosceso(-a)

step up vb, 1 (speed up), accelerare. 2 (a campaign), intensificare

sterling n (currency), lira nf sterlina

stick (on) vb, incollare

sticky label n (offce), etichetta nf autoadesiva

stipulate vb, stipulare

stock n, 1 (goods), 'stock' nm, magazzino nm; **in stock** (fin), in stock, in magazzino; **take stock**, fare l'inventario; **stock turnover** (fin), rotazione nf dello stock; **be out of stock**, essere sprovvisto(-a). 2 (stock market), azioni nfpl; **stock market** (fin), borsa nf; **stock option** (fin), opzione nf d'acquisto azionario

stock vb, tenere a magazzino; **we no longer stock . .**, non teniamo più a magazzino . .; **we stock all items in the catalogue**, teniamo a magazzino tutti gli articoli del catalogo

stockbroker n (fin), agente nm di cambio

stockist n (mktg, sales), grossista nm

stockpile, n, riserva nf di materiali

stocktaking n, inventario nm

stolen adj (transp), rubato(-a)

stop vb, 1 (stop doing something), fermare vb. 2 (prevent), impedire. 3 (travel, stop at) fermarsi a . . . 4 (naut), fare scalo. 4 **stop work** (pers), interrompere il lavoro

stopover n (trans), scalo nm

stoppage n (of work), (pers), interruzione nf del lavoro

storage n (transp), 1 (own materials), immagazzinamento nm; **storage space**, luogo nm d'immagazzinamento. 2 (warehousing service), deposito nm

store n, 1 (shop), negozio nm. 2 (for storage), deposito nm

store vb, 1 (gen), (keep), tenere a magazzino. 2 (keep in warehouse), depositare, tenere a deposito. 3 (comp), mettere in memoria

stow vb, 1 (gen), mettere a posto. 2 (in a ship), stivare. 3 (fill up), riempire

strategy n, strategia nf

streamline vb (production, a company), razionalizzare

strength n (materials), resistenza nf

strengthen vb, rinforzare

strengthened adj (imp/exp), rinforzato(-a)

stress n (health), pressione nf, 'stress' nm

stress vb (insist, point out), insistere

strict adj (discipline), severo(-a), rigido(-a)

strike n (pers), sciopero nm

strike vb (pers), scioperare, fare sciopero;

strong adj, 1 (gen), forte. 2 (materials), resistente. 3 (powerful), potente. 4 **strong room**, camera nf blindata

structural adj, strutturale

structure n, struttura nf

study vb, studiare

style n, stile nm

subcontract vb, subappaltare

subcontracting n (pers), subappalto nm

subcontractor n (gen), subappaltatore nm

subject n, soggetto nm

subject to adj, soggetto(-a) a

subscribe to vb (a journal, a service), abbonarsi a . . .

subscriber n (to magazines), abbonato(-a) nm/f

subsidiary n (company), società nf

consociata

subsidise vb, sovvenzionare

subsidy n (fin), sovvenzione nf

substandard adj, di qualità nf inferiore

substitute n (materials), imitazione nf; **leather substitute**, imitazione pelle

substitute vb, (goods), sostituire, **please substitute plastic for aluminium**, si prega di sostituire la plastica con l'alluminio

suburb n, periferia nf

subway n (gen), (underpass), sottopassaggio nm

succeed vb, riuscire a . . . **he succeeded in . .**, è riuscito a . . .

success n, successo nm

successful adj, riuscito(-a), di successo, che ha successo

sue vb (law), citare in giudizio

suffer vb, soffrire

suitable adj, 1 (gen), adatto(-a); **a suitable location**, un luogo adatto. 2 (convenient), conveniente; **is this a suitable time?**, è un'ora conveniente?

sum n, somma nf

summarise vb, riassumere

summary n, sommario nm; **make a summary of the report**, per fare un sommario del rapporto

summon vb (law), citare in giudizio

summons n (law), ingiunzione nf, citazione nf

supermarket n, supermercato nm

superstore n (mktg, sales), ipermercato nm

supervisor n (pers), sovrintendente nm

supplementary adj, supplementare; **supplementary charge**, spesa nf supplementare

supplier *n* (gen), fornitore *nm*

supply *n*, fornitura *nf*; **supply problems** (gen), problemi *nmpl* di fornitura; **a supply of . .**, una fornitura di *nf* . .; **supply and demand**, domanda e offerta *nf*

supply *vb*, fornire

support *n* (gen), appoggio *nm*; **the project has the support of . .**, il progetto ha l'appoggio di . . .

support *vb* (gen), appoggiare; **support a proposal**, appoggiare una proposta

surcharge *n*, sovraccarico *nm*

surface mail *n*, posta *nf* normale

surge *n*, ondata *nf*, impeto *nm*; **a surge in imports**, un'ondata di importazioni; **a surge of anger**, un impeto d'ira

surrender *vb* (documents), consegnare; **surrender the documents to . .**, consegnare i documenti a . . .

surrender value *n* (fin), valore *nm* di riscatto

survey *n* (gen), studio *nm*; **market survey**, studio di mercato

survey *vb* **(damage)** (ins), esaminare i danni

survey *vb* **the market**, fare uno studio del mercato

suspend *vb* (stop), sospendere; **suspend payments** (fin), sospendere i pagamenti *nmpl*

switch *n* (elec), interruttore *nm*

switch off *vb*, spegnere, fermare

switch on *vb*, accendere, mettere in marcia

switchboard *n* (offce), centralino *nm*; **switchboard operator** (offce), centralinista *nm/f*

synthetic *adj*, sintetico(-a)

system *n*, sistema *nm*

T

table *n*, 1 (of figures), tabella *nf*; **the table shows the sales figures for this month**, la tabella mostra le cifre di vendita per questo mese. 2 (furniture), tavolo *nm*, tavola *nf*

table *vb* (put on agenda), mettere in agenda

tacit *adj*, tacito(-a); **we have the tacit agreement of the manufacturer**, abbiamo l'accordo tacito del fabbricante

tackle *vb*, (deal with), affrontare; **I would like to tackle the problem of . .**, vorrei affrontare il problema di . . .

tactic *n*, tattica *nf*; **their usual tactic is to . .**, la loro tattica abituale è di . .; **negotiating tactic**, tattica *nf* di trattativa

tag *n*, 1 (gen, informal), prezzo *nm*; **the price tag for this type of operation is very high**, il prezzo per questo tipo di operazione è molto alto. 2 (label showing price), cartellino *nm*

tail lift truck *n* (transp), camion *nm* con sponda elevatrice

tailor to *vb*, adattare in funzione di . .; **we can tailor our service to your exact needs**, possiamo adattare il nostro servizio in funzione dei vostri precisi bisogni

tailor-made *adj*, fatto(-a) su misura

take *vb*, 1 (gen), prendere. 2 (volume), contenere; **the tank can take 5000 litres**, il serbatoio può contenere 5000 litri; **take into account**, prendere in considerazione; **take after**, assomigliare; **take back**, riprendere; **we are willing to take back the unsatisfactory goods**, siamo disposti a riprendere le merci non soddisfacenti; **take a bath**, fare un bagno; **take care of . .**, aver cura di . .; **take to court** (law), portare in tribunale; **take a degree**, laurearsi; **take down**, smontare; **stands must be taken down within 24 hours of the end of the exhibition**, gli stand devono essere smontati entro 24 ore dalla fine dell'esposizione; **take it easy**, prendersela con comodo; **take an exam in . .**, sostenere un esame; **take legal action**, citare in giudizio; **take a load to . .**, (transp), trasportare un carico a . .; **take notes/minutes**, prendere appunti; **take off**, I (planes), decollare. 2 (garments), togliersi. 3 (go up) andare su; **sales are taking off**, le vendite stanno andando su; **take on (staff)**, (pers), assumere (personale); **take over** (a company), rilevare; **Schilke GMBH have been taken over by . .**, Schilke GMBH è stata rilevata da . .; **take over (from)**, succedere, essere il successore; **Mr Jones has taken over from Mrs Smith in your sector**, nel vostro settore il Signor Jones è il successore della Signora Smith; **take place**, aver luogo; **the conference will take place on . . . at . .**, la conferenza avrà luogo il . . . a . .; **take steps (to)**, prendere provvedimenti; **take to**, darsi al . .; **he takes to gambling**, si da al giuoco; **take up** (an option), accettare (un opzione)

takeover n (of a company), rilievo nm; **takeover bid** (fin), offerta nf di rilievo; **make a takeover bid**, fare un'offerta di rilievo; **to receive a takeover bid**, ricevere un'offerta di rilievo

talk vb, parlare

talk n, **give a talk on . .**, fare una conferenza su . ., parlare di . . .

talks npl, I (gen), discussioni nfpl. 2 (fin), trattative nfpl; **have talks with . .**, avere trattative con . . .

tamper vb, I (with goods), manomettere; **the boxes have been tampered with**, le scatole sono state manomesse. 2 (with documents), alterare; **these papers have been tampered with**, questi documenti sono stati alterati. 3 (with people), corrompere; **they have tried to tamper with a witness**, hanno tentato di corrompere un testimone. 4 (with animals), drogare; **tamper with a horse**, drogare un cavallo. 5 (interfere or meddle), immischiarsi; **do not tamper with his business**, non immischiarti nei suoi affari

tangible adj (acct), sensibile, tangibile

tank n (imp/exp), serbatoio nm

tanker n (transp) I (road), autocisterna nf. 2 (naut) nave nf cisterna. 3 **petrol tanker**, petroliera nf. 4 (rail), vagone nm cisterna

tape n, I (sound recording), cassetta nf. 2 (video recording), video nm

tape recorder n, registratore nm

tape vb (record sound), registrare

tapering rates, npl, tariffe nfpl a scalare

target n, obbiettivo nm; **be on target**, raggiungere l'obbiettivo; **sales target**, obbiettivo vendite; **target market**, mercato nm d'obbiettivo; **target price**, prezzo nm d'obbiettivo

target vb (mktg, sales), prendere di mira; **the new product targets the under 21s**, il nuovo prodotto prende di mira le persone al di sotto dei 21 anni

tarpaulin n (transp), telone nm impermeabile

task n, compito nm

taste n (food), gusto nm; **a new taste**, un nuovo gusto

taste vb, **1** avere un sapore, sapere, (di); **the mixture tastes very sweet**, questo miscuglio ha un sapore molto dolce; **this mixture tastes like honey**, questo miscuglio sa di miele. **2** (sample), gustare; **we will want to taste several bottles before buying**, vorremmo gustare parecchie bottiglie prima di acquistare

tax n, tassa nf, imposta nf; **tax consultant** (fin), consulente nm fiscale; **tax disc** (vehicles), bollo nm; **tax-free** (fin), esente da tasse; **tax relief** (fin), sgravio nm fiscale; **tax year** (fin), anno nm fiscale

taxable adj, tassabile, imponibile

team n, squadra nf

tear vb (materials), strappare

teaser n, **1** (gen), persona nf irritante, persona dispettosa. **2** (sales), 'stuzzichino' nm

technical adj, tecnico(-a); **technical sales representative** (mktg, sales), tecnico-commerciale nm

technician n, tecnico nm

technique n, tecnica nf

technology n, tecnologia nf; **it incorporates the latest technology**, incorpora la tecnologia più avanzata; **it uses advanced technology**, usa una tecnologia avanzata

telegraphic address n, indirizzo nm telegrafico

telegraphic transfer n (fin), trasferimento nm telegrafico

telemarketing n, marketing nm per telefono

telephone n, telefono nm; **telephone answering machine**, segreteria nf telefonica; **telephone call**, telefonata nf; **following your recent telephone call**, a seguito della vostra recente telefonata;

receive a telephone call from . ., ricevere una telefonata da . .; **telephone sales** (mktg, sales), vendita nf per telefono

telephone vb (gen), telefonare

teleprinter n, telestampante nf

telesales n (mktg, sales), vendite nfpl per telefono

television n (set), televisione nf; **on TV**, alla televisione, (colloquial) alla tivi; **television programme**, programma nm televisivo

telewriter n (comp), telescrivente nf

telex n, telex nm; **telex machine**, macchina nf telex; **telex number**, numero nm di telex

telex vb, inviare un telex; **telex a company**, inviare un telex a una società; **telex an order to . .**, inviare un ordine per telex a . .; **please telex details of the load**, si prega di inviare per telex i particolari del carico

temporary adj, temporaneo(-a); **temporary address**, indirizzo nm temporaneo; **temporary employment** (pers), impiego nm temporaneo

tend to . . . vb, tendere a, avere tendenza a

tendency n, tendenza nf; **it has a tendency to . .**, ha una tendenza a . . .

tender n (an offer), offerta nf d'appalto; **invite tenders**, chiedere offerte d'appalto

tender vb (offer a price), sottomettere un prezzo; **tender for a contract**, concorrere per un contratto, fare offerte d'appalto per un contratto

tentative adj (agreement), provvisorio(-a)

terminal n (electr) morsetto nm

terminate vb, terminare; **terminate a contract**, terminare un contratto

terms *npl* (gen), condizioni *nfpl*;
terms of payment, condizioni di
pagamento

territory *n* (mktg, sales), territorio
nm

test *n*, prova *nf*

test *vb*, esaminare, provare

thank *vb*, ringraziare

think *vb*, pensare

third *n* (fraction), (maths), terzo *nm*;
third party, fire and theft (ins),
assicurazione *nf* per danni contro
terzi furto e incendio

thirdly *adv*, in terzo luogo

thorough *adj* (research, report),
profondo(-a)

threat *n*, minaccia *nf*

threaten *vb*, minacciare

three (number), tre; **three times as
high/low as . .**, tre volte più alto(-
a)/più basso(-a)

threshold *n*, soglia *nf*; **reach the 5%
threshold**, raggiungere la soglia del
5%

thriving *adj*, **1** (gen), prospero(-a).
2 (of a business), florido(-a). **3** (of
plants), robusto(-a)

through bill of lading *n*, polizza *nf* di
carico diretta

through flight *n* (transp), volo *nm*
diretto

through train *n* (transp), treno *nm*
diretto

tick *n* (on a form, document), visto
nm

tick *vb* (documents), spuntare; **please
tick the appropriate box**, si
prega di spuntare il quadratino
appropriato

ticket *n*, **1** (travel), biglietto *nm*. **2** (on
goods), etichetta *nf*

tide *n*, marea *nf*; **high tide**, alta
marea; **low tide**, bassa marea

tidy up *vb*, mettere in ordine

tie up *vb* (capital, resources), investire

tight *adj*, **1** (gen), stretto(-a). **2** (law),
severo(-a). **3** (fin), scarso(-a);
money is tight, il denaro è scarso

tighten up *vb*, serrare

tightrope *n*, corda *nf* tesa

timber *n* (gen), legname *nm* da
costruzione

time *n*, tempo *nm*, ora *nf*, momento
nm; **as time goes on**, col passar
del tempo; **local time**, ora locale;
a suitable time for a meeting,
un momento adatto per una
riunione

timetable *n* (gen), orario *nm*

tin *n* (container), latta *nf*

tip *n*, **1** (information, help),
informazione *nf*. **2** (the end of
something), punta *nf*. **3** (pile of
waste), deposito *nm* rifiuti.
4 (gratuity), mancia *nf*

tip *vb*, **1** (give information), dare
informazioni. **2** (a load), scaricare.
3 (give gratuities), dare la mancia

title *n* (gen), titolo *nm*; **title deed**,
titolo di proprietà

token ring network *n* (comp), rete
nf ad anello a gettone

tolerance *n*, tolleranza *nf*

tolerate *vb*, tollerare

toll *n* (road), pedaggio *nm*

ton *n*, tonnellata *nf*

tonnage *n*, tonnellaggio *nm*

tool *n*, attrezzo *nm*

top *n*, **1** (best), migliore *nm/f*.
2 (highest point), sommità *nf*, cima
nf; il punto *nm* più alto. **3** (of a
container), coperchio *nm*. **4 come
top . .**, essere in testa

top *vb* (beat), superare; **this year
profits will top £5m**, quest'anno i
profitti supereranno i 5 milioni di
sterline

total n, totale nm; **a total of £23,664 . .**, un totale di £23,664

total adj, totale; **total quality management**, gestione nf di qualità totale

total vb, 1 (reach a total of) raggiungere il totale; **it totals 373**, raggiunge il totale di 373. 2 (add up figures), fare il totale

touch n, contatto nm; **get in touch (with)**, contattare; **please get in touch with our office in . .**, si prega di contattare il nostro ufficio a . . .

tour n (of factory), giro nm, visita nf

tourism n, turismo nm

tourist n, turista nm/f

tow vb, rimorchiare

town n, città nf

TPND, **theft, pilferage, non-delivery** (imp/exp), furto nm, piccolo furto, mancata consegna nf

TQM (pers), gestione nf di qualità totale

trackball n (comp), 'trackball', pallina nf di comando

track record n, 1 (gen, pers, CV) esperienza nf; **have a good track record**, avere una buona esperienza; **no track record in . .**, nessuna esperienza in . . . . 2 (company results), risultati nmpl; **the company has a very successful track record**, la società ha dei buoni risultati

trade n, 1 (professional activity), mestiere nm; **trade union**, sindacato nm. 2 (comm), commercio nm; **export trade**, commercio di esportazione; **foreign trade**, commercio estero; **international trade**, commercio internazionale; **trade day** (mktg, sales), giorno nm riservato ai commercianti; **trade mark**, marchio nm di fabbrica

trade adj, commerciale; **trade balance**, bilancio nm commerciale; **trade fair**, fiera nf commerciale; **trade magazine**, giornale nm commerciale; **trade press**, stampa nf commerciale; **trade supplier**, fornitore nm commerciale

trade (in) . . . vb, commerciare in . .; **the company trades in plastics**, la società commercia in plastica

trading account n (fin), conto nm profitti; **the trading account shows a small deficit for the month of . .**, il conto profitti mostra un piccolo deficit per il mese di . . .

trading estate n, zona nf commerciale

trading year n (fin), esercizio nm commerciale

traffic n, traffico nm; **road traffic**, traffico stradale; **traffic light**, semaforo nm

trailer n (transp), rimorchio nm

train n (transp), treno nm; **goods train**, treno merci; **express train**, espresso nm; **passenger train**, treno viaggiatori

train vb (pers), addestrare

training n (pers), addestramento nm; **training centre** (pers), centro nm d'addestramento

transaction n, trattativa nf

transfer n, trasferimento nm

transfer vb (fin), trasferire; **transfer money from account NW . . . to account NZ . .**, trasferire denaro dal conto NW . . . al conto NZ . . .

transferable adj (fin), (securities), trasferibile

transhipment n (transp), trasbordo nm

transit n (transp, ins), transito nm; **in transit** in transito; **goods damaged or lost in transit**, merci *nfpl* danneggiate o smarrite in transito

translate *vb*, tradurre

translation *n* (imp/exp), traduzione *nf*

transmit *vb* **(to, from)**, trasmettere (a, da)

transparency *n*, trasparenza *nf*

transport *vb*, trasportare

transporter *n* (company) (transp), trasportatore *nm*

travel *n* (mktg, sales), viaggio *nm*; **business travel**, viaggio d'affari; **regular travel** (pers), spostamenti *nmpl* frequenti; **travel agency**, agenzia *nf* di viaggio; **travel expenses**, spese *nfpl* di viaggio; **travel insurance** (ins), assicurazione *nf* di viaggio

travel *vb*, viaggiare

traveller *n*, viaggiatore *nm*; **business traveller**, viaggiatore d'affari; **traveller's cheque**, assegno *nm* per viaggiatori

trend *n*, tendenza *nf*

trial *n* (law), giudizio *nm*, processo; **trial period**, periodo *nm* di prova

trip *n*, viaggio *nm*; **be on a trip to Venice**, essere in viaggio per Venezia

triple *vb*, triplicare; **profits have tripled**, i profitti si sono triplicati

true *adj*, vero(-a)

trust *n* (gen), fiducia *nf*; **we have complete trust in our agent, Signor Garcia**, abbiamo completa fiducia nel nostro agente, il Signor Garcia

trust *vb*, aver fiducia; **you may trust Ms Smith completely**, può avere completamente fiducia nella Signora Smith

try *vb*, **1** (attempt), tentare; **we will try to find the model you want**, tenteremo di trovare il modello che voi desiderate; **we will try to have the order ready for the end of the month**, tenteremo di avere l'ordine pronto per la fine del mese. **2** (sample, try out), provare; **you may try the machine for one week at no expense**, potete provare la macchina gratuitamente per una settimana

TT, telegraphic transfer (fin), trasferimento *nm* telegrafico

TUC, Trades Union Congress, federazione *nf* dei sindacati britannici

turn down *vb* **a proposal/an offer**, respingere una proposta/un'offerta

turn on *vb* (machine, light), accendere (una macchina, la luce)

turnover *n*, **1** (acct) giro *nm* d'affari. **2** (stock), rotazione *nf* (dello stock)

twice *adv*, due volte; **twice as high/low as . . .** (maths), due volte più alto/più basso(-a)

type *n*, tipo *nm*; **a new type of machine**, un nuovo tipo di macchina

type *vb*, dattilografare

typewriter *n*, macchina *nf* da scrivere

typist *n*, dattilografo(-a) *nm/f*; **typist's chair**, sedia *nf* per dattilografo(-a)

tyre *n*, pneumatico *nm*

U

UK, United Kingdom, Regno *nm* Unito

ultimatum *n*, ultimatum *nm*

unadvisable *adj* (not wise), inopportuno(-a), non consigliabile

unanimous *adj*, unanime

unanimously *adv*, unanimemente

unanswered *adj*, senza risposta; **our letter of complaint has remained unanswered**, la nostra lettera di reclamo è rimasta senza risposta

unapproved *adj*, disapprovato(-a)

unauthorised *adj*, non autorizzato(-a)

unavailable *adj*, **I** (gen), non disponibile. **2** (useless), inutile

unbranded *adj* (mktg, sales), senza marchio

unchanged *adj*, immutato(-a)

unconditional *adj*, incondizionato(-a)

unconfirmed *adj*, non confermato(-a)

uncorrected *adj*, non corretto(-a)

undamaged *adj*, **I** (ins), non avariato(-a). **2** (gen), in buone condizioni

undelivered *adj*, non consegnato(-a)

under *prep*, **I** sotto, al di sotto di; **under 15%**, al di sotto del 15%; **under the bed**, sotto il letto. **2** (according to); **under the terms of . .**, secondo le condizioni di . . .

undercut *vb*, (sales), offrire a un prezzo minore; **undercut competitors**, offrire a un prezzo minore di quello dei concorrenti;

undercut the competition, offrire a un prezzo minore della concorrenza

underdeveloped countries *npl*, paesi *nmpl* sottosviluppati

underestimate *vb*, sottovalutare

undersigned *adj*, sottoscritto(-a); **I, the undersigned . . . declare . .**, il sottoscritto/la sottoscritta . . . dichiara . . .

understand *vb*, **I** (gen), capire; **I understand the problem**, capisco il problema. **2** (hear), sentir dire; **we understand that you are currently dealing with an agent in Rome**, abbiamo sentito dire che voi al momento state trattando con un agente di Roma

understanding *n*, **I** (gen), comprensione *nf*; **I am grateful for your understanding**, le sono grato(-a) della sua comprensione. **2** (agreement), accordo *nm*, patto *nm*; **we accept on the understanding that . .**, accettiamo a patto che . .; **we have reached an understanding**, abbiamo raggiunto un accordo

undertake to *vb*, promettere, impegnarsi a

undervalue *vb*, sottovalutare

underwrite *vb*, **I** (gen), sottoscrivere. **2** (ins), (to share risks), assicurare

uneconomical *adj*, non economico(-a)

unemployed *adj*, disoccupato(-a)

unemployment *n*, disoccupazione *nf*

uneven *adj* (results), non uniforme, irregolare

unexpected *adj*, inatteso(-a), imprevisto(-a)

unfair *adj*, ingiusto(-a), sleale; **this is unfair**, questo è ingiusto; **unfair competition**, concorrenza *nf* sleale

unfavourable *adj*, sfavorevole; **the**

results are unfavourable, i risultati sono sfavorevoli; **the outlook is unfavourable**, la prospettiva è sfavorevole

unforeseen adj, imprevisto(-a)

uniform adj, uniforme

union n, 1 (gen), unione nf. 2 (trade union), sindacato nm; **union representative** (pers), delegato nm sindacale

unit adj, unitario(-a); **unit cost**, costo unitario; **unit price**, prezzo unitario; **unit trust** (fin), società nf d'investimento

unit n (of goods), unità nf

unlawful adj, illegale

unlikely adj, improbabile; **it is unlikely that economic conditions will improve now**, è improbabile che le condizioni economiche migliorino adesso; **in my opinion the situation is unlikely to change for the time being**, secondo me è improbabile che la situazione cambi per il momento

unload vb (transp), scaricare

unofficial adj, non ufficiale, ufficioso(-a)

unpack vb, 1 (suitcases), disfare (le valige). 2 (parcels), disimballare

unpaid adj, 1 (bills), non pagato(-a), non saldato(-a); **there is an unpaid bill for . .**, c'è una fattura non pagata per . .; **our invoice N 38382 is still unpaid**, la nostra fattura N 38382 non è stata ancora saldata. 2 (charity work), **unpaid work**, lavoro nm di beneficenza

unsaleable adj, invendibile

unserviceable adj, inutilizzabile; **the equipment is now unserviceable**, l'attrezzatura adesso è inutilizzabile

unsold items npl, articoli nmpl invenduti; **according to the agreement unsold items may be returned**, secondo l'accordo gli articoli invenduti possono essere restituiti

unsuitable adj, inadatto(-a)

untrue adj, falso(-a), inesatto(-a)

unused adj (goods), non usato(-a)

up adv, **be up 2%**, essere in aumento del 2%; **be 5.000.000 lire up**, essere in aumento di 5 milioni di lire; **go up**, andar su

upgrade vb, 1 (gen), migliorare, modernizzare. 2 (pers), promuovere, aumentare lo stipendio

upswing n of prices, sbalzo nm dei prezzi

upturn n, ripresa nf, incremento nm

upward trend n, tendenza nf al rialzo

urban adj (gen), urbano(-a)

USA, United States of America, Stati nmpl Uniti (d'America)

use n, uso nm

use vb (gen), usare

used adj, 1 (second-hand), usato(-a), di seconda mano. 2 be used to, essere abituato(-a) a; **I am used to getting up early in the morning**, sono abituato ad alzarmi presto al mattino

user n, utente nm

user-friendly adj, di facile utilizzazione

USP, Unique Selling Proposition (mktg, sales), vantaggio nm unico del prodotto

usual adj, usuale, abituale

utility n (comp), programma nm utilitario

V

vacancy n, posto nm vacante

vacuum-sealed adj, sigillato(-a) sottovuoto

valid adj, valido(-a); **valid from . . . to . . .** (tickets), valido dal . . . al . . .

validity n, validità nf

valuable adj, prezioso(-a), costoso(-a)

value n, valore nm; **face value**, valore nominale; **be good value**, valere

value vb, 1 (appreciate), apprezzare. 2 (estimate the value), valutare

valued adj, valutato(-a); **valued at £5,000**, valutate a 5000 sterline

van n (transp), furgone nm, camionetta nf

variable adj, variabile; **the demand is very variable**, la domanda è molto variabile; **the quality of the goods is very variable**, la qualità delle merci è molto variabile

variation n, variazione nf

vary vb, 1 (change something), modificare; **we can vary the contents according to the customer's needs**, possiamo modificare il contenuto secondo le necessità del cliente. 2 (subject to change), variare, cambiare; **the price varies according to the season**, il prezzo varia secondo la stagione

VAT, **value added tax**, TVA, imposta nf sul valore aggiunto

VC, Vice Chairman, vice presidente nm

VCR, video cassette recorder, registratore nm per video

vehicle n, veicolo nm

vending machine n (for drinks), distributore nm automatico

vendor n, venditore nm/venditrice nf

Venn diagram n, diagramma nm di Venn

venture capital n, capitale nm di partecipazione

venue n (gen), luogo nm di riunione

verbal adj, verbale

verify vb, verificare

vessel n, 1 (transp), nave nf. 2 (container), recipiente nm

veto vb, mettere il veto

VGA n (comp), VGA

via prep, via

vice chairman n (pers), vice presidente

vice president n (pers), vice presidente

video n (film), video nm; **promotional video**, video promozionale

video vb, fare un video

view vb, 1 (property), esaminare. 2 (a film), vedere

view n, vista nf; **in view of . .**, in vista di; **in view of the cost of raw materials . .**, in vista del costo delle materie prime. . . .

virus n (comp), virus nm; **virus protection**, protezione nf da virus

visit n, visita nf

visit vb, visitare

visitor n, visitatore nm

voluntary adj, 1 (freely chosen), volontario(-a). 2 (unpaid), **voluntary work**, lavoro nm di beneficenza

vote n, voto nm

vote *vb*, votare

voucher *n*, buono *nm*

W

wage(s) *n(pl)* (pers), paga *nf*, salario *nm*; **wage freeze**, blocco *nm* dei salari; **wage increase**, aumento *nm* dei salari

wagon *n* (transp), vagone *nm*

wait *n*, attesa *nf*

wait *vb*, attendere, aspettare; **I will wait for confirmation of . .**, aspetterò la conferma di . .; **I will wait for you at the airport**, l'aspetterò all'aeroporto

waiting room *n* (gen), sala *nf* d'attesa

waive *vb* (a right), (ins), rinunciare

waiver *n* (ins), rinuncia *nf*

walk out *vb* (stop work), scioperare

walk-out *n*, sciopero *nm*

walkway *n* (between exhibition stands), passaggio *nm* pedonale

wall chart *n* (offce), grafico *nm* da muro

want *vb*, volere, desiderare

warehouse *n*, magazzino *nm*; **warehouse warrant**, bollettino *nm* di deposito, nota *nf* di pegno

warehouse manager *n* (transp), responsabile *nm/f* di magazzino

warehousing *n* (transp), magazzinaggio *nm*; **warehousing charges**, spese *nfpl* di magazzinaggio

warn *vb*, avvertire; **please warn your driver that there is a strike at the port . .**, vi preghiamo di avvertire il vostro autista che c'è uno sciopero al porto . . .

warning n, avvertimento nm; **receive a warning about . .**, ricevere un avvertimento su . .; **send a warning letter to . .**, inviare una lettera d'avvertimento a . . .

warrant vb, garantire, giustificare

warranty n, garanzia nf

waste n, spreco nm, scarto nm; **waste products**, prodotti nmpl di scarto

waste vb, sprecare

waterproof adj (imp/exp), impermeabilizzato(-a)

waterproof vb (gen), impermeabilizzare

waybill n (imp/exp), lettera nf di vettura, foglio nm di via

weak adj, debole

weaken vb, indebolire

week n, settimana nf

weekly adj, settimanale; **weekly deliveries**, consegne nfpl settimanali; **weekly magazine**, rivista nf settimanale

weekly adv, settimanalmente

weigh vb, pesare

weight n (imp/exp), peso nm

weighted adj (calculations), ponderato(-a); **weighted average**, media ponderata

weld vb, saldare

wet adj (transp), bagnato(-a)

wharf n, banchina nf, molo nm

wheel n, ruota nf

white adj, bianco(-a); **white goods** (mktg, sales), elettrodomestici nmpl

wholesale adj (mktg, sales), all'ingrosso; **wholesale price**, prezzo nm all'ingrosso

wholesaler n (mktg, sales), grossista nm

wholly-owned subsidiary n, società

nf interamente controllata

wide adj, largo(-a), ampio, vasto; **the box is 16 cm wide by 12 cm long**, la scatola è larga 16 cm e lunga 12 cm; **a wide selection of . .**, un'ampia selezione di . .; **a wide range of . .**, una vasta gamma di . . .

widen vb (gen), allargare, ampliare

width n, larghezza nf

win vb, 1 (gen), vincere. 2 (gain), guadagnare. 3 (conquer) conquistare

wind up vb (a company), mettere in liquidazione

with prep, con; **with particular average**, con avaria particolare

withdraw vb, 1 (money), prelevare, ritirare. 2 (person), ritirarsi

without prep, senza prep

witness n (law), testimone nm; **eye-witness**, testimone nm oculare; **act as a witness** (law), agìre da testimone

witness vb (law), 1 (gen), testimoniare, fare da testimone. 2 (be present), essere presente. 3 (sign as a witness), firmare da testimone; **witness a document**, firmare un documento da testimone; **witness an accident**, essere presente a un incidente

wood n, legno nm

wooden adj, di legno

wool n, lana nf

woollen adj, di lana

word n, parola nf, voce nf, vocabolo nm

word vb (an agreement), esprimere a parole

wording n, testo nm; **according to the wording of the contract** secondo il testo del contratto

word-processing n, trattamento nm del testo; **word-processing software**, software per il trattamento del testo

work n, lavoro nm; **work in hand/work in progress** (acct), lavoro in corso

work vb, **1** (machines, method of operation), funzionare; **the demonstration will show how the machine works**, la dimostrazione illustrerà come la macchina funziona. **2** (gen, employees), lavorare; **work for . . .** (pers), lavorare per . .; **work under . . .** (pers), lavorare sotto la direzione di . . .

work out vb, **1** (calculate), calcolare. **2** (find a solution), risolvere

workforce n (pers), personale nm lavorativo; **the company has a workforce of 1,200**, la società ha un personale lavorativo di 1200 persone

working capital n (fin), capitale nm liquido; **working capital turnover** (fin), giro nm del capitale liquido

working conditions npl (pers), condizioni nfpl lavorative

working day n (gen), giorno nm lavorativo

works manager n (pers), direttore nm d'officina

worldwide adj, mondiale

worth n, valore nm

worth, be worth vb, valere

worthwhile, be worthwhile vb, valere la pena; **it is not worthwhile to go now**, non vale la pena andare adesso

WP 1 (comp), **word processor**, 'wordprocessor', macchina nf per trattamento di un testo. **2** (comp), **word processing**, trattamento nm del testo

WPA, wpa, with particular average (ins), con avaria nf particolare

wrap vb, avvolgere, imballare

wrapped adj (imp/exp), avvolto(-a), imballato(-a); **wrapped in wood wool**, imballato(-a) nei trucioli di legno

wrapping n, materiale nm da pacco

writ n (law), mandato nm

write vb, scrivere; **write a report**, scrivere un rapporto; **write to someone**, scrivere a qualcuno

write off vb, **1** (acct), (progressively), ammortizzare. **2** (bad debt), defalcare

write off n (ins), perdita nf totale; **in our opinion the vehicle is a write off**, secondo noi il veicolo è una perdita totale

writing pad, blocco nm note

wrong adj, sbagliato(-a); **they sent the wrong goods**, hanno inviato le merci sbagliate; **wrong items** (gen, imp/exp), articoli nmpl non ordinati; **wrong price** (gen, imp/exp), prezzo nm incorretto

wrong, be wrong vb (opinion, judgement), avere torto; **I think we are wrong in this case**, penso che abbiamo torto in questo caso

W/W, warehouse warrant n (imp/exp), bolletino nm di deposito, nota nf di pegno

X Y

X-ml, X-mll, ex-mill (imp/exp), dalla fabbrica *nf*

X-ship, ex-ship (imp/exp), merce *nf* sbarcata dalla nave *nm*

x-stre, ex-store (imp/exp), dal magazzino *nm*

x-whf, ex-wharf (imp/exp), franco banchina

x-whse, ex-warehouse (imp/exp), dal deposito

x-wks, ex-works (imp/exp), dallo stabilimento

yacht *n*, panfilo *nm*, yacht *nm*

yard *n*, **1** (measurement), iarda *nf*. **2** (area outside factory buildings), cortile *nm*

year *n*, anno *mn*, annata *nf*; **year in year out**, un anno dopo l'altro; **a good working year**, una buona annata lavorativa

yearly *adj* (gen), annuale

yearly *adv*, annualmente

yield *n*, **1** (fin), reddito *nm*. **2** (crop), raccolto *nm*

yield *vb*, produrre, rendere

Yours faithfully, distinti saluti *nmpl*; colgo/cogliamo l'occasione per porgere i miei/nostri più distinti saluti; mi/ci è gradita l'occasione per porgere i miei/nostri più distinti saluti

Yours sincerely, distinti saluti *nmpl*; colgo/cogliamo l'occasione per porgere i miei/nostri più distinti saluti; mi/ci è gradita l'occasione per porgere i miei/nostri più distinti saluti

Z

zero *n*, zero *nm*; **above/below zero**, sopra/sotto zero

zero fault *n* (quality management), nessun errore *nm*, nessuno sbaglio *nm*

zero hour *n*, ora *nf* zero

zero potential *n*, potenziale *nm* nullo

TEACH YOURSELF BUSINESS FRENCH
Barbara Coultas

Now that the European market place is truly with us, thousands of business people are finding that they need to be able to say more than just 'Bonjour, Monsieur' if they are to survive. If you are one of them, and you've never learnt French before, or if your French needs brushing up, this is the ideal course.

Barbara Coultas has created a practical course that is both fun and easy to work through. She explains the language clearly along the way and gives you plenty of opportunities to practise what you've learnt. The course structure means that you can work at your own pace, arranging your learning to suit your needs.

The course contains:
- A range of units of dialogues, culture notes, grammar and exercises
- Further units of cultural briefings – in French to give you more practice
- Verb tables
- A quick reference list of key phrases
- An extensive French–English vocabulary

By the end of the course you'll be able to participate fully and confidently in meetings, on the shop floor, on the telephone or in the bar after work.

This title is also available in a book/cassette pack.

TEACH YOURSELF BUSINESS SPANISH
Juan Kattán-Ibarra

With 300 million speakers, the Spanish language is the key to some of the biggest markets in the world, and to compete in them you'll need to know more than just 'hola!'.

If you've never learnt Spanish before, or if your Spanish needs brushing up, this is the ideal course. Equally, if you are taking an evening class or a BTEC award, it is the perfect companion.

Juan Kattán-Ibarra has created a practical course that is both fun and easy to work through. He explains the language clearly along the way and gives you plenty of opportunities to practise what you've learnt. The course structure means that you can work at your own pace, arranging your learning to suit your needs.

The course contains:
* Sixteen units of dialogues, culture notes, grammar and exercises
* Eight further units of cultural briefings – in Spanish, to give you more practise!
* A pronunciation guide
* Verb tables
* An English-Spanish glossary of business terms
* An extensive Spanish–English vocabulary

By the end of the course you'll be able to participate fully and confidently in meetings, on the shop floor, on the telephone or in the bar after work.

This title is also available in a book/cassette pack.

TEACH YOURSELF BUSINESS GERMAN
Andrew Castley and Debbie Wagener

Now that the European market place is truly with us, thousands of business people are finding that they need to be able to say more than just 'Guten Morgen' if they are to survive.

If you've never learnt German before, or if your German needs brushing up, this is the course for you.

Andrew Castley and Debbie Wagener have created a practical course that is both fun and easy to work through. They explain the language clearly along the way and give you plenty of opportunities to practise what you've learnt. The course structure means that you can work at your own pace, arranging your learning to suit your needs.

The course contains:
- A range of units of dialogues, culture notes, grammar and exercises
- Further units of cultural briefings – in German to give you more practice
- A pronunciation guide
- Verb tables
- An English–German glossary of business terms
- An extensive German–English vocabulary

By the end of the course you'll be able to participate fully and confidently in meetings, on the shop floor, on the telephone or in the bar after work.

This title is also available in a book/cassette pack.